WHAT OUR FRIENDS SAY:

"The PolitiChicks' collection of essays is a necessary must read for today's constitutional conservative. The 2016 presidential election cycle isn't the end, it marks a beginning. It's the beginning of America accepting the challenge of Benjamin Franklin on September 17, 1787 -- "A Republic if you can keep it". And the only way we restore, keep, maintain, and advance the seminal ideal of liberty in this Constitutional Republic is to evidence the courage, passion, and intellect to support and defend its founding principles. God bless Ann-Marie Murrell, Morgan Brittany and their PolitiChicks writers; we certainly need that clarion call to arms!" — **Lt. Col. Allen B. West** (US Army, Retired), author of *Guardian of the Republic*

"After decades of near-universal Leftist hegemony, American conservatism is newly resurgent, and people are hungering for the truth after being inundated with lies and distortions from the establishment propaganda media. That's what makes *PolitiChicks: A Clarion Call to Political Activism* so valuable. On politics, education, parenting, Islam, and numerous other issues, these true feminists cut through today's fog of misinformation and disinformation to provide solid facts and a reliable basis for the political action in which all freedom-loving Americans need to be engaging today. Every conservative woman — and conservative man — should read this book and absorb its lessons, and pass on a copy to liberal friends who are open to a dose of clear thinking." — **Robert Spencer**, author of the *New York Times* bestsellers *The Politically Incorrect Guide to Islam (and the Crusades)* and *The Truth About Muhammad*

"When I first heard of the PolitiChicks, I thought it might be a group of college girls out to have some fun talking about politics. I found out that the PolitiChicks were a group of brilliant and opinionated professionals who were stirring up a storm of activism for conservative ideas. They come armed with wit, depth, and perspective. PolitiChicks.com has inspired many to stand up and speak up. These essays will hopefully cause *you* to get in the game!" —**Mike Huckabee**, former Governor and presidential candidate

"A must read blueprint for conservatives interested in changing the world, not just talking about it." —**Dan Bongino**, author of *Life Inside the Bubble*

"Passionately Patriotic PolitiChicks, Ann-Marie, Morgan Brittany and their cadre of contributors, light up the political scene with their pursuit to shine light so others can see the Truth."— **AlfonZo Rachel,** author and activist

"The PolitiChicks provide not only an urgent wake-up call, but also the crucial vehicles to Americans to speak up and fight for their civilization. An ambitious, commendable and heroic achievement." —**Dr. Jamie Glazov,** author and host of *The Glazov Gang*

"These collected essays, led by the lovely and brilliant PolitiChicks Ann-Marie and Morgan, comprise a record of how everyday citizens can lead others to respect our Constitution, in the face of advancing leftist tyranny. Be inspired, as I have been, by their courage, their intelligence and their humor, and use your voice! Even if you are not a Peabody-Award-winning international film and television star, you can make a difference. And the PolitiChicks can show you how." — **Nick Searcy,** actor

"I have been following the PolitiChicks for years. I enjoy the unique way they approach the issues affecting not just women, but men and children from all walks of life. The book is filled with great essays written by grassroots activists about how to effectively combat the attack on Americanism. Great read, don't pass it by." — **Joe Messina,** author and radio host of *The Real Side with Joe Messina*

"Activism was not my intention. When government overreach threatened my family, like many Americans I was shocked into action. I found to my surprise and delight the solutions are in our Constitution. The Founders knew tyrannical, oppressive, and big government is a constant threat to families and freedom. They secured for us the tools for the fight: our faith, our rights, our voice, our vote, and running for office. New comers to activism find many elected officials have compromised their principles, succumbing to cronyism. The activist must rip out corruption by the roots. Get trained, join other activists and never, never, never quit." — **Sharron Angle,** author and activist

"Ann-Marie Murrell, Morgan Brittany, and all of the PolitiChicks contributors fights tirelessly for America in the spirit of the great founders of our country." — **Mark Isler**, radio host

"When your fear of being judged or ridiculed for believing in things like "God & Country", "Law & Order" and "Respect & Honor" takes over your willingness outwardly represent those values then the ones who are trying to suppress, deter or undermine them become empowered to act out in more Godless, Lawless and disrespectful ways. I feel like we're seeing an overall suppression of goodness in our society due to the lack of genuine respect that exists within those who should be exuding it the most. In today's "LIKE" and "SHARE" world, Ann-Marie and her love of country make her a shining star from whose book we all should take a page. From one Patriot to another, It's an honor to watch her: STAY THE COURSE...FINISH THE FIGHT!" —**Dave Bray**, lead singer *Madison Rising*

"President John F. Kennedy once said, *"Today we need a nation of minutemen; citizens who are not only prepared to take up arms, but citizens who regard the preservation of freedom as a basic purpose of their daily life and who are willing to consciously work and sacrifice for that freedom. The cause of liberty, the cause of America, cannot succeed with any lesser effort."* Ann-Marie Murrell's Politichicks.com offers a place for citizens-turned-activists to come together and answer that call, advancing the cause of freedom on a platform that knows no boundaries. It's citizen-activists who are quickly replacing the old media as the vanguards of a new generation." —**Tim Donnelly,** former CA Assemblyman & gubernatorial candidate

"I've been reading Ann-Marie and PolitiChicks pieces right from the start. Always clear-eyed, common sensical and right (and I do mean right) on." —**Evan Sayet**, author of *The Kindergarden of Eden: How the Modern Liberal Thinks*

PolitiChicks:
A Clarion Call to
Political Activism

A Collection of Essays from the Writers of
PolitiChicks.com

PolitiChicks: A Clarion Call to Political Activism

Dedicated to American conservatives who are learning to find their political voices.

Be courageous. Be passionate. Be truthful.

And go ahead and talk about religion and politics in public; they do.

We also dedicate this to our first fallen PolitiChick, Maureen Mullins; we miss you everyday.

CONTENTS

PART THREE: EDUCATION

PART FOUR: ISLAM

PART FIVE: PARENTING

PART SIX: RELIGION

ACKNOWLEDGEMENTS

A SPECIAL THANK-YOU to our families and friends, and all of the wonderful people who have been supportive of PolitiChicks.com from the beginning. We wouldn't be writing this book without you.

We want to acknowledge Dr. Sarah Condor for conceptualizing this book and for encouraging and helping Ann-Marie Murrell put it together.

A few VIP's of PolitiChicks.com are Daniel Greenfield and Dr. Jamie Glazov. Thank you, gentlemen, for your courageous activism and for inspiring us daily. The respect we have for you is boundless.

Tim and Rowena Donnelly, James Patrick and Mary Riley, Evan Sayet, AlfonZo & CJ Rachel, Rob and Brinka Lowe (CastingNewLives.com), Tom Bendure, Frederick and Carolyn Eichelman, thank you for everything.

Tom Lehner, Robert H. Patrick, Zel Mitzel, Darla Gardner, and so many other social media warriors, thank you for your daily work promoting PolitiChicks. And thank you to Marc Langsam for your photos, and to Alan Mercer for the photo of Morgan Brittany on the cover.

Because there are so many co-authors of this book, we can't individually thank as many people as we'd like but you know who you are.

We also thank all the visionaries who blazed the trails before us. We hope we have made you proud.

FORWARD by Daniel Greenfield

Resistance.

Radicals want a constant state of war. Living this way comes naturally to them. The same isn't true of us.

Conservatives value tradition and family. It isn't the peace activists of the left who rush from rally to rally who truly want peace, but the soldier, the police officer and the patriot.

The radical dream is to squat in khakis on a throne of bones while waving the red flag. Their greatest dream is to make everyone do what they want.

Ours is to be left alone.

Resistance doesn't come naturally to us. Most conservatives would rather be working on their farm or reading to their children in the bedroom. They don't want to march on Washington D.C. or lead a revolution.

All the time that George Washington, our first president and our first conservative president, the man after whom the town at the center of the massive government was named after, was toiling at the tasks of government, he was pining after the simple life back in Mount Vernon.

His letters constantly reference the "vine and fig tree", the simple life free of the battles for power.

As conservatives, we want our own vine and fig tree. A life in which government would leave us alone and allow us to have the life that we want, to run our small businesses and care for our families.

Many who are natural conservatives never get involved because they share Washington's distaste for the struggle for power. Many more are eager for someone else to take the burden off their shoulders. They want to sign a petition, write a check and have someone else solve the problem for them.

The contributors to this volume have recognized that they must take on the burden. Like Washington and so many after him, they are serving their country, their communities and their families by fighting for their right to be free.

For their right and for our own.

They recognize that they can't just count on someone else to do it for them. They know that they have to go out and do it themselves.

When I last saw Ann-Marie, it was at an event in defense of freedom. It had clearly not been an easy trip for her. But she went anyway. All of the contributors to this volume, including myself, have their personal challenges, the areas of their life that they put aside for this cause.

But the cause is no less than that of human freedom.

I know many conservatives who have despaired and burned out. The women and men you will be reading in this volume have not. They strive and persevere. They fight on. For all of us.

It's a lot to ask of anyone. And yet the age asks it of us.

We were not born into an age in which we could just quietly drift along the current.

We must seize the oars or we will all drown. And we must do it with courage and integrity.

We have our models and our heroes. But we must also remember that all of them, even George Washington, were people just like us. There were times when they despaired. And many times when they wanted to go back home to their vines and fig trees and let someone else fight the battle.

It's their humanity that makes them heroes. And each one of us can be heroes too.

It isn't comic book superhuman skills that make a hero. It's commitment.

The people of PolitiChicks are committed. The contributors you will read in this volume are committed. And they can show you how you can be committed too. They can show you how you can make a difference. Not just for yourself, but for all of us.

This fight did not end with this election. Our battle for freedom is an enduring one. It has gone on for all of our history and for all of human history.

By writing and by speaking out, by sharing and by standing up, we can all join the good fight.

Join us.

PART ONE: POLITICS

The Democrat Party is a house of cards and one strong gust of wind will take them down.
*– **Morgan Brittany***

1

WHAT IS A "CONSERVATIVE"?

by Sonya Sasser

Since the beginning of the 2016 GOP primary, many Americans have been debating the true meaning of Conservatism. Not only that, but some are also debating whether or not Conservatism even has a place in the United States anymore, much less a home in the Republican party. Needless to say, many Constitutional Conservatives are feeling as though they are in exile.

To truly understand Conservatism is to recognize that its voice is the very conscience of America and the distinct alarm that sounds when we begin to deviate from the core principles that made our nation so exceptional. Without Conservatism to remind of us our core (Judeo-Christian) values, the United States would not only morph into a dark and empty shell of her former self, but the absence of her light would cause the rest of the world to thrust into great darkness and extreme chaos.

Conservatives recognize that the United States is indeed that "shining city on a hill," as President Ronald Reagan used to infamously describe.

As Senator Ben Sasse [1] so eloquently defined Conservatism:

> *"America is the most exceptional nation in the history of the world because the U.S. Constitution is the best political document that's ever been written. Because it says something different than almost any people and any government has believed in human history. Most governments in the past have said "Might makes right," and "The king has all the power and the people are dependent subjects."*

And the American Founders said, "No, God gives us rights by nature and government is just our shared project to secure those rights." Government is not the author or source of our rights. We don't 'make America great again' by giving more power to one guy in Washington, D.C., We make America great again by recovering a Constitutional Republic where Washington is populated by people who are servant-leaders who want to return power to the people and to the communities."

Contrary to modern-day Progressives, Conservatives hold steadfastly to the idea that power ultimately belongs to the people (not any king), and that our government was an institution established by God to be a servant that helps secure the God-given rights of its citizens (which include "Life, Liberty, and the pursuit of Happiness").

Conservatives recognize the entire purpose of government is to protect the most precious human rights that are given to people by their Creator ("endowed by their Creator with certain unalienable rights"), according to the Declaration of Independence upon which this country was founded, and they sound the alarm when government begins to forget its own purpose.

So, it comes as no surprise when power-hungry politicians attempt to silence the Conservative voice.

Sonya Sasser is a National Spokesperson for PolitiChicks, along with owners Ann-Marie Murrell and Morgan Brittany. Sonya has gathered enormous amounts of research for PolitiChicks.com and has conducted exclusive interviews with many conservative activists and authors. Sonya is a Christian, a wife, a mother, a registered dietitian, and a fashion and fitness guru. If you ask Sonya why she spends so much time on the political battlefield, her response will most certainly be, "I do it for my children."

2
"DON'T DRINK THE KOOL-AID!" STUDY OF AN AMERICAN SOCIALIST

by Ann-Marie Murrell

This man was all about "the People" and began his career as a community organizer.

Despite greatly benefiting from it, he despised capitalism and denigrated "millionaires and billionaires". He gathered the trust of the poor and oppressed by claiming he was a religious man. Only after establishing their trust and devotion did he admit he was an atheist. [2]

Democrat politicians and dignitaries lauded him, including California Governor Jerry Brown, San Francisco Mayor Willie Brown, Walter Mondale, gay activist Harvey Milk, and former first lady Rosalynn Carter, all of whom either donated money or attended testimonial dinners for him.

He claimed in a sermon that Jesus was a communist.

He was friend to many of the United States' worldwide enemies, including the Nation of Islam, communist leaders, dictators and terrorists like Angela Davis. In fact he was once described as a combination of "Martin King, Angela Davis, Albert Einstein...Chairman Mao."

He was an excellent fundraiser and collected money from people throughout the world.

He hired media specialists to dispute any negative allegations made against him, including rumors that he was gay.

He idolized Mao Zedong and carefully studied how Mao was able to overthrow the Chinese government.

No, he's not Bernie Sanders, Barack Obama, or any number of progressives in America today; he was "Don't Drink the Kool-Aid" Jim Jones, founder of the Peoples Temple and the leader of one of the largest mass-suicides in history.

Jim Jones was obsessed with creating a 'socialistic utopia'

in America and he realized the easiest way to manipulate the masses was by infiltrating religion. "How can I demonstrate my Marxism? The thought was, infiltrate the church," Jones said, [3] and soon after he created The Peoples Temple Christian Church Full Gospel. At a time when segregation was still occurring in America, Jones' church was interracial and attracted thousands of poor and disadvantaged people.

After Jones was given tax-exemption status for his Peoples Temple church, he began openly telling outsiders that he was an atheist and communist. He admitted in an article that he had learned the way to achieve social change through Marxism in the United States was to "mobilize people through religion." In one of his California sermons, Jones said, "If you're born in capitalist America, racist America, fascist America, then you're born in sin. But if you're born in socialism, you're not born in sin."

Jim Jones' ultimate goal—much like the organizers of Occupy Wall Street–was to create a 'socialist utopia' in the U.S. but when he realized that wasn't going to happen, he moved to a strip of land in Guyana which he renamed "Jonestown". Everything finally came crashing down when Jones learned that California Congressman Leo Ryan was coming to Guyana to investigate Jonestown for possible human rights violations. Jones ordered some of his followers to murder Rep. Ryan, three journalists and a defecting Temple member [4] in an ambush on a Port Kaituma airstrip. Backed into a corner, the master manipulator convinced his followers to participate in a "revolutionary suicide" by drinking cyanide-laced grape Flavor-Aide. Jones had borrowed the term by Black Panther leader and Peoples Temple supporter Huey P. Newton [5] who said, "the slow suicide of life in the ghetto ought to be replaced by revolutionary struggle that would end only in victory (socialism and self determination) or revolutionary suicide (death)."

On November 18, 1978, 909 inhabitants of Jonestown, 303 of them children, were found dead in and around a pavilion, including Jones who had died from a self-inflicted gunshot to the head. The Jonestown suicides were the greatest single loss of American civilian life in a non-natural disaster until the 9/11 attacks.

"We didn't commit suicide; we committed an act of revolutionary suicide protesting the conditions of an inhumane world," Jones said in a tape recording made during the event.

In 2010 Jim Jones' adopted son, Jim Jones, Jr. was on the Oprah Winfrey show. [6] He said, "I'm part of an organization that tried to build a new world. Nine hundred people died, and I miss them every day. But I also recognize that they tried. They tried something—they failed horrifically—but they tried, and out of that, I've taken a lot of pride to realize that I'm Jim Jones Jr. I can't hide from that."

Ann-Marie Murrell is the creator, owner, and Editor-in-Chief of PolitiChicks.com. She was the recipient of Front Page Magazine's Glazov Gang Ronald Reagan Award and is co-author of the bestselling book, "What Women (Really) Want". Ann-Marie is a regular on talk radio and has appeared on dozens of television shows including Fox & Friends, Hannity, the Dr. Phil Show, The Mike Huckabee Show, Lou Dobbs, C-SPAN, Stuart Varney & Company, Newsmax TV, CNN, MSNBC, and more.

3

THE DEMOCRAT PARTY
IS A HOUSE OF CARDS

by Morgan Brittany

With the chaos continually surrounding Hillary Clinton—either for her missing emails, Benghazi, or the Clinton Foundation antics – throughout the Democrat presidential primary of 2016 the party looked like an anthill that had been stepped on and the ants were left scattering. Progressive pundits, news organizations and Washington insiders scrambled to put out the perpetual fires surrounding their only hope for 2016, Queen Hillary. Even Hollywood began to abandon her. According to Newsmax,[7] during the primary top donors like Norman Lear and others were speaking out about looking elsewhere to put their support for 2016.

It was almost comical how desperate Hillary supporters became, trying to defend the indefensible. They made excuses for the private server, the deleted emails, and the fact that *she decided* what was going to be turned over to the state department along with everything else that she lied about. They didn't even go near the Clinton Foundation scandal in order to keep it away from the media's full attention.

So why are Democrats always in such a panic mode? The eye-opening fact occurred in 2016 when Hillary Clinton was their only chance - their only hope, despite how they saw her position as a teetering house of cards.

The truth of the matter is that the entire Democrat Party is forever teetering on the brink of ruin. You may not know it by their bluster and noise, but it is a fact that they are not the party they once were - and much of the blame goes to the Clintons and Barack Obama.

Look at the other two candidates they put up for the 2016 presidential primary: Self-avowed communist Bernie Sanders, and Governor of Maryland, Martin O'Malley (who?). You can see that when they show their cards, they've got nothin'.

But after such a disastrous, eye-opening presidential primary, the die-hard Democrat unions, with their tactics of strong-arming and voter fraud, and even the media, began to silently panic over the realization that the tide is turning.

Bottom line, the Democrat Party is looking old and tired. They are parading out the same old faces, the same old talking points, the same old tired attacks against the Republicans and people are done with it. Not only that, but the same old strategy of lying over and over again and hoping the American people won't notice is grating on everyone's nerves.

People are fed up with the Brian Williams media types re-inventing their own history to make themselves more important. They are tired of the Clintons and Obamas who think that they are above the law and entitled to different treatment than everyone else. They are done with the demonization of our law enforcement agencies across this country, and they are sick to death of American citizens taking a back seat to people who break the law, come here illegally and reap the rewards of our tax dollars—and all of this is brought to you by the Democrat Party.

In fact, the entire party is skating on thin ice and they better wake up. Don't they see that Al Sharpton is not an asset to them, and those old-school politicians like Nancy Pelosi and Elijah Cummings would be better off not speaking? As in ever again, anywhere, for any reason?

With Leftists at the helm, we have seen a rise in chaos around the world. Terrorism is rampant, and we don't command respect anymore. Ever since Obama made his first bow to Saudi King Abdullah, we have become weak in the eyes of the world. Putin, Iran, ISIS, they all just steam roll right over us and we do nothing. The Democrats knew that Hillary was not the answer and that she would only make things worse; but like I said, they had no one else.

The reality is, the Democrat Party is a house of cards and one strong gust of wind will take them down.

Morgan Brittany is the co-owner and a National Spokesperson for

PolitiChicks. Morgan has been a film, television and stage actress for over 50 years appearing in over 150 television shows including the original cast of "Dallas". Morgan has been married for 31 years and has 2 children. In 2001, she became one of the first openly outspoken conservatives in Hollywood. She has appeared many times on Sean Hannity's Great American Panel for Fox News, Dennis Miller's television show, and many conservative TV and radio programs across the country.

4
CLARIFYING PARTY BRANDING
FOR THE POLITICALLY CONFUSED

by Leslie Deinhammer

For the casual observer of news, navigating the political landscape has proven increasingly difficult with the influx of modern day semantics. Political parties, it seems, rebrand themselves with every 24-hour news cycle. Liberals call themselves progressive. The self-proclaimed and open-minded call themselves independents. Conservatives come with qualifiers – their conservatism is either fiscal or social. Republicans are too busy posturing over who is the next Ronald Reagan to redefine.

Identifying party affiliation begins to get truly difficult when liberals and conservatives cajole under the cloak of moderateness for fear of being labeled either fringe, extreme or radical. Party identity proves to be quite confusing for the apolitical.

Newscasts are littered with a hodgepodge of swappable names – Blue Dog Democrat, Tea Partier, Centrist, Libertarian, and other nomenclatures. News outlets make the assumption that viewers are well versed enough in the political landscape to decipher revolving party definitions. Outlets opt to gloss over party complexities without clarity or consideration for viewer confusion.

For the record, here are the definitions:

Blue Dog Democrats [8] are southern state Democrats with a Conservative voting record.

Tea Partiers [9] are limited government proponents who favor responsible taxation.

Centrists [10] are interchangeable with **Moderates**. [11] Moderates, who in theory oppose extreme views or actions, often align with their Centrist colleagues, who propose policy that fit the current need, to advocate for votes in the interest of political expediency rather than in the interests of their constituents (i.e., budget legislation).

Libertarians [12] are for individual liberties, including more lenient drug policy, and free markets.

Party committee chairs go to great lengths to frame their brands to escape the negative stereotypes that accompany them. Branding matters, even in the political realm.

For example, Republicans would rather not be branded as bigoted, callous or arcane.

Many in the Party have come to the realization that if their brand cannot be resuscitated, it must be rebranded or scratched entirely. In the hopes of appearing more lucid like their progressive counterparts, those wise to the stereotypical negativity are leaving the Party in droves for Libertarian pastures.

With the political landscape in a constant state of flux, new, fresh voices emerge; each jockeying to redefine the Party brand under his or her leadership. With focus on more centralized government with the onset on mandated healthcare and increased social spending, President Obama transformed President Clinton's center left Democrat Party hard left. [13]

Having determined the changing hands of leadership as the definitive factor in Party affiliation, brand and direction, deciphering the labyrinth of the political spectrum still projects to be complex in perpetuity. Deciphering party direction proves even more daunting during the election cycle when candidates seek to appear more populist than partisan.

Politics have become more about branding Parties, issues and personalities, than about policy. Intricacies of issue stance have become increasingly inconsequential to the larger brand and are often lost in its shadow. Consumers have their favorite brands and are often loyal to them. The campaign consulting class banks on it.

Leslie Deinhammer is a writer, chaplain, and proud wife of a Marine Corps veteran. Leslie writes on topics of politics, human rights and faith.

5
CLINTONS: LIVING ABOVE THE LAW IN AMERICA

by Becky Noble

One of the many beautiful things about America is that the law of the land is just that. No matter if you are the CEO of a million dollar company down to the janitor at that million-dollar company. We fought a war for this very principle. Before America's independence from Britain, if you committed a crime or some other infraction, and you were a good buddy of the King, chances are that things would go a lot easier for you than if you were just the average tricorner-wearing colonist.

Since the founding of the nation, even with that idea for the most part in place, there have always been a handful of well-connected people who always seem to slide by, to skate. Are they that charming, are they expert manipulators of the truth, do they know the right people, or all of the above?

Over the years we have learned that the dubious system is firmly in place, and if your name happens to be Clinton - doesn't matter if it is Bill or Hillary - the sky's the limit and the world is your oyster.

It is not a new phenomenon. Long before the couple from Hope, Arkansas enchanted the nation, the citizens of Arkansas were well acquainted with the "legal and otherwise" escapades of the Clintons. [16] From the bungled Whitewater land deal, to Hillary's cattle futures windfall, to those long searched for Rose Law Firm records (which just POOF, appeared out of nowhere in the White House), the close inner circle made sure that no Clinton would ever be held accountable for any questionable activity.

When Bill Clinton became president, the cycle continued, and with the assistance of an always-willing liberal media, the Clintons would be investigated, questioned, and interviewed. But the long arm of the law never seemed to be long enough to ensnare that crafty duo.

Then came the night of September 11, 2012 when the U.S. Consulate in Benghazi Libya was attacked by terrorists. Four people, including a United States Ambassador, were killed. The Obama administration, with Hillary Clinton as Secretary of State, told the world the "spontaneous" attack is because of an offensive YouTube video. Years later we learned that virtually everything Americans were told about the attack was a lie. We also learned that not only was Hillary Clinton using unsecured servers to send and receive sensitive classified information, she lied repeatedly and ad nauseum about it all. The entire case was handed over to the FBI, but despite possible multiple felonies committed the FBI dropped the case and Hillary became the Democrat presidential nominee. Once again, a Clinton skated beyond the law.

So let's review. Over time we have learned that the concept of *equal treatment under the law* does not apply if you are a Clinton. FBI Director James Comey [17] all but told us that if this were any other American, they would have surely earned themselves an orange jumpsuit. But not Hillary. Not only does Hillary get away with anything/everything because of her name, she *expects* to be above the law.

Sadly, when you lose one of the basic tenets your society was founded upon, why would you not assume others are to follow?

The American people have watched Bill and Hillary Clinton wiggle out of every bit of legal mayhem that has come their way, with their willing media accomplices clearing the path for them. Meanwhile, Americans are tired, fed up, and angry that the Clinton double standard has been proven true for decades.

It is clear that the Clintons will not go away quietly; in fact, they seem gleeful in all they've been able to accomplish, legal or not. It is a crime spree that needs to come to an end.

***Becky Noble** is a Blogger, Writer, and radio talk show host in St. Louis Missouri. She writes two of her own blogs and hosts her own Internet talk show, "Conservative Cauldron Radio" on BlogTalkRadio.com. She is married to Randy, who is an author, and they are the parents of Jezzie, a 50lb Border collie who thinks their house is hers.*

6

THE APOLOGY DEMOCRATS OWE AMERICA

by Monty Morton

As a young boy growing up in the 1950's and 60's, I remember hearing about how my maternal Grandfather, in the early 1900's, came to America through Ellis Island. As I grew up, I was fortunate to have two living Grandparents; however, my Grandfather was a stoic individual, an immigrant from Russia, uneducated, but with strong hands and a will to succeed. He truly was the quintessential immigrant; a man who felt that America afforded him an opportunity that if he worked hard, he could make his way in life. He believed in the common man, and my Grandfather was a common person - a housepainter.

Grandpa saw America as a country with mutual obligations. Long before JFK's iconic statement of "Ask not what your country can do for you, ask what you can do for your country," my Grandfather knew that if he took care of his family, he was also making a contribution to this new land. Yet, being the 'common man' that he was, he identified with a political party that also was for the 'common man.' Grandpa was a Democrat. My Grandfather was so much a Democrat that when Franklin Roosevelt died, he broke down and cried.

But something happened; Grandpa's America was changing, and changing fast. In 1964 Lyndon Johnson announced his 'Great Society.' It was a laudable objective, a plan whose goal was to eliminate poverty and racial injustice. There were new programs that addressed education, medical care, poverty, urban issues, and the like. In 1965 the poverty rate in America was at about 14%. According to the U.S. Census Bureau, the poverty rate in 2014 was...wait for it...14%! Nothing has changed. In the 50 years since LBJ's pronouncement, depending on which statistic is used, America has spent between $15 and $20 Trillion Dollars combating the War on Poverty. According to the Heritage Foundation, the money spent of The War on Poverty is three times the cost of all U.S. Military Wars since the

American Revolution.

By no means am I being dismissive as to goals of those programs, however politicians soon learned that if you throw money at people, 'you have voters for life!" It begs the obvious question, "Has America betrayed Blacks and the poor?" Perhaps the worst thing about it is that most poor people are just having a hard time, and looking for a little help to make life easier for themselves and their families. However, between being poor, failing schools, and some cities overrun with crime, it's no wonder that life for these people is tough. Little do these people realize that the 'progressive help' they are being offered is akin to a drug dealer offering free samples.

In 2010, Mayor Cory Booker of Newark, New Jersey, a city stricken with failing schools and poverty, got a pledge of $100 Million from Mark Zuckerberg to fix the schools. In the first two years, $20 Million had been spent on Unions, consultants and activists. According to a New Yorker article, the principal of Central High, and a Councilman, became the leading opponents. They were able to convince parents that white people were trying to take their city back, and that charter schools were the same as colonizing. It was the same year that the union demanded $31 Million in back pay for the two years teachers worked without raises, plus another $41 Million had to be set aside for a principal's contract and other labor expenses. It's a sad story. It shows how poverty-crime cities are stuck. It's tragic because those opponents knew that Charter Schools would be good, but put their own interests and the dependency of others first. It gets worse.

What do Detroit, Baltimore, Milwaukee, St. Louis, New York, Chicago, and Gary, Indiana have in common? Those cities are among the cities with the highest homicide, murder and crime rates along with the higher than average incidences of poverty. Since 1962, those cities have had 42 Democratic Mayors, and only three Republican Mayors. It has been the policies of the left e.g. the expansion of welfare, class dependency, and an implosion of the family unit that has led to the crime and joblessness. For example, welfare pays for girls to have babies out of wedlock. According to NBC News "Women's

Health," 72% of black women who have babies are unwed mothers. In the larger cities like New York, Baltimore, and D.C., being on welfare is equivalent to earning between $10.90 and $14.00 an hour. When Obama eased the 'work requirements' for Welfare, something that Bill Clinton tightened up, Obama made people more dependent, and ensured more votes for the Democrat Party.

It's apparent that wherever liberal policies have proliferated, even among able-bodied people, misery and dependency follows.

Democrats owe America an apology, but I don't think that will ever happen. Perhaps if Grandpa were alive, he might get an apology.

Monty Morton, upon receiving his degree from UCLA, began a 40 plus year career in the Financial Services Industry. In 1989, he co-founded a full service Pension Consulting Firm. Monty has been a keynote speaker at industry events, lectured, and has taught Personal Finance at a local College. Along with his real estate partner, Monty developed the first 'High-End' residential retirement hotel in the San Fernando Valley. Monty is now retired, lives with his wife of 45 years in Agoura Hills, California, and has eleven grandchildren.

PART TWO: HISTORY

Washington's ragtag American army was certainly a tireless minority. It was outnumbered, outmanned, and out-resourced by the most powerful military in the world. Yet, it eventually prevailed. Not to mention the fact that these irate men had a damn good General. – **Sonya Sasser**

1
HISTORY IS CHANGED BY THE FEW

by Sheri Sharp

Throughout the 2016 presidential primaries, conservatives and constitutionalists have wrangled with the stark reality that true conservatism is relegated to the minority in this country – at least for the time being. On the Democrat side, Hillary Clinton is a staunch progressive with absolutely no ideals remotely construed as conservative. Donald Trump had little history of promoting conservative ideals and principles.

Throughout the eight years of perhaps the most anti-American Presidential Administration in U.S. history, we experienced a stagnant economy and a doubling of federal debt. Internationally, we witnessed chaos and newly emboldened adversaries. Domestically, we faced a fire-hose of outrageous political correctness and progressive agendas that take the place of morality, decency, privacy, and common sense.

We live in tumultuous times, and our country strays further from both its founding principles and individual freedom. However, neither leading Presidential candidate is the antidote for what ails us. Make no mistake; the cause of the slippery slope we find ourselves on is a complete and often contemptuous disregard for the intent and meaning of our Constitution — by many leaders and some citizens.

Dennis Prager wrote, [1] *"...America was founded to be an idea, not another country". In the same article, Prager also cited Margaret Thatcher: "Europe was created by history. America was created by philosophy".* As conservatives, we cannot be deterred when teaching the philosophy of this country's founding. It is clear that neither major political party today represents conservatives or the Constitution. Conservatism appears to be the only political philosophy in America today that wholly supports and represents the Constitution.

The philosophy of America, envisioned by our Founders, is limited government, freedom, all men being created equal, unalienable (God-given) rights, separation of powers, and the notion of a government receiving its powers from the consent of the governed. Calvin Coolidge, in a speech [2] on the 150th anniversary of the Declaration of Independence in 1926, emphasized the anti-Constitutional and anti-American ideals of progressivism. Coolidge said, *"If all men are created equal, that is final. If they are endowed with inalienable rights, that is final. If governments derive their just power from the consent of the governed, that is final. No advance, no progress can be made beyond these propositions. If anyone wishes to deny their truth and their soundness, the only direction in which he can proceed historically is not forward, but backward toward the time when there was no equality, no rights of the individual, no rule of the people. Those who wish to proceed in that direction cannot lay claim to progress. They are reactionary."*

Unfortunately, Coolidge's assessment in the denial of our founding truths is upon us. Progressives are not making "progress"; they are moving us backwards and claiming it to be "progress". They are driving America toward the ever-changing and chaotic ideas of man, and away from the unalienable rights from God. They are not making us "equal" nor do they intend to produce equal opportunity. Rather, they force changes in behavior and even thought with legal strong-arm tactics that end up making some more equal than others.

With Obama as the nominal head of this progressive philosophy, the people no longer rule. We witness almost weekly examples of government over-reach and illegal use of Presidential authority. We live in a time where more and more Americans look to the government to solve their problems, to eradicate speech and actions they oppose, and to supply their every need. Too many appear willing to give up their freedom in return.

Our nation was not founded on the idea that citizens should look to government to solve their problems or to silence those they oppose. They sought to create a nation of citizens who have equal opportunities, not equal outcomes. They understood and advocated that God created our rights, not man. The honorable Justice Janice Rodgers Brown said [3] in her

Heritage Foundation-sponsored 2015 Joseph Story lecture:

"So we must ask ourselves: What were the ingredients of that mortar, that binding spell, that gave us statesmen like Adams and Madison, judges like Marshall and Story, and presidents like Washington and Lincoln? What made America possible and limited government conceivable? And can we, a polity so greatly changed, recapture the optimism and certitude of the Founders in a world of Big Government and judge-made rights none of them could have imagined? Or was a republic peopled by free men a naïve and childish dream to which we wiser, more sophisticated grown-ups should bid good riddance? Though America seemed a miracle, was it only a product of its time, destined to fail as the sensibilities that produced it faded from the national conscience?"

The principles of our nation's founding were neither childish nor naïve, and I'm sure Justice Rodgers would agree. We know that maintaining freedom has always been difficult, and sometimes must be fought for against great opposition. This is where we conservatives and Constitutionalists are today! We are fighting against two parties that sometimes speak of the Constitution, but seem unaware of what it really says.

I passed a local church near my home just the other day. The front sign read: "History is Changed by The Few". We are the few. As conservatives, championing our Constitution and freedom is our role, and I believe that our time in history has come.

Sheri Sharp is a busy stay-at-home mom with a professional background in Telecommunications Executive Management. Sheri attended the University of Oklahoma where she earned a Bachelor of Science degree in Electrical Engineering and received her Masters of Business Administration degree from Oklahoma City University. Sheri is married to a retired US Navy Officer (Carrier-Based Aircraft) and has two daughters that keep her busy.

2

"LIBERTY ONCE LOST, IS GONE FOREVER"

by Carolyn Elkins

"History has informed us that bodies of men, as well as individuals, are susceptible of the spirit of tyranny." Thomas Jefferson [4]

"There is danger from all men. The only maxim of a free government ought to be to trust no man living with power to endanger the public liberty." John Adams [5]

So much happened during the 8 years of the Obama administration that it sometimes became overwhelming. As a writer, when I have a hard time expressing myself politically I turn to those whose wisdom exceeds my own. I also tend to look critically at myself. I don't hold any fancy titles or have multiple diplomas hanging on my walls; I'm a stay at home mom trying to raise her child the best I can. I also wasn't born in America; I've actually only been a legal citizen for a short time. So how is it that an ordinary, average person has the right to lecture those who have Ivy League backgrounds, or have lived their entire lives in America?

What I have – what all Americans have - is a great burden for this country and for the people who have given so much to preserve her. Not just our men and women in uniform (although they are never far from my heart and thoughts) but also all people who care about this country.

That being said, it's difficult to understand how people who profess to love America can elect (and reelect) politicians who want to transform her. Or perhaps worse, when they don't care who they elect as long as there is something in it for them. And how many politicians truly love America? It seems too many have made politics their lifelong career and care more about their prestige than they do about keeping their oaths to uphold and protect the Constitution...the Law of this country.

A poll [6] conducted a few years ago showed that only half of protestant pastors have a Biblical worldview. They didn't believe in doctrines such as the sinless nature of Jesus, the literal existence of Satan, the omnipotence and omniscience of God, salvation by grace alone, and the personal responsibility to evangelize. How can someone follow a calling to do something they don't even understand or believe in? It is much the same with politicians and their electorate who perpetually keep them in office.

Over the past few years as a political researcher/writer, I've come to understand that today's problems in America stem from two sources: a lack of belief and a lack of historical understanding of America.

America's very foundation was built upon these words from the Mayflower Compact: [7] **"For the Glory of God, and Advancement of the Christian Faith."** If one is to read the Colonial compacts [8], early government charters, codes and covenants, one would see that Biblical belief and the ideas of freedom are reiterated throughout all of these documents. The men who founded America knew of and held true to the Biblical ideals and freedoms in the Magna Carta [8] as well. Many claim that the Founding Fathers were Deists at most, but looking at their words–not only the Declaration of Independence and Constitution, but also their private words, letters and speeches– we know that these men clearly understood the Nature of God and His hand in the foundation of Government.

In a speech to the Constitutional Convention [9], Benjamin Franklin observed,

"I've lived, Sir, a long time, and the longer I live, the more convincing Proofs I see of this Truth — That God governs in the Affairs of Men. And if a sparrow cannot fall to the ground without his Notice, is it probable that an Empire can rise without his Aid? We have been assured, Sir, in the Sacred Writings, that except the Lord build the House they labor in vain who build it. I firmly believe this, — and I also believe that without his concurring Aid, we shall succeed in this political Building no better than the Builders of Babel: We shall be divided by our little partial local interests; our Projects will be confounded, and we ourselves shall

22

become a Reproach and Bye word down to future Ages..."

God is mentioned four times in the Declaration of Independence:

He is Nature's God, Maker of Nature's Laws, and Legislature.

He is our Creator, our Founder.

He is Supreme Judge, and Judiciary.

He is Divine Providence, the Executive.

Our Founders knew that "Nature and Equality" could only be truly represented in a limited government, which has a separation of powers, and they knew the giver of liberty: *"God who gave us life gave us liberty."* Thomas Jefferson [10]

Again from Thomas Jefferson [11], *"That these are our grievances which we have thus laid before his majesty, with that freedom of language and sentiment which becomes a free people claiming their rights as derived from the laws of nature, and not as the gift of their chief magistrate."*

Government by consent of the governed [12] is the first guarantee of limited government and freedom, which is why We the People are meant to have power <u>over</u> those who govern us.

Our Founders knew that when people are free to pursue their own industries and secure prosperity [13] for themselves and their families, they would be vigilant about whom they elect, to ensure that the general welfare of our communities was promoted. If the general welfare of our local communities is as good as, or better than our own, we can be sure our liberties will not be restricted.

They gave us a representative Constitutional Republic [14], which would continue to give government enough power to protect our liberties, but not so much as to take them away. They knew this type of limited government with checks and balances is one in which freedom is granted to each individual and where small groups of 'nobles' or privileged class would not gain tyrannical power over the rest of the people.

The basic duties of our government are laid out in the Preamble to the Constitution: *"We the People are to have power over the government."* Our first duty was to establish justice because America is a nation of just laws as given in the

Constitution.

"Ensuring domestic tranquility" ensured that people would get along and be safe, so community laws were established to keep peace. Providing for the common defense is the main duty of the federal government. America is a sovereign nation, and our federal government is charged with ensuring the safety of the citizens by defending in cases of attack by others, or by securing and making sure people follow the laws to enter into the US.

The most misunderstood part of our Preamble is *"to promote the general welfare".* This meant that we would ensure that those who governed us would promote and protect our liberties and leave us free to pursue our goals which benefit society, and that we would hold onto these for ourselves and our children. And again from Thomas Jefferson, [15] "A rigid economy of the public contributions and absolute interdiction of all useless expenses will go far towards keeping the government honest and unoppressive."

Too many people have wrongly succumbed to the idea that government handouts are a duty of the federal government and that the government is the giver of rights.

Patrick Henry, my favorite Founding Father, once said, [16] *"Guard with jealous attention the public liberty. Suspect everyone who approaches that jewel. Unfortunately, nothing will preserve it but downright force. Whenever you give up that force, you are inevitably ruined."*

My burden is for this country that I love and call home. I see our "jewel of liberty" in danger, not only by a government out of control, but by so many who would be willing to trade it for what is offered to them in the form of government handouts. *"Dependence begets subservience and venality, suffocates the germ of virtue, and prepares fit tools for the designs of ambition."* Thomas Jefferson [17]

Our liberties and our rights are inalienable, which means they are not transferrable, can't be given away, and can't be taken. Our Freedoms, as embedded in our Bill of Rights, are God given – and our Founders knew that.

"It is the greatest absurdity to suppose it in the power of one, or any number of men, at the entering into society, to renounce their essential natural rights, or the means of preserving those rights; when the grand end of civil government, from the very nature of its institution, is for the support, protection, and defense of those very rights; the principal of which, as is before observed, are Life, Liberty, and Property. If men, through fear, fraud, or mistake, should in terms renounce or give up any essential natural right, the eternal law of reason and the grand end of society would absolutely vacate such renunciation. The right to freedom being the gift of God Almighty, it is not in the power of man to alienate this gift and voluntarily become a slave"
–Samuel Adams [18], The Rights of the Colonists, November 20, 1772

If you give the government power to grant rights, you also give them power to take those rights away. History has shown us tyrannical systems of government in which the majority was ruled over by a minority of men who decide who does and doesn't get fed. They decide who gets to work and where; who gets to keep their property, and who doesn't. Throughout the ages, millions have suffered at the hands of dictators who have the power to decide who gets to live and who dies. And yes, even in light of our own country's healthcare debates, our own leaders potentially have the power to decide who gets a lifesaving operation and who does not.

Too many people who were born in America don't realize just what a beacon of freedom our country has been to people all over the world. Millions have come to escape government tyranny and for the chance to live freely; to pursue their dreams unhindered and live their lives without fear. People outside America understand how valuable freedom is, and so did our Founders as they broke free from tyranny themselves.

Finally, we as a free people absolutely must preserve what so many have fought and died for. Aren't those who have given, and who continue to give today, worth fighting for here on the home front?

We are Americans. Despite what anyone says, America is

and has always been exceptional. It has always been the greatest of nations. It is not simply a nation of "free stuff" - it is a nation of freedom! Do something to save this nation. Read about our Constitution [19] and why it is the most perfect political document known to man. Understand the reasons for our Declaration of Independence [20], and the intent of the founders when they formed a limited Representative Constitutional Republic.

"If virtue and knowledge are diffused among the people, they will never be enslaved.

This will be their great security." Samuel Adams [21] Or as Thomas Paine described in his essay, **The American Crisis**, [23]

"Tyranny, like hell, is not easily conquered; yet we have this consolation with us, that the harder the conflict, the more glorious the triumph. What we obtain too cheap, we esteem too lightly: it is dearness only that gives every thing its value. Heaven knows how to put a proper price upon its goods; and it would be strange indeed if so celestial an article as FREEDOM should not be highly rated."

Carolyn Elkins' articles for PolitiChicks.com have been shared by Mark Levin, NewsBusters and New Media Journal. Carolyn is a guest writer on The Right Scoop and PolitiBrew under the name American Duckie. Born in Canada, but now a proud U.S. citizen, Carolyn is the founder of the Constitutional Freedom Party, a completely grass roots organization whose foundation is on God and the Founder's intent for a Constitutional Republic.

3

THERE CAN BE NO CAPITALISM, NO REPUBLIC, WITHOUT INDEPENDENCE

by Dr. Sarah Condor

The European Union as we know it was not established until 1993 in Maastricht. You may recall that Margaret Thatcher argued strongly against it. [30] People who have opposed the current vote to exit the Union are not familiar with its history. Rather, they have been scared by the big government junkies and politicians who think the world would not turn without their treaties and agreements.

I lived and studied in England from 1990 to 1995. I visited England many times after that, especially when I worked for the European Community in Brussels in 1996-7. I was also employed by the government to teach the history and "magnificence" of the EU to the employees of the National Bank, Supreme Audit Office and other grand governmental establishments.

I also spent two years traveling and working all over England. From Newcastle to Plymouth, from Exeter to Canterbury, people were proud to be British. They absolutely hated having to abandon their currency, the Pride of their Kingdom, and submit to the government in Brussels. They were proud of their "splendid insulation," their independence from "the Continent." They would say: "That's the way we do it, not like on the Continent," placing a disparaging accent on the last word...

Subsequently, I worked in Brussels at the very core of the European Union, *Directorate Generale*. To my surprise and bewilderment, I had a very similar experience with Belgian people, who absolutely hate and detest the EU government, which, they say, sucks them dry and leaves them out – EU officials' starting salary is 3 times that of an average Belgian citizen! They travel by cabs and shop in special stores around the

EU district. Belgian people in that district are better off – from *boulangeries* to pharmacies to clothes and shoe stores... "They look down on us," my Belgian friend told me. "People like you," she continued, "they come and go, well dressed, caring nothing for what we want." How "common Americans" feel about Washington D.C. today, it seems to me, is very similar...

From the Coal and Steal Community in 1951, [31] EU has developed not just into a single market area with free movement of goods, but also into the Schengen passport-free area without borders. There is no doubt in my mind that this development (especially the 2009 Lisbon Treaty, which created a "legal personality" and a host of unelected, permanent officials, growing the government in Brussels ever larger) [32] contributed significantly to the current development. Had there been no Schengen, there would have been no Muslim Invasion.

Just like Obama in 2009, in 2012 the European Union received the Nobel Peace Prize for "having contributed to the advancement of peace and reconciliation, democracy and human rights in Europe." How absurd is this? First, they give it to a novice politician with no record of achievement but a trail of apologies, which caused the rise of Terrorism and Islamic Fascism in the world; then to a body politic (for lack of a better term) for something accomplished by FDR, Truman and Reagan (end of World War II and Cold War). Will the gathering of senile professors in Stockholm be taken by surprise when Sweden referendum falls the way the British did?

There can be no capitalism without independence. There can be no republic in a borderless world of universal socialism. The Muslim Invasion of Europe was the last straw. I am only surprised that it has taken so long...

Sarah P. Condor-Fisher, Ph.D., Esq., LL.M. grew up in communist Czechoslovakia. At 17, she was apprehended crossing the border, cross-interrogated by the KGB & jailed. She studied philosophy at University College London. She holds a BA & MA in English & a Ph.D. in American Literature & Literary Criticism. She is a practicing CA attorney with her own law firm & has published over 50 books. She is also a former Olympic swimmer, Miss World & Miss USA in natural bodybuilding (INBA).

4

THE OFFICIAL REJECTION OF THE DECLARATION OF INDEPENDENCE AND THE CONSTITUTION

by Lainie Sloane

The United States Declaration of Independence begins: When, in the course of human Events, it becomes necessary for one People to dissolve the Political Bands which have connected them with another and to assume among the Powers of the Earth, the separate and equal Station to which the Laws of Nature and of Nature's God entitle them, a decent Respect to the Opinions of Mankind requires that they should declare the causes which impel them to the Separation.

Perhaps, based upon the opening of the Declaration of Independence, could it be possible that the time has come once again for a moral people to separate themselves from the godless laws that are perverting the land?

Again, the Declaration of Independence begins: *When, in the course of human Events, it becomes necessary for one People to dissolve the Political Bands, which have connected them with another...*

What course of human events compels the division among us from the unity that has historically linked Americans as one People? Perhaps this passage from the Declaration of Independence may shed some light: *...and to assume among the Powers of the Earth, the separate and equal Station to which the Laws of Nature...*

The founding Fathers understood that there were certain natural laws or as they put it, Laws of Nature, that were self-apparent and it was based upon the establishment of these Laws of Nature, that the entire legitimacy of their secession from England was based. In other words, if something goes against nature's law, it is not a valid reason for those who would be subjugated to submit to or tolerate.

Wikipedia defines natural law as follows: Natural law, or the law of nature (Latin: *lex naturalis*), is a system of law that is purportedly determined by nature, and thus universal. Classically, natural law refers to the use of reason to analyze human nature—both social and personal—and deduce binding rules of moral behavior from it.

Therefore, our Constitution and our government stand upon the clear understanding that some things are natural laws given by ... nature's God, meaning nature's laws come from nature's God who designed a normality and properly functioning system in nature as opposed to those nonfunctioning systems which pervert the natural order of nature's law which we recognize as being unnatural (i.e., perverted).

Our Founding Fathers understood the natural order of things and credited nature's law to a Law Giver. If we deviate from the natural order and natural law, then we denounce the natural order of things in preference of unnatural or a perversion of that entity upon which our government and laws were built. By weakening that foundation and rejecting the natural order of things in favor of unnatural preferences, we doom our society, laws, government, social institutions and the reason for our existence.

Be aware America—we have crossed that path and there is no one who can defend our reluctance to continue down a path of sanity, preferring instead to travel the path of perversion to our assured demise. Regarding all earthly systems, be it forces of nature or forces of government, we are now to assume among the Powers of the Earth, the separate and equal Station to which the Laws of Nature and of Nature's God entitle them. To reject natural order and the Laws of Nature upon which our society is built, it is now shaken to its foundations, and the mortar of natural law and nature's God is quickly being eroded, thus preventing that solid base upon which no nation can flourish without.

It would behoove us to remember that the last part of our Declarations of Independence's admonishment that justifies the breakdown, or a decent Respect to the Opinions of Mankind (,) requires that they should declare the causes which impel them to the Separation (,) and that cause is brought on by the rejection of the natural order as laid out in our Constitution, but even more important, it is the profound rejection of the authority who created that natural law.

Consider this path we have chosen and realize that today we can no longer justify our independence from England based upon the Declaration of Independence and its precepts. We cannot blame anyone else for our tragedies, because it is us who have rendered the very principals upon which it exists as null and void.

It happened so subtly that few people noticed at first. Little by little, morality and freedom started to crumble. It came first in government, in education, in the media—and finally it began to shake our families and our lives.

Law and government have become the means of licensing moral perversions of all kinds. Education has become the enemy of religious truth and values. And the media have provided the means for propagating the change.

"A Christian Manifesto" is literally a call for Christians to change the course of history—by returning to biblical Truth and by allowing Christ to be Lord in all of life… –Intro to A Christian Manifesto by influential Christian thinker and author, Francis A. Schaeffer, copyright 1981.

Lainie Sloane began her grassroots political activism as a Teen Age Republican (TAR). She was awarded an Indiana Honorary Indiana Secretary of State. Lainie worked in management at Sony Pictures, Walt Disney Company, and various production companies. She co-hosted a Blog Talk Radio show, and is now an editor for AvingtonHouse Publishing. She resides in Indiana with her husband, Dr. J.P. Sloane, and their daughter, Shannon.

5
AN INTERVIEW WITH "BONHOEFFER" AUTHOR, ERIC METAXAS

by Julie Klose

On several occasions I have been asked, as a mother of three and a former pre-school teacher, why I would venture into the political blogging world. It's difficult to really put it into words but the easiest way for me to describe it is to simply mention the name of Dietrich Bonhoeffer. I began to have this pull into the political world but it wasn't until I read Eric Metaxas' book **Bonhoeffer** that I realized it was more of a calling on my life. I suddenly was completely grateful for my faith and my love for God and the freedom I was given to express this faith in America. However, at the same time I began to notice the encroaching changes in this country that were limiting this freedom. Suddenly, I saw this freedom through the eyes of my children and realized, that boldly standing up for religious liberty was important even if done simply through the blogging world.

The story of Dietrich Bonhoeffer's life has taught me the importance of religious liberty but it is also a reminder that faith in God is the cornerstone of life itself. I recently had the opportunity to interview Eric Metaxas and I am grateful for his ability to tell stories like Bonhoeffer that change hearts and minds. The following is my interview.

JK: People are really responding in a positive way to the life story of Dietrich Bonhoeffer. Through all the interviews you have done and the people you have talked to, why do you think people are resonating with his life story?

Eric Metaxas: You really need to go to my website at EricMetaxas.com because there is so much to stay about that and I say them in many different speeches. The short version is that almost everybody recognizes the parallels with what is happening now. It is shocking because I didn't put the parallels in there on purpose. The first parallel is the religious liberty issue, that you have a big state beginning to push a church around and the church never really having had to deal with that and doesn't know how to deal with it. They don't know how to stand up quickly enough and before you know it they have been neutralized and boxed out. A lot of people can see that happening here and there is a rising tide of secularism, which fundamentally violates the Founders' sacred idea of religious liberty. When that is violated all liberties are compromised. This is something people are waking up to because of the story of Bonhoeffer. Also, we need heroes and Bonhoeffer was a real hero and people want to be inspired and people are being inspired dramatically.

JK: You also wrote "Amazing Grace" about William Wilberforce and his heroic battle to end the slave trade. Both Wilberforce and Bonhoeffer were men who brought their faith outside the walls of the church to fight injustice. They were in many ways seen as radicals of their day. Do you think the church of today has lost that radical Christianity?

Eric Metaxas: I think the church of every era has lost that radical Christianity and there are people that God uses to attempt to reawaken it. There are always prophets. In the Old Testament, you have prophets calling the people of God to be the people of God. How is it that the people of God never are the people of God but in name only? But the prophetic voice comes through someone or through a number of people to wake up the church. That's exactly what Wilberforce was in his generation.

There were others but he was one of the main voices. He was speaking to a dead church across Great Britain and saying you call yourself a Christian nation and here is what it means to be Christian. He called the church to itself and in a way he called the nation to itself. Same thing with Bonhoeffer, except he was less successful and he was crying out like a Cassandra and the people did not heed his voice. I think there are voices now calling the church to wake up. I think the voice of Bonhoeffer through my book is calling the American church to wake up and stand against encroaching government.

JK: At CPAC, you outlined the importance of religious freedom in this country. You referred to the HHS mandate in requiring religious groups to provide contraceptives and abortificiants. Now we have Hobby Lobby vs. Sebelius going before the federal court. Why is it important as Christians to pay close attention to this federal case?

Eric Metaxas: This is a classic example of how we have forgotten this idea of principles. This particular case may not affect us but in the bigger picture it will affect us dramatically because it is an issue of fundamental religious liberty. If the government can push around anybody and tell them, "We don't care what you believe or what your faith teaches. We don't care, tough luck. You better do what we tell you to do', then once it starts to do that, it is game over or it's the beginning of the end of the game. Because that's what it is to be an American. That is being taken away under ridiculous pretenses.

It's amazing that the government sees an issue on their side that they think is a principle of women's rights. That's absurd! It is not women's rights, otherwise people of faith would be all for it. It's sort of sexual license and it is big government. This case and others like it are determining our future as a nation. If we don't stand up against it as one, we will rue the day that we did nothing.

JK: You also talked about the political ramifications to religious freedom in redefining marriage. Now we have bakers and wedding photographers having to choose between their faith and their convictions over their jobs and livelihoods. This is a heated debate and frankly it feels like we (Christians) are losing the battle. How do we stand up for religious liberty and traditional marriage while (to quote you from last year) "expressing the truth in civility and love"?

Eric Metaxas: We can express the truth in civility and love and people who don't like it can say that we are not expressing it in civility and love. It's really not an issue if we can convince everyone that it is in civility and love. If someone is against same sex marriage as the law of the land, which I am, do people appreciate the struggle that someone who is dealing with same sex attraction go through? Do their hearts break for someone who has to deal with that struggle? If we are not with those people appreciating that, then how can we really talk to them and cavalierly express our opinions? Our hearts have to break at the very least so that we know this is difficult for everyone.

This is not an easy thing that we can just say this is wrong and move on. Even if we differ politically, we can express that we generally do care about the struggles that people are going through. However, I do think we have to be clear about what we believe and be clear that there is religious liberty in this country and we ought not to be forced to celebrate something that we find goes against our faith.

JK: What is the biggest misconception about religious freedom in this country?

Eric Metaxas: I think most people have no idea about what religious freedom means. I barely did two years ago. It is only recently that I have had some sense of what that is. I think that is true not just about religious freedom but a lot of the things that make America what it is. We haven't had civics classes where past generations have really understood what it means to be an American. We are not familiar with these ideas, we take them for granted, and think we will always have them. Suddenly we realize they are being taken away. Well, it's because we haven't appreciated them for all these decades.

Religious liberty is misunderstood. It simply means that the Founders said that everyone in America should have the freedom to practice and exercise their religion. Not to believe it but to exercise our beliefs- to act on our beliefs. It's not about believing privately in your head, privately in that building, or simply about freedom of worship. It is freedom of religion where you can live out your faith boldly. In fact, not only do they say we should be able to do that but it is at the heart of the genius of the United States of America. If we don't have people freely acting out their beliefs, eventually that will be the end of America. Religious liberty is the salt and light that has made us the great nation we are in a whole number of ways. We have taken it for granted and we need to wake-up to what it is and we need to begin to stand against those encroachments.

(William Wilberforce, Dietrich Bonhoeffer, and many of the other people that Eric Metaxas has either written or shared about have the common theme of courage and faith. Metaxas has also demonstrated courage and faith in telling these kinds of stories. Perhaps, it is time that we live out these characteristics in our own lives and step beyond the walls of the places we worship for that truly is what religious liberty is all about.)

Julie Klose *is a freelance writer and blogger. Julie covers all topics related to US and foreign politics but is particularly passionate about social issues. She is pro-life and has interviewed different people and organizations within the pro-life movement. Julie has been featured on several radio shows for her conservative opinions.*

PART THREE: EDUCATION

There are only so many examples of curriculum that you can look at before you begin to ask the question, "Why?" Why are the powers-that-be doing this? Why have they changed the educational boundaries so much?

*– **Macey France***

In the olden days, teachers were considered among the chosen, and they were respected and treated with honor.

*– Retired teacher **Lou Ellen Brown***

1
COMMON CORE IS <u>NOT</u> ABOUT EDUCATION
PART ONE: THE CURRICULUM

by Macey France

When I first started researching the Common Core and learning about the good, the bad and the ugly, [1] I had a gnawing feeling that something wasn't right. That the Common Core was going beyond the traditional educational reform that we've seen in the past.

There are only so many examples of curriculum that you can look at before you begin to ask the question, "Why?" Why are the powers-that-be doing this? Why have they changed the educational boundaries so much?

Let me introduce you to one of the ladies I am blessed to know here in Oregon. Lidia Larson is a mom who is fighting the Common Core like me. The difference between Lidia and myself is that she has the patience and wherewithal to do the research beyond the normal human capacity to do it. She spends countless hours chasing that "why?" question until she gets the answer.

Lidia discovered a very helpful website that has shown us a lot of answers. The name of this site is Invisible Serf's Collar. [2] The author also wrote a book documenting education's evolution and all of the reforms that have come and gone and failed. I highly recommend reading this book, which the author put on hold so she could blog about the events of the Common Core initiative, real time. The book's title is, ***Credentialed to Destroy: How and Why Education Became a Weapon***. [3]

You do not need to read the blog or the book to follow this series I am going to be writing but it will give you a rich historical sense and an idea of why our search began heading in a different direction. My intention is to draw out the picture of why many others and I are saying that the Common Core is not about education. At the end of the series you can decide what you think it's about but I guarantee you the answer will not be that it is about education.

Due to Lidia's determination to find the answers we now have the documents that lay it all out directly from the mouths of the people in charge.

I will begin with the curriculum that we have begun to see in the form of worksheets and materials that make it home and the assessments the kids will be taking.

I've always maintained that the Common Core Standards are ambiguous at best and confusing to boot. Why would you want a child to come to the conclusion that 4 x 3 = 11? Why would you want a very young child to be reading complex informational text and then answer questions about that text that are almost unanswerable. This kind of ambiguity is done on purpose. Don't think there is single thing the people who are in charge of this mess are doing that is *not* intentional.

Why would you want to constantly bombard a child with ambiguous and tenuous situations? The simplest answer is probably the correct one and that would be that by introducing them to these untenable situations you are at the very least, getting them comfortable with the ambiguity.

Putting aside the fact that the questions are asking kids to infer what an author was intending, which is ridiculous, let's focus on the answers provided.

After reading the Smarter Balanced Assessment sample test for English Language Arts for the 6th grade, the first question I can argue is that any one of the answers they provide is correct. So how are these things going to be graded? Is each answer worth a certain amount of points? I don't believe that you have to pick the exact right answer. I believe they are trying to see how a child's mind works. The answer a student picks says a lot about the way their brain is making connections, no?

Isn't that what they mean when they talk about "dispositions"? Have no doubt that is the aim here. To see how the child answers and what part of the brain they are using for this "higher order thinking." These are just two of the things you will hear about in the Common Core standards. We need to promote critical thinking and higher order thinking. What you may not see is the part about dispositions. I will unveil that further in another article.

For now keep in mind that dispositions are defined as "'mindsets (sometimes referred to as behaviors, capacities, or habits of mind) that are closely associated with success in college and career." Higher order thinking [4] is defined as "*critical, logical, reflective, metacognitive, and creative thinking whose processes are activated by when the individual encounters unfamiliar problems, uncertainties, questions or dilemmas.*"

If you read this piece put out by the Harvard Graduate School of Education [5] you will see what I am talking about: "*The Common Core will mean fewer "bubble tests" and more performance tasks that require analysis and reasoning.*" – See here, we are not just asking a child to pick an answer and it is either right or wrong. We want a peek at how their brain works and how they got to that answer.

Another quote: "*These expectations are aimed at ensuring that all students develop the knowledge, skills, and **dispositions** they need to succeed in the global economy and society...*" (Emphasis added by author.)

How do they measure what a child's disposition is, I ask? By giving curriculum and assessments created to measure how a child thinks rather than whether or not they have gotten the correct answer or learned any real content.

The Common Core goes much deeper than just curriculum. While the curriculum is a small part of the puzzle, it is a very important part.

If a student works on traditional mathematical algorithms and learns the black and white rules of punctuation and grammar for English Language Arts then their brains are receiving information and filing it away to be used in the future, perhaps even to be recalled when doing a traditional assessment. The horror!

In reading the book I mentioned above you will see the aim is to use the part of the brain that bypasses rational or analytical thought in favor of an emotional response not based on facts.

The ambiguous questions are to see what concepts the

brain falls back on, and to fully ensure that a child is thinking "properly" and using parts of the brain that the educrats want to be used, they must be immersed in this curriculum.

Macey France *is considered one of the nation's leading experts on all-things-Common Core. She is the co-founder of* **Stop Common Core in Oregon***, working with parents to teach & promote advocacy for their children's education. Macey has spoken about Common Core for various news outlets across the nation & her PolitiChicks article about* **The Bluest Eye** *was discussed on a panel on Al Jazeera America and was nominated for a CPAC Blogger Award. Macey is a wife and stay at home mom of two boys.*

2
COMMON CORE IS NOT ABOUT EDUCATION
PART TWO: BEHAVIORS

by Macey France

States had to jump through many hoops to be able to apply for Race to the Top funding. [6] Of course we know that one of those things was the disastrous Common Core.

If you read your state's Race to the Top application you might not have noticed a small part about behavior systems. In order to apply for the funding from the federal government your state had to implement a Positive Behavior Intervention and Support system, or PBIS. [7]

Every school that receives federal dollars had to make sure that they had the proper behavioral system in place. These behavioral systems include names that you may have heard before.

Of course, some schools have been using a form of PBIS for years, but the government wanted to make sure that *all* schools were using behavioral intervention systems. The easiest way to do that is to tie it to funding.

Or, if you're Barack Obama, you can use your phone and pen and make it an executive order. That's right. He did. [8]

According to NASP Resources [9] the whole PBIS system is based on the theory of behaviors and keeping track of them all the way through to outcomes: *"PBS plans are **individualized** and **data-based** and include procedures for monitoring, evaluating and reassessing the process."*

For someone who has been reading a lot about "individualized learning" and "individual determination" and knows the amount of data collected on students these days, that sentence is very frightening.

An interesting document you can download and read is A K-12 Federal Policy Framework for Competency Education, [10] put together by Competency Works, a part of Knowledge Works.

So we have schools recording behaviors of the child. If they are good, bad or indifferent it all goes into a database. This information goes to the state and then on to the federal government.

Why does the federal government give a hoot about how your child behaves in the classroom? Perhaps they figure they have "invested" money through the Race to the Top grant and want to see the return on their "investment?"

You give a child ambiguous curriculum and watch how it affects their minds. You then assess the way the child's brain processes that curriculum and what it says about their values, behaviors and beliefs.

And we know this is true and is absolutely the goal of PBIS, Common Core, and all the data collected because we found a man named David T. Conley. [11]

Conley is the man responsible for the definition of College and Career Readiness that the Common Core so proudly touts. In fact, Conley's organization, Educational Policy Improvement Center or EPIC, [12] received grants from none other than the Bill and Melinda Gates Foundation [13] to work on this definition and all the trappings therein. He also heads up the Innovation Lab Network, or ILN, [9] that is a project of the Council of Chief State School Officers. The states currently involved with ILN include: California, Iowa, Kentucky, Maine, New Hampshire, Ohio, Oregon, West Virginia and Wisconsin.

EPIC even has a page devoted to something called "metacognition." [14] They do much work in this area. Some valuable information to be found on EPIC's website [15] include:

Metacognitive Learning Skills refer to any student--level variable that is not subject-specific (e.g., math, science, or reading), including:

1. Personality and motivational factors;
2. Experiential and contextual intelligence;
3. Social skills and interests; and
4. Adjustment and student perceptions.

Another fascinating tidbit:

"...Need to know much more about how students manage the learning process, and how their beliefs about themselves as learners affect their ability to understand and retain content knowledge. By elevating noncognitive information to an equal position relative to content knowledge, we may find the missing link needed to close the achievement gap more rapidly and effectively for the many students who possess the cognitive ability to improve their capacity to learn, but are limited by a lack of effective learning strategies and the appropriate mindset. As a first step down this road, educators, researchers, and policy leaders must be willing to rename "noncognitive measures" as "metacognitive learning skills."

To the average reader that bolded sentence might seem like an awesome idea. Let's dig into kids' brains and see what behaviors and values make them tick so we can close that achievement gap. That's probably why they bolded it. That way you really focus on what they see as "good."

To someone seasoned in reading the things that are not supposed to stand out as much this sentence is much more telling: "educators, researchers, and policy leaders must be willing to rename "noncognitive measures" as "metacognitive learning skills."

Why rename it? Could it possibly have anything to do with the fact that educated people might read it for what it actually is, a way to get inside the student's brains and see what the very essence of who they are is and how that was formed? Can you say creepy with a capitol C?

If not, then visit the EPIC website for some major goose bumps. [16] It outlines things that are to be watched, learned about, and monitored on our children. A small disclaimer at the bottom notes, *"Our definition of metacognition includes thinking skills that are not specifically content-based."* Basically almost everything mentioned are things that I see as something the school really has no right to teach. They are things children should be learning at home from their families. Values and expectations at home are more important to my children then what is expected at school, although school would have you believe differently.

The Social & Personal Responsibility heading is another interesting tidbit. In all of the documents we have found we noticed that they constantly use the term College, Career and Citizenship ready. That's right. You can see above they want your child to be citizenship ready. They want to direct students to become environmental granola kids! And they better be volunteering at the local Planned Parenthood, too.

Resource Utilization clearly came from Linda Darling-Hammond [17] who said at one time that the object of education is to teach students how to utilize the government programs available to them.

Do you think that message is too clear to send to the parents? They probably don't want parents to realize that they want the kids to develop into their idea of what a citizen should look like so they cut that all-important "Citizenship" off and just call it College and Career Ready. Yet it remains in all of the documents that outline their plans.

Who needs to learn content?? 2+2=4 and America became a country in 1776 are examples of content a kid might learn in school. Conley must guffaw over that one! Why do kids need to know this? Why do we need to teach this? According to EPIC, we really don't! Learning valuable content has nothing to do with gauging attitudes, behaviors and beliefs, now does it?

And just to be clear that none of this is just "theory" I will tell you that we uncovered a presentation that Conley made to the Oregon Education Investment Board about these very metacognitive factors.

How do you measure them? You get together with Linda Darling-Hammond and you create systems for assessment of deeper learning!

Deeper learning [18] is not as smart and pretty as it sounds. It is not content knowledge. It's the "metacognitive" or personality, behavior and belief portions of what makes up a child. Ambiguous curriculum, positive behavior systems, school climate surveys (measure your perceptions and personal opinions about how the school culture), assessments designed for "deeper learning" or, more accurately, measuring the values, attitudes and beliefs...all combined say nothing about actual education do they?

I have no doubt that this will be making an appearance here in Oregon soon. And all other states that Conley has his finger in through the Innovation Learning Network.

Adding that to the fact that Oregon's new Chief Education Officer, Nancy Golden, [19] is president of the board of EPIC, David Conley's baby, well, I can see that we are already, in fact, on that very slippery slope.

When you put all the parts of the Common Core initiative together it does not add up to being good education.

If people are not the total sum of their parts the same is true for Common Core. The Core proponents would have you believe that the sum of the CCSS parts = a grand 21st century education. When in fact, the sum of all the initiative's parts = an evil way for the powers that be to get inside American school children's minds, hearts and souls.

Give them the Common Core curriculum, which will prepare them for ambiguity and make sure their minds fall back on an emotional response. That's the wedge that will open up their mind.

Make sure you turn the structure of the school day into a Positive Behavior System where kids are encouraged to be one of a larger group and not stand out. They can't even to stand up for someone else without getting in as much trouble as the bully.

This teaches kids to join the rank and file and never step out of line.

Assess them at every turn to make sure that the connections their brains are making are emotional and reactive and completely bypassing rational thought. Watch to be sure that they aren't getting content knowledge and pay attention to what answers they choose and what those tell you about how that child thinks.

And finally, record everything, including data from pre-k on through workforce. [20] Everything about your child will be kept in a database. From what snacks he or she ate in preschool to what age they began to read. How they interact with other students and teachers and what extracurricular activities they do. Know their family's background, income, and voting status. See how their brains work in what answers they pick on assessments. Note any behavior problems and compare their data to other kids' data to foresee perhaps what may become of them as they get older.

Make this data accessible to 3rd party vendors and to the state and federal government.

And what is the government and their big business cronies going to do with all of this information? They'll have a virtual army of kids that grow up with no content knowledge and who run highly on emotion. They'll be perfect lemmings that will never step out of line.

What's the government going to use that army for?

3

WHAT IS SOCIALISM (REALLY) ABOUT? A FORMER CZECH EXPLAINS

by Dr. Sarah Condor

What is Socialism? Most of those who grew up in the capitalist West and do not entirely dislike the idea would answer, *social equality, of course, what else?* Some of the more radical ones would say "spreading wealth" or equality...

However, those are just words, phrases void of meaning, because there is no such thing as "equality" – we are all different. Equality of something? Perhaps. Equality of opportunity, equality of chance, and equality in the right to compete: Get in the ring and fight!

Although it dates back as far as Plato [21], modern socialism took root with the French revolution: Equality, Liberty, and Fraternity. Ah, those French, they have always had a penchant for pretty sounds and idealism. They gave us the Statue and with it came, well, a Trojan present, it seems, for the world is swarming with poor, huddled masses today. They have all heard of our Freedom, but what is it? Certainly not giving everybody what they want and letting them do as they please.

Yes, as someone who grew up in socialism, I can tell you what it is, what it results in – socialism, the very opposite of democracy. Let me tell you why.

Socialism consists of:

1) Censorship, total control of speech, political correctness regulated by the government,
2) Central planning, by design from above, based not on the needs of the people but on what the demagogue in power says that (his) people need,
3) Limited freedom of movement,
4) Limited ability to achieve and prosper (speak of Pursuit of Happiness, ha!), and

5) Regulated market, thus limited economy and ability of the state (GDP, prosperity) to grow.

If you are able, capable, want to compete and conquer; if you are creative and want to exercise your freedom; if you are an intelligent, intellectual person who wants to think for himself–socialism is not for you.

If you are someone who just wants to be and let be, has minimum interests in life and wants only a shelter and something to eat, a mandatory vacation once, twice a year, guaranteed minimum wages, no matter what you do or how hard you work (or do not work), long hospital lines with the same fed-up "doc" at the end of the day, grocery lines packed with hangdog faces, shabby houses no-one cares for (because everything belongs to everyone), oh well, then socialism is for you.

Beware: You can get there by electing your demagogue. You can get back only by a violent revolution, by overthrowing him and abolishing and demolishing the tyranny, for that is what socialism is. Naturally, you will be walking the tightrope of anarchy at all times during your struggle to re-acquire, re-conquer the freedoms you so blithely gave away.

Adjectives like "intellectual" or "catholic" are terms of insult and opprobrium in socialism, for it is the proletariat, the "working class" that stands above all doctors and lawyers and architects. "True Architect is the people," says the Demagogue. "The individual does not matter! People got killed? What difference does it make? I rule the people! They elected me to rule! Make no mistake, I am in power!"

Elections? There is one party and one Rule in socialism. Elections exist, to be sure, but they consist of coming to the ballot box to openly show support to the One. If you do not, he will crush you. You may "disappear" overnight without anyone ever hearing from you again. You think that Secret Police cannot enter your house without your permission? You think that you have to have right to an attorney? You think they cannot arrest you for looking dirty at a cop? Think again. **Socialism is a police state.** You have no idea what it means? Orwell's *1984* is much too real for me to ever read again...[22]

Let me tell you about the "state of equality." Socialism desires equality. Equality consists of a state of equal outcome, where everything is based on the need for an equal outcome. If you are a doctor and work twelve hours a day, your salary is the same as that of a shop assistant who works eight hours a day. As a shop assistant once told my mother (a physician who spent seven years of her life working shifts as a nurse while studying medicine at night): "We all have one mouth and two hands, why should you get paid more than I?" Teach that to two generations of people and it will take four generations to alter their children's thinking – if ever.

Plato had it right: democracy may easily turn into a totalitarian regime – because the power is vested in the people and the people may give it away – to a populist demagogue. It is the demagogue who will promise blue from the sky to them: education will be for free, healthcare will be for free, houses and accommodation will be provided by the government... What else do you want? Yes, that will be for free too and that one too.

What follows? The moment the demagogue acquires power he will take away a few rights, just a few, such as by modifying the First Amendment, what you can say and what religion is allowed. You have to speak "equality" be "politically correct" and, above all, "make no mistake." The Second Amendment follows suit, for by taking away your means of self-defense, the demagogue becomes invincible. Of course, the demagogue will ask "you the people" for an armed car, guard and military detail at all times by his Palace. That is taken for granted and is promptly provided. Do democratic leaders not have the same?

The next step is to bite off the First Amendment a little more and have you worship the Party of the Demagogue; abandon all other Gods, all other idols. He is your God, He is your Idol. Have you ever heard of a personality cult? Stalin cult? I could mention someone else too... In 1986, I visited Rumania (one of the few allowed countries on the permitted Party "vacation list"). The streets were not lined with trees but with portraits of Ceausescu and communist mottos, even in the country. Good sounding mottos too: "Through Peace to Prosperity!" or "With Soviet Union to World Peace!" or "Communism Our Goal!" or "Through Socialism to Glittering Tomorrows!"

I grew up among these mottos, too. But the people were even worse – totally indoctrinated. Naked children begging by the train. Why, I also came from socialism. Yes, but we were more to the west, we still had what to eat... The stores in Rumania in 1987 consisted of rows of toilet paper, rows of cans of beans, alcohol and an old man trying to sell dry, inedible stinking fish. The Black Sea was barren, dark, as if it reflected the country that shored it. Milk was provided in exchange for special tickets, which were distributed only to families with children once a month... Do I have to go on?

I was unlucky enough to suffer an ear infection while in Rumania. Had it happened at home, in Czechoslovakia, my mother (as a doctor) could have called an ear specialist and we could have brought her a bottle of wine and some chocolates. That way we would not have had to wait in line and she would surely have given me the one ointment prescribed by the state. Of course, there was a better one but it was manufactured in Switzerland and was not even available on the black market. You'd better not fall sick.

What happened in Rumania? There was a doctor who spoke German so we could get by. Her office looked like the holding cell where I later spent a few nights after my arrest for trying to "run away" from those kowtowing communist weasels. On the floor, there were a couple of rugs and a bucket, something you might use for washing a car. Next to it stood a small iron table with a tray and a couple of iron instruments, pliers, needles – I was surprised there was no hammer...

She looked at me, called on her bodybuilder nurse who grasped my head and said something in Rumanian that sounded like a Hitler speaking to his staff. Out of the corner of my eye, I saw this huge dirty syringe; I mean something you would use for a horse, holding probably half a liter of liquid. She stuck a large needle on it (which lay in the open in plain sight next to the pliers in the tray) with her bare hands and pushed the whole thing into my ear. The bodybuilder nurse was holding my head. Then they started squeezing the liquid into my ear. I felt it in my toes. The pain was unimaginable! I could not hear for three weeks thereafter... Well, my father gave her ten German Marks, all we had for emergency purposes (black market money), and I was "discharged."

The free healthcare you get in socialism is worth precisely what everything else you get "for free" is worth. You had better study medicine yourself or have a doctor in the family – else, in any case, just hope that you never need socialist healthcare. I did have an advantage, as I say, my mother being a physician, but we still had to bring bribes to the office and they could only do so much in terms of the communist market cures and medication...

In socialism, all competition in the market disappears: there is governmental monopoly on drugs, cars, and food... If you want something better, you want the greengrocer to "save" and put aside three bananas for your children for Christmas, you have to find a way to "befriend" the grocer. I remember my father cutting thin slices of a banana on a small breadboard, arranging them on a plate with tiny squares of a Cuban orange. It was Christmas Eve and I was allowed to eat half the plate myself.

My parents had each one-quarter, about four slices of banana and a quarter of an orange. I know, it is hard to believe, but that is how I grew up: from flu to scarlet fever to bronchitis, to rickets – I was a sickly child, mainly because my parents were "intellectuals" with few contacts to the "working class" people who lived in the country and had their own chickens and even a cow and a pig... They ate rabbits and once we were invited (by one of my mother's patients) to a "pig killing" – which was a wonderful thing: I had a sausage for the first time in my life. And the boiled and fried pieces of fat tasted so good!

If I say that the socialist market consists of monopolies and lack of competition, that does not quite describe what my experience does, does it? I still have to say that costs are established by the government, as is the product, the same for everyone – one or two brands of the car, television set, even the house furniture. You go visit your schoolmate at home – they will have exactly the same furniture from the same company (which supports the Regime, the Party and has acquired the much-desired governmental monopoly) – consequently, everything looks familiar to you. You feel at home everywhere. Isn't that wonderful?

Yet, you do not have a home. Your home, your privacy, your dignity has been taken away from you. After a while, you cannot imagine anything else... Not until you take a peek into a West German catalog someone has smuggled into the country... Not until you (surreptitiously, at low volume at night) listen to the Russian-jammed Radio Free Europe...

Here is another aspect of socialism. Socialism is a police state. If a policeman stops you, you have to do as he says, go with him, stay locked up without any rights until he lets you go or you proceed to prison from which they pick you up and put you in front of a three-judge panel. Hopefully, these minions of the Regime will let you go...

Of course, if you have had the audacity to say something untoward about the government or the Demagogue – why, that is worse than a murder! Political prisoners are prisoners of free speech, the greatest evil of capitalism. The minimum sentence for "attacking the Regime" was 20 years, usually of hard labor, in a uranium mine (by then totally "mined out" by the Russians) or in a coalmine. Years later, after the "Velvet Revolution," I had a boyfriend who had these rather large black spots around his spine and lower and upper back. I asked him where they came from, what were they. He said he was doing forced labor in a coalmine for two years, a deep black coalmine in Northern Moravia. I asked no more.

Today, I look at the modern demagogue who grew up with all advantages of capitalism and what he – indeed, she too – knows about socialism is limited to sociology studies, books describing those wonderful ideals of Marx, Engels, Lenin and their followers). This Modern Demagogue says: I am a "democratic socialist" – just to confuse you. If it has "democratic" or "democrat," it must be good, mustn't it?

Allow me to explain: social democrats in western European political systems are innocent only because they play their "social role" and function as part of a multi-party parliamentarian political system. What is more, they are "social" democrats, not democratic socialists – a difference not without insignificance! The latter, a democratic socialist, obviously means that this Modern Demagogue is a socialist first and uses the "demos" – i.e. people – only as an adjectival premodifier to personal power, the power of a populist demagogue who will turn "demos" (people) into "agony" (struggle) at the very first opportunity, the moment they transfer their power to Him: the "Struggle of the Proletariat," Marx called it.

In a two party representative government, the danger of democracy turning into a totalitarian regime is much greater than in a multi-party parliamentarian system, where all powers and factions are kept in check by all the other powers and factions. As freedom is indispensable to democracy and it is also "to a faction as air is to fire", [3] we must treat democracy not as a stable system, a huge majestic animal without any natural enemies, but as a fragile, beautiful creature, a gentle lady, who can be swayed and lured, led astray and – violated – by a mob.

A mob is what people become in the hands of a socialist demagogue. There is no more "We the People." People do not matter. Mottoes and icons matter, banners and slogans that you must shout too – or else...

I shiver when I see it, I can smell it a thousand miles away. When you have seen the **Heart of Darkness**, [24] it alters you forever. "We the Mob, We the Mob!" is ringing in my ears. Ah, but that was not the old communist T.V. – that was NBC. Really? Just think in silence, do not let it out; for if you refuse to be subdued, suppressed, refuse to conform and give away your rights and liberties for some larger abstract "good," off to the mine with you! [24] Make no mistake about it: an individual "makes no difference!"

That is what socialism is about. Believe me, I have been there before – and I am not going back. [25]

4

HOW A HANDFUL OF OKLAHOMANS (INCLUDING ONE POLITICHICK) TOOK ON COMMON CORE AND WON!

by Julia Seay

The following [26] have been paying millions on messaging for Common Core: Bill Gates, U.S. Chamber of Commerce, National Governors Association (which is a private club of Republicans, Democrats and Corporations that have no business making policy for states since they are not accountable to taxpayers), GE, Exxon, Federal and State Departments of Ed, et.al.

Despite all the money spent, parents along with a few courageous teachers are winning the argument by showing the facts. In the words of Winston Churchill: "Never, never, never give up!" Never give up fighting statists that think the world would be a better place if you would let them be in charge of your life. Never drop your kids off at school and not check up on what they are being taught. Never believe a shiny brochure over a home-printed handout.

They had to pass it to see what was in it. They have spent money trying to indoctrinate educators, money on shiny brochures to tell parents and communities about how wonderful CC is, money to try to make people believe that states have the new "Oklahoma/Alabama/Colorado Academic Standards" which we immediately proved were nothing but Common Core under a new name. They spent money on TV ads, newspaper editorials, lobbyists, campaign donations, created new agencies like Stand on Children in many states... They named it Stand for Children, but they don't stand for children so we appropriately renamed them.

They spent money with the National PTA because they thought they could purchase some grassroots. The Teachers Unions all got donations to "like" Common Core. They have given campaign donations and created PACS to get statists elected in State Legislatures. The list is endless, but much of it can be found on the Gates Foundation donation page [28] if you like to research. They are still at it, even in Oklahoma. But even with their millions, they are losing the argument.

Just imagine if there was an even playing field, and the parent-researchers had the funds to spend informing folks that the Corporate Crony Educrats have. Not only are we not paid for the hours of research and time spent travelling the State, attending Legislative Committee Meetings and interim studies, other than having some very understanding and supportive husbands we have no budget. Zip, zero, zilch, nada. I know from my time on the board of Restore Oklahoma Public Education*, we have the same $30 in our account that was there when I signed on almost four years ago. From time to time we pass the plate to collect some gas money, and sometimes folks pick up the tab for some printing or for dinner, and our awesome Oklahoma Labor Commissioner Mark Costello threw in half and helped grassroots get the money together for our Common Core is Not OK t-shirts for our rally, but that was about it for our budget. Once some ladies from western Oklahoma gave us a big basket of homemade bread, jams and other goodies. We were in Heaven!

When Common Core began to hit Oklahoma classrooms, groups of parents and teachers and citizens started popping up all over the state, we got the attention of more legislators and BOOM, we finally got a repeal bill passed, and then confirmed by our State Supreme Court. Amazing. I love the tagline "Band of Mothers" given to us by Joel Gehrke of National Review.

Their $Millions vs. our gas money makes this Rasmussen poll a miracle, and should encourage parents and educators everywhere. We are winning. They own the media and we are still winning. They take our tax dollars and use it against us, but we are still winning!

From Rasmussen Reports [27]:

"Breaking the numbers down further, less than one third of Republicans thought Common Core would improve education, while 55 percent did not. A separate poll released last week by Pew Research revealed that conservatives of all stripes reject the national standards by a more than two-to-one margin, putting establishment GOP bigwigs such as Jeb Bush firmly on the fringe."

It is time to visit the school board meetings, both local and state. It is time to visit your State Legislators and inform them. It is time to visit local Chamber of Commerce members. Most have no idea. They believe the shiny brochures, if that is the only source of information they have. You might overcome the campaign donation promises of your State Chamber if you rationally show them what Common Core Standards with all the strings attached really consist of, and the impact they will have on the future for their children. You might win over the majority of the members of your local chamber. Legislators are just people. Businessmen and women have families. You need to get to know them anyway, and inform them. And you can.

Find your state's group of #stopcommoncore parents and teachers and join! Educate yourself! In addition to PolitiChicks, visit websites like www.restoreokpubliceducation.com, http://americanprinciplesproject.org/, and http://truthinamericaneducation.com/ along with many others, and you will be armed and ready to educate the educators, school board members and legislators. All these resources give you links to prove the facts.

It is time to hold Governors on both sides of the aisle accountable. They all seem to be in agreement that they should collect our children's data to sell to/share with "stakeholders" to pick and choose their future employees rather than to educate your children to become all that God created them to be.

They will be giving legislators and educators shiny brochures; the Governor will be sending staff, the corporations want to nudge them into training children to be their future workforce rather than their competition, and if parents and teachers don't rise up, they will just quietly legislate your freedom away until they own your children. Oh, whoa. Was that radical? Think I'm crazy? Look up the YouTube video of Arne Duncan stating that he wants your children 14 hours a day, 7 days a week and 12 months a year.

Governors are pushing it into our states, like Governor Fallin (R-OK) [30] whose education agenda as Chair of the National Governors Association sounded like a speech of Hu Jintao, President of China. BEWARE. She eventually signed our repeal bill, but not without a big fight.

They know they can outspend us by zillions, and really thought they would squash us like bugs. They assume they can outlast us. This has been going on for a very long time under one name or another. Arm yourself with truth, and do not let them get away with lies. It is absolutely ludicrous that parents and teachers don't want high standards for their children. Do not let anyone get away with stating that premise! Set the record straight.

In spite of the odds, in spite of their endless money spent on messaging and perceived power, we are winning! The truth is winning. Join the fight. Shine the light.

*Restore Oklahoma Public Education was renamed Reclaim Oklahoma Parents Empowerment after the OK Common Core repeal bill was signed into law. It became apparent that there would never be permanent change until parents stood up and reclaimed their role as primary educator in their children's lives whether they choose public, private, or homeschool.

Julia Seay was instrumental in eliminating Common Core from the state of Oklahoma via Restore Oklahoma Public Education. Julia is a Christian wife and mother who worked in courtrooms and conference rooms, and then became involved in her local public school system. She was formerly on the board of Restore Oklahoma Public Education, dedicated to affect education legislation. Julia is currently on the board of Gateway Women's Resource Center, a non-profit ministryW.

FROM THE 1800'S TO TODAY: TWO GENERATIONS OF TEXAS TEACHERS

by Lou Ellen Brown

In the olden days, teachers were considered among the chosen, and they were respected and treated with honor. For a variety of reasons, the life of a teacher was deserving of every bit of respect, as the teacher was not always available in small communities, and might have to share her time with more than one schoolhouse. Also, schoolhouse might have been just that: an unused house turned into a schoolhouse.

My mother and one of her sisters were teachers in the late 1880s and early 1900s. They both took the state test and my aunt scored higher and got the older students, while my mother did not do well enough at math so she got the younger students. They did always have the same meeting times and places, and sometimes they had to spend the night in the home of one or another of the students. Sometimes one of their brothers could take them on a wagon, and sometimes they might have to ride horseback. My mother didn't really like having to ride a horse, so she most often was taken by wagon and left with a nearby family for a week or more. It was not unusual that payday might include a live chicken or other edibles.

At the schoolhouse, winters were hard, and because school was not always held during the farming and harvesting season winter school was easier to attend, for teachers and students. Often both sisters taught the older and younger classes and there might be only a few of any age. Mom and her sister followed the family, as they were sharecroppers or workers at one of their more prosperous relatives' farms. Everyone worked at whatever was available, but teachers did not have many alternatives as to where the schoolhouses were, and took what they could find. Their best reward was when they were valued for what they were doing to make the future somewhat better, as not everyone in the rural areas of Texas was near enough to a school to attend, and reading was a gift of great price to those children who really wanted to learn. In those days, reading and writing at a fourth grade level was pretty special, and doing simple math meant that someone in the family was able to cipher, doing arithmetic, and could help with family finances, if there were any.

And so it went for a time for my mother and aunt, and at one point the family from the piney woods of East Texas followed the family workers with railroad jobs out to the wild and wooly West Texas. It was there that my mom and my aunt met their husbands, and because the teaching positions were held for a privileged class, they married and put down their teaching tools.

Why did they have to quit? It was a simple rule of survival. The women who were not married and did not want to be married, or could not attract a husband were spinsters or old maids or widows and had no other means of support than to be teachers. My aunt went on to college later and did keep a teaching job as times began to change. Towns were growing, farms were still in need of workers and my mom became a wife and eventually a mother of three, one son and two daughters.

The three of us, proud of what our mother had done, in our turns became teachers.

For all of the years, forty three in all, I kept my mother's old hand ringing school bell somewhere in my classroom, and as I write, it is on a shelf in the room where I am writing this tribute to her, for it was her life, her story, that led the family to do whatever it took to provide with honor for those who loved us or needed us, and to serve as beacons to light someone's eyes with new dreams of their own.

Lou Ellen Brown is a 4th generation Texan. She taught high school 43 years in all 5 geographic regions of Texas. She is a Certified Lay Minister in the Methodist Church. Lou Ellen has been very active in her community and served two terms as president of the Sesame Literary Club. Lou Ellen and her husband, Gene, are also the parents of Ann-Marie Murrell and writer Lisa K. Brown.

PART FOUR: ISLAM

Islam is the only socio-political-legal-religion that only allows for Allah and world denomination—if not through peace and subterfuge—then through the force of arms. There is no wiggle room in the Qur'an or Hadiths for tolerance. - **Dr. J.P. Sloane**

1
THE ISLAMIC WAR ON WOMEN

by Carolyn Elkins

Leftists in the West must be getting pretty perturbed about the continuous Muslim rapes happening worldwide. There are so many ways to look at the spate of rapes perpetrated on Western women by Muslims, while also remembering that Muslim women and children have been suffering the same insidious acts against them for centuries.

When one thinks of American leftists with their many years of propagating a fake Republican War on Women while spreading the "Islamophobe" narrative every time people dare to question Islamic crimes, it's amazing that they are virtually silent when their two main pet causes clash.

As western liberal women lament Christian Conservatives and equate us to the Taliban because we don't want to pay for their birth control and abortions, they seem to clam up when women and girls are getting acid thrown in their faces, stoned, whipped, raped, sold as sex slaves, and murdered in predominantly Islamic countries. Where are the Sandra Fluke's and Gloria Steinem's when it comes to a woman's right to live without being violated and treated less than animals by the men who keep them?

Germany has Angela Merkel [1] as their advocate... well, no, not helping women but as an advocate for Muslim refugees. You know, those 20- 30 something military-aged men that the west claims are in desperate need of refugee status. It's amazing that the powers-that-be have the power to shut their borders, but instead, not only have they thrown out the welcome mat, now that the raping and pillaging has begun in earnest, these governments are turning on their own citizens.

It's not as if there are no records of abuse toward women in the Muslim world where the West can claim ignorance. Egypt is the worst country to be a woman followed by Iraq, Saudi

Arabia, Syria, and Yemen. Many Islamic countries rank the worst [2] when considering employment for women, marital abuse, rape, honor killings, stoning and sexual slavery among other practices. While Muslim women fare better in Western countries, the steady flow of 'migrants' from Muslim countries is bringing much of the Muslim and Arabic practices with them including their deplorable treatment of women.

One has to wonder, with the indifference of western politicians and leftist organizations when it comes to Muslim practices (such as FMG and sexual slavery), do they believe practices such as bacha bazi (boy play), [3] which is the rape of young boys in Afghanistan, or child marriage of other Islamic counties, is a "cultural" thing? Many Arabic and North African Muslims men are importing their own cultural thing [4] called taharrush gamea, [5] which is like gang raping on steroids when one considers the victims are being raped or sexually assaulted in public areas by large crowds of men while others look on.

The rapes that occurred in Cologne and other places on New Years Eve in 2016 5 are reminiscent of the sexual assault of Chicago Tribune reporter Kim Barker, who was sexually assaulted in Pakistan in 2007. And the same happened in 2011 to CBS News correspondent Lara Logan, who was brutally gang raped in Egypt. A year later, British journalist Natasha Smith [6] was sexually assaulted.

I have to wonder, where are these women now, and are they speaking out? In the past, at least with Kim Barker, she equated her experience of rape as a "tool of war", which in her view [7] has nothing to do with Islam...And yet women in Europe, who are now experiencing what women in Muslim countries have experienced, are not journalists in a Muslim war zone--they are in their own nations which are being turned into war zones because of the Muslim men their own governments willingly imported.

What really bothers me about the relative silence from the left is that they continually try to pass the narrative that this has "nothing to do with Islam" and that we - as Westerners - must be sensitive to Muslim's feelings. Not only are they silent about what's happening to women and children, they are willingly being conquered by Islam while mocking and berating anyone who tries to *warn* about Islam.

It's evident across Europe, when Churches are removing their crosses and other Christian symbols [8] so as to not offend Muslim migrants. And in many cases it is suggested that western women need to dress 'less provocatively' to avoid being raped in their own cities. [9] Dress less provocatively? Seriously? Since when? Liberalism has been the bastion of sexuality for decades. It's seen in entertainment, advertising, and education. How far Leftist women have come since the days of encouraging women to burn their bras. Soon, they will be encouraging women to don the burka.

In 2015, after the San Bernardino, California Islamist attack, [10] Obama's Attorney General and many Democrat representatives crafted a hate crime bill [11] in which someone could be criminally charged if a Muslim 'feels' verbally or emotionally abused. The same type of bill has been used in Europe for years. [12]

As Europe continues to bow to Islam and allow more refugees into their countries, the U.S. and Canada are willfully trotting down the same road. As we accept more Muslims into our country, it makes sense to think that liberals will not only continue to ignore and/or cover up brutal sexual attacks, but blame women for it. Ironically, Leftists are now responsible for allowing a real Muslim War on Women – and Lord help them if any of them become their next victims.

2

ACCOMMODATION, SUBMISSION, AND INSPIRATION: AN INTERVIEW WITH FRANK GAFFNEY

by Lydia Goodman

In July 2016, I had the opportunity to interview Frank J. Gaffney, Jr., following a panel discussion on Security and Counterterrorism at The Bridge, The Annual Conference of the Persecuted Church. Frank Gaffney is the Founder and President of the Center for Security Policy in Washington D.C. The Center is not-for-profit, non-partisan educational corporation established in 1988. Under Mr. Gaffney's leadership, the Center has been nationally and internationally recognized as a resource for timely, informed and penetrating analyses of foreign and defense policy matters. He is also a great friend of PolitiChicks.

LG: In the hour prior to meeting with you, I was given a first-hand account by a teacher at a private military school and college that a classroom had recently been converted, dedicated, and consecrated as a prayer room for Muslim students. This occurred after school hours and without any teacher or parental input. How common is this?

Frank Gaffney: I think you will find that this kind of incremental civilization jihad is occurring, not only in academic institutions, but in the financial sector, the media, military, and government. You will find that each of these areas has been subjected to 'influence operations' in which people demand some kind of concession or accommodation. It usually starts in an innocuous way but, inevitably; they become more aggressive.

LG: By bringing it to light, what can people do once they are aware of the actions of the school administration or, for that matter, in any sector you mentioned?

Frank Gaffney: Here's the point. Getting rid of people who engineered this is a necessary step but, mark my words, they will turn this into a national controversy if anyone tries to do this. A friend of mine is on the board of a military academy in Vermont, actually a college, where the administration had an applicant who they knew was Muslim. She was accepted by the school and then announced after her acceptance that she wanted to wear the hijab under her uniform as one of the cadets. They (the administration) wrestled with this for a very brief period of time and decided they would make this accommodation. Her father, it turns out, holds the number two position in CAIR in Florida. This is a perfect example of how this works. Nobody had ever done that before, somebody is now asking for it, and they (the administration) worry that if they don't do it they will be sued by the Justice Department or have other problems. It's much easier to go along with it...until the next demand.

LG: In your opinion, why do jihadists hate the Western world so much?

Frank Gaffney: That was a question introduced right after 9/11. The truth of the matter is that they hate us because they are indoctrinated in the belief that inevitably we are to be subordinated to them. Getting from here to there is just a matter of tactics and time and if they can do it violently that's the most efficient way. If they can't, because at the moment we are too strong, then they will try to change perceptions through various techniques to bring us around to the point where they can accomplish this goal of subordination.

LG: In the panel discussion, you discussed NAIT. Please explain what it is and its purpose.

Frank Gaffney: NAIT is a basic mechanism. For example, the German government expressed concern over how many people were coming into their country so the Saudi government said, "We will build you 200 mosques to accommodate them". NAIT is a vehicle that the Muslim Brotherhood created as an offshoot of their largest front organization called the Islamic Society of North America. Its purpose is essentially to work as a pass-through for funding. The Saudis will put money into the Muslim World League which then makes grants to the North American Islamic Trust (NAIT) to enable it to either build or take-over mosques. Their mortgages, their financing, and everything else that goes along with it is funded by this organization.

One of my friends actually had two of his mosques that he helped establish taken over by NAIT. He believed the form of Islam being presented was the way it should be practiced and he was comfortable with the program. The next thing you know, he was not welcome there because it had become a Sharia adherent program. Unfortunately, this case is just systematic of the infrastructure building by NAIT that happens to mosques in the Islamic tradition. They aren't houses of worship anymore or, at least, exclusively houses of worship. Mosques are being used for community political activities and, in quite a number of cases, have become places where people are being trained and recruited to jihad. The French and the Belgians have both recently stumbled into this. Some are being used as arsenals, literally, with stocked weapons. My feeling about it is, as I made the point earlier, is that when you look at how these jihadists who have engaged in so-called "lone wolf" activities, you will find that they were all tied to one or another of these type of mosques.

LG: So, would you consider NAIT a type of satellite system?

Frank Gaffney: It is more than a satellite system. They are incubators. It is what you will get a lot more of as they feel more emboldened. For example, what little surveillance activity that was being done by the NYPD was cancelled by Mayor De Blasio. These are the type of actions that's really putting us at risk, I'm afraid. These decisions are not only creating an opportunity for jihadism to grow, but they are also giving an incentive to have more people engaged--confident in the knowledge that they will get away with it.

LG: What should one primarily know about the tactics of jihadists?

Frank Gaffney: This is one of the most important take-aways: Whether we dress it up as political correctness or as multiculturalism or as sensitivity to diversity or as giving people their "safe spaces", whatever we think of it, there is another term used by the jihadis and that is "submission". When they see "infidels" submitting, they have, under this doctrine of Sharia, a very clear mandated response to redouble the effort, as the Quran puts it, to make them feel more subdued. The object of the exercise is submission.

Lydia Goodman has written numerous PolitiChicks articles on world human rights issues, in an effort to focus attention on the atrocities perpetuated against people of faith. She has conducted exclusive interviews with Israeli author Lela Gilbert; activist and lead singer of KANSAS, John Elefonte; Todd Daniels of International Christian Concern, and Bob Fu of China Aid, among other notable subjects for PolitiChicks.com. Lydia has also appeared on radio and television as a guest commentator.

3
A NEW YORKER RECALLS 9/11/01

by Jin Ah Jin

The morning of September 11, 2001 our phone rang. It was my children's grandparents on the line; they usually didn't call so early so I was a bit worried something may have happened to them. I had just dropped of my two girls at school and was feeding my baby daughter breakfast.

My husband at the time groggily told me a plane had hit the World Trade Center. My response was, "Don't worry, it was made to withstand planes hitting it." You see several months earlier I had spoken with my friend, Taesun Hong, a world-renowned architect who at the time was a partner at Yamasaki Associates with Mr. Minoru Yamasaki, the architect had designed the World Trade Center. I had asked him the question about "what if" an airplane hit the World Trade Center and he had explained to me the core and the way it was built.

We told the grandparents not to worry and started getting ready for our day when the telephone rang again. Another plane had hit the second Tower. I rushed out of my chair to turn on the television as my heart started racing, muttering, "Something is not right." As the television came on, we saw the Towers on fire and the replay of the planes.

My heart pounded, watching. This was not right. Something was not right. It was all wrong! My eyes stayed glued to the television, watching the scene, looking for my friends. I had worked in both Towers during the late 80s for two different banks and the third company I had worked for had offices there as well; thus I had been in and out of both buildings quite frequently.

I watched as the people came running out of the smoking buildings, the firemen and policemen. I watched in horror as they showed human beings jumping out of the windows to their deaths, thinking over and over "this can't be real" while at the same time praying that my friends were safe.

As we watched the replay over and over, they began reporting that there was another plane that had been headed for D.C. and had just hit the Pentagon. My heart quickened. We lived just 20 miles away from the Pentagon. My neighbor, one of my good friends, worked there; I was her emergency contact. My husband went to check on my friend and, thank God, she was home and had taken the day off! I started calling my friend at the Samsung building directly across from the Towers and no one was answering the phones.

I was barely holding it together as they flipped back to one of the Towers as it started falling down--and I couldn't hold back anymore.

My daughter clung to me as I sobbed, not knowing what was going on or why I was crying. My husband came over and we all held each other in shock as my body just shook, tears streaming down my face. We saw the people running, ash clinging to their faces and bodies. I could not take my eyes off the devastating scene--and then my body almost went into shock as we saw the second Tower burn.

I sat in front of the television all day crying listening for any bit of news I could get. President Bush had come on and he had broken down in tears, too. This was crazy. What world are we living in? Will we be alive tomorrow? The questions, the uncertainty running through my brain and my heart, about our future and our lives began hitting home.

All day, I thought of the faces of all my colleagues and the people I had met during those days working in the Towers. I thought of the walk down pathway from the subway to the news shop in the downstairs mezzanine, where the sunny smile of the beautiful man from Jamaica used to greet me every morning as we chatted about how the day would go. The jokes, the office parties, the office breaks and hanging out after work with those friends at South Street Seaport...I thought of Christmas Eve day when it started snowing and the way it looked out of my office window, looking at the other Tower. So many memories hitting me like a hurricane.

Who were these people? Who were these awful people that wanted to kill so many innocents? And for what purpose?

Wives, sisters, mothers, brothers, fathers, sons, daughters, uncles, aunts, and friends--all beloved by someone.

Later of course, we found out it was the same people that had tried bombing the Towers before by putting a bomb in a truck in the parking garage.

When you live in NYC and work in certain buildings, you get used to the bomb threats so it's no big deal and things happen all the time and you go on with your day. This was not the ordinary day.

As I continued watching the news coverage that day, I again tried calling my friend and colleague at Samsung where I was an events contractor. She finally answered and told me how everyone was at the windows, crying, and you could still hear her tears as my tears started flowing again. Neither of us could believe it but we knew the reality of what had just happened. She said the smoke and the fire was still going on but everyone was afraid to move. They had all checked on their families but were told to remain in the office until they knew if it was safe to leave. We hung up the phone. I had a meeting there on September 12 but we canceled it to the 13th.

On the 13th I drove up to NYC to pick up my friend. It was quieter but you could see the devastating effects on people's faces. You could still see the smoke and the ash. We drove across the GW Bridge then went on to Samsung Headquarters office building in Ridgefield Park. I stood at the window looking over the river to the smoke and the missing outline of a place where I had once spent the majority of my waking hours. Again, the tears came quickly.

We did our business and I drove home. It was a long drive full of memories. Thousands of people had just perished. Time could never wash that away.

As I write this, my stomach is churning and hurting again. My tears are streaming down my face. The faces of my friends are running through my mind and heart and I feel such a terrible loss. I also feel like, it could have been me, if I had not decided to take a different course in life. I also feel guilt at being alive and they are not. Once again, all these years later, it still hurts.

And of course we now have two 9/11 anniversaries to

mourn—New York in 2001 and Benghazi in 2012, all at the hands of Islam. You would think things would have changed and gotten better; that we would have made the world safer—but it is the exact opposite.

Jin Ah Jin assists in local minority grassroots politics in her state of Virginia, working as a volunteer for Mercy Corps raising awareness for the health and poverty of women and children in North Korea, and for the Korean American Association of Greater Washington, D.C. area. More importantly, Jin is the mother of 6 children. She says her passion for service is led through her children's eyes.

4

ARMENIAN GENOCIDE: MORE THAN 100 YEARS OF SILENCE AGAINST CHRISTIAN PERSECUTION

by Susan Swift

"Why, after all, speaks today of the extermination of the Armenians?" – **Adolph Hitler**, Obersalzberg 1939 [13]

It has been over 101 years since the Armenian Genocide, part of the larger genocide when the Islamic Ottoman Empire murdered 3.5 million Armenians and Greeks from 1914-1923 [14] because they were Christian. Hitler's Obersalzberg Speech– given shortly before invading Poland and undertaking the murder of 6 million Polish Jews and Christians to create "lebensraum"– revealed how emboldened he felt by the world's silence at the Armenian Genocide. Today, that silence continues as Islamic groups persecute, murder and ethnically cleanse Christians throughout the world.

And throughout his presidency, Barack Obama refused to identify radical Islam as the cause, instead bashing Christians for being on their "high horse" and "unloving". Even on the 100th anniversary, President Obama refused to use the word "genocide" to describe the slaughter of 3.5 million Christians, lest he offend Islamic Turkey. [15]

The Armenian Genocide 4 remains mostly ignored by history, in part eclipsed by the horrific devastation of World War I and later World War II and the Jewish Holocaust, and in part due to political aversion at ruffling the feathers of NATO "ally" Turkey, which continues to deny the Genocide [16] and attack anyone mentioning it, including most recently courageous remarks on the genocide by Pope Francis. [17] The Mainstream Media also has been complicit in this evil silence. The New York Times refused to use the term "genocide" until 12 years ago. [18] In today's Mainstream Media, Islamic atrocities against

Christians virtually do not exist. Instead, an odd-sounding group named "Boko Haram" murders and kidnaps "village girls", [19] or "al Shabaab" massacres Kenyan "university students", [20] or an acronym "IS" or "ISIS" engages in mass murder, rape and enslavement of "Yazidis" [21.] Carefully scrubbed from most accounts is that the perpetrators are Muslims and the victims are Christians because they are Christian. Similarly, the Armenian Genocide is rarely if ever presented as the Islamic Ottoman Empire ethnically cleansing Christians from what is now Turkey, a monstrous feat successfully accomplished with absolutely no adverse consequence from the rest of the world.

Also ignored is that, as genocides go, the Ottomans were uniquely brutal. Unlike their coldly efficient Nazi successors-in-crime, the Ottomans Islamists did not only seek to exterminate a religious group, they did so with brutish sadism. They engaged in systematic mass rape of Christian girls and women. [22] One historian noted how Christians would be marched into the desert, stripped naked, and left to suffer prolonged painful deaths, and how the Ottomans "drowned people in rivers, threw them off cliffs, crucified them and burned them alive." [23]

Does crucifixion and burning alive sound familiar? It should because it's happening today in parts of the Middle East. [24] Yet unlike the rarely publicized Armenian Genocide, Islamists now videotape and publicize their atrocities against Christians, so apparently unafraid they are of consequence or retaliation. And why should they be afraid? Who will punish them? Democrats? Are you kidding? Which has he given more attention to: a police shooting of a store robber in Missouri, or the ethnic cleansing, beheadings, mass rape, forced enslavement and persecution of Christians throughout the Middle East?

In 1922, the Ottoman Islamists [25] marched into the Turkish coastal city of Smyrna, a city originally settled by Greeks in 700 B.C. that had grown to become the most prosperous and opulent city in the Ottoman Empire. Its "problem" was its large population of Greek and Armenian Christians. So in 1923, the Ottoman military set fire to and destroyed the city, murdering nearly 100,000 Christians in the process. [26]

Susan Swift is a former movie star, lawyer, wife, and the mother of seven children. In 2010 Andrew Breitbart invited Susan to write for his young website Big Journalism. Susan graduated magna cum laude from UCLA's Department of Theater Arts, then attended Pepperdine Law School where she graduated with honors. As a lawyer Susan joined the LAPD legal defense team in the Rodney King federal civil rights lawsuit, receiving a special award from the LAPD Booster Association.

5
RADICALIZATION FROM START TO FINISH

by Dr. Sarah Condor

How does radicalization start? Radicalization is a process of becoming an extremist, one who follows an idea, which is attractive to him or her because it is "winning" and speaks to their inner selves. It is – a calling.

Radicalization penetrates the human soul from two directions: from within, and from without. It is a process we all know very well. We have all been radicalized in certain respects: I am radical about what I read and watch. I am radical about what I eat and drink. I am also radical about how I think about politics and ideology – because I grew up in one and know it close and personal.

Radicalization is not any different from our "conversion" to some activity we love. I love to swim, so I join the team, we swim together. We are keen on it and feel a familial bond when we get together and compete. It springs from within because we all need some form of persuasion, some grand and noble idea to follow. It is one of the greatest and noblest of human characteristics. As such, it is also supported from without, because there are already followers and societies that accept us as their members.

Radicalization can be good and productive if it is based on an idea that advances humanity. Edison was a radical, so was Ford and Rockefeller. To think of it, Jefferson, Hamilton, Madison, even George Washington were radicals – rebels, mavericks, radicals all! The term "radical" means strong headed and persuaded of one's own right and of the value of what one says and does. In a way, Donald Trump is a radical – except his "radical philosophy" is that of "America First", and it does not kill or hurt anybody.

Radicalization is not something one is subjected to and must accept. I grew up in a society that wanted to radicalize me, make me into a communist, and blindfold me to the Free World. I was taught communism, I had to wear a communist uniform, go to communist manifestations where I was supposed to shout: "With Soviet Union Forever and Never Any Other Way!" The more they forced it into me, the more I resisted.

What happens today is no different. It takes place online and in mosques but there is little difference in terms of its appeal as an *ideology*. By being secreted, it is made even more attractive. People in the West are radicalized precisely because they are not forced into it the way I had been. They find it appealing as a cult and an ideology.

Islam is not a religion of peace for one simple reason: it is not able to defend itself against this radicalization. The majority may be "peaceful Muslims" but they are but followers. It is the radical minority that rules and prevails, because they are the leaders, they set the direction of the whole "nation" or "House" of Islam, if you will, in the same way the communist "papalashe" set the direction for entire nations when I was growing up.

The way to defeat radicalization, and thus radical Islam, is *not* by trying to trace every single convert and look for needles in a haystack but by making the ideology itself unpopular, uncool, unattractive, and show that it has failed or that it leads to nowhere.

This must be done: 1) by eradicating them physically (not here but at the root), 2) by having stronger propaganda, 3) by ostentatiously displaying our cultural superiority.

First, physical eradication. This is clear and requires very simple strategy, a pincer maneuver supported from the air. Untie the hands of our military and they will do the job in a week or two. Just cut them loose and let them do their jobs.

Further, do the same with the police and FBI at home. Let them choose the means and ways, and let them "profile" if they deem it necessary. Profiling means composition of details into a picture. For that, you have to be a great fact-finder. Modern detective work started with Sherlock Holmes and if you can say one thing about Sherlock: he was a great profiler, detail and fact-finder.

Second, propaganda is a concerted media effort, which must begin by promulgating our uniqueness and pointing out disadvantages and drawbacks of the typical Sharia society, which is a backward totalitarian theocracy and for which there is no room in a civilized society. We all can contribute to the blogs like this one and make ourselves heard in a persuasive way.

However, the main propaganda must come from the government. Perhaps we should have a propaganda center within the CIA whose purpose it would be to only make movies, videos, write blogs and post well-informed, targeted internet propaganda.

Third, we should all fly American flags – not just at home, but abroad. I would swamp the Middle East with American flags, pictures of Hollywood and little bric-a-brac souvenirs showing our American greatness. I would do the same with all media in the Middle East. When I was growing up, the Russians were constantly jamming Radio Free Europe and BBC World Service. Instead, they were feeding us pre-digested, censored "news" about the greatness of the Communist World. There's a thought...

When President Obama called them a "JV Team," [27] he was right in one respect: they are inferior fighters with no military education, and they are also too inexperienced and young to know what life is really about. Someone who believes in "Paradise and 77 virgins" is mentally undeveloped and intellectually retarded.

Finally, the House of Islam must stop teaching Quran literally. No religion is to be taken literally; all religions are allegories and guides to our lives. There may be real elements and stories in them, but the substance is to guide us to a productive and peaceful existence. To paraphrase Hayek, "It is always the most painful experience when we find out that the ideal we have blindly followed led us to the very opposite we wanted to achieve." In this case, two misguided Muslim fanatics ended up splattered on the street like road kill. They will be buried in shallow graves where no one will visit them but a stray dog that will go there to mark its stone. Paradise? No--it is the end of radicalization.

6

THE ROMANCE OF ISLAM IN THREE STAGES

by Dr. J.P. Sloane

Stage One: The Courtship

The first stage of the Islamic struggle (jihad) is deception, referred to in Islam as taqiyya. It is used when the Muslim community is in the minority and cannot muster any political or physical numbers to defend itself against any non-Muslim adversaries. During the first 13 years in Mecca, when Muhammad first started promoting his new religion—and was outnumbered—he wisely offered conciliatory language. Below is one of those conciliatory verses in the Koran which Muslim defenders love to quote when critics of Islam point out the over 164 jihadi verses found in the Koran:

There is no compulsion in religion. The right direction is henceforth distinct from error. And he who rejects false deities and believeth in Allah hath grasped a firm handhold which will never break. Allah is Hearer, Knower (Sûrah 2:256)

Unfortunately, at the beginning of his ministry, Muhammad had only convinced less than 100 people to accept his new religion—mostly friends and family. One of the very earliest conciliatory instructions given by Allah—while Muhammad was weak and had very few followers—was addressed to the nonbelievers in Mecca:

Say: "O disbelievers! Worship not that which you worship; Nor worship you that which I worship. And I shall not worship that which you worship. Nor will you worship that which I worship. Unto you your religion and unto me my religion" (Sûrah 109:1-6).

Desperate to make Islam spread, Muhammad solicited the help of his uncle (Abu Talib). He asked Talib to hold a meeting behind closed doors with the leaders of the Quraysh tribe to suggest that his tribe begin to say, "There is no God but Allah."

Muhammad believed their cooperation would help him conquer the non-Arab tribes (al-Tabari, Volume VI, p. 96, 1178).

The idea was to speak peace and coexist with the public at large while trying—at the same time—to gather an army to overthrow his adversaries. Muslims refer to this type of deception as taqiyya or permissible lying when Muslims are weak and their lying promotes a favorable outcome regarding Islam (Sûrah 3:28).

This did not go well with the Quraysh who rejected the idea and resented the fact that while they were tolerant of Muhammad's new religion, he insulted theirs. This growing animosity led to Stage Two when Muhammad had to seek refuge in the oasis village of Yathrib.

Stage Two: The Spurned Lover

We now enter Stage Two, which we will refer to as the spurned lover syndrome. In this stage, we embark upon a more defensive jihad mentality by Muhammad. At this point, Muhammad must have felt like a spurned lover when his tribe and the other inhabitants of Mecca rejected his new religion. Now relocating to Yathrib, perhaps Muhammad thought his new religion of Islam was more compatible with the Jews and Christian in the area. A lot of what Muhammad taught included stories that claimed to be—if not true to form—of biblical origin. The Jewish tribes of Yathrib—along with the Christians in the region—believed Muhammad when he told them how he and his small band of Muslim followers were victims of the majority in Mecca because they were persecuted for their religious belief, which was very similar to the religion of the inhabitants of Yathrib's monotheistic believers; consequently, the villagers of Yathrib offered Muhammad and his followers support.

As is usually the case, the spurned lover turned to more sympathetic ears and sobs about how mistreated he was and forced to leave his home, when all he wanted to do was bring love and blessings to his intended bride (the Quraysh tribe) who he was trying to woo.

Like any sympathetic friend who only hears one side of the story, it appeared to the inhabitants of Yathrib that the spurned lover was indeed poorly treated. It was during this time that—-coincidently—Allah too changed his mind about being tolerant, so he abrogated the previous conciliatory revelations he gave to Muhammad in favor of more militant ones:

Sanction is given unto those who fight because they have been wronged; and Allah is indeed Able to give them victory; Those who have been driven from their homes unjustly only because they said: Our Lord is Allah - For had it not been for Allah's repelling some men by means of others, [and thereby protecting the] cloisters and churches and oratories and mosques, wherein the name of Allah is often mentioned, would assuredly have been pulled down. Truly Allah helps one who helps Him. Lo! Allah is Strong, Almighty" (Sûrah 22:39-40, clarification mine).

Yet contrary to what Muhammad told the people of Yathrib, the hostility did not start out against him, but rather it was he who attacked the religion of the Meccans. This behavior is a continuation of Stage One (taqiyya stage), which, as we saw above—is the permissible lying/deception stage—when Muslims are weak and outnumbered and play the "persecution or victim card:"

(Muhammad) declared Islam publicly to his fellow tribesmen. When he did so, they [the polytheists of Mecca] did not withdraw from him or reject him in any way, as far as I have heard, until he spoke of their gods and denounced them (al-Tabari Vol.VI, p.93, bracketed clarification mine).

We (the Meccans) have never seen the like of what we have endured from this man (Muhammad). He has derided our traditional values, abused our forefathers, reviled our religion, caused division among us, and insulted our gods. We have endured a great deal from him (al-Tabari, Vol.VI, p.101).

As Muhammad gained strength during this time in Yathrib, he began using the tactic of terrorism by attacking caravans from Mecca. He attacked seven caravans and the Meccans did nothing in retaliation. During the days prior to Muhammad and his new religion of Islam, the Arabs observed what was known as the "sacred months" which consisted of a four-month festival in Mecca—which should not be confused with the Islamic "sacred month"—that came later. For the duration of the pilgrimage to Mecca, all tribes and religions were to observe a truce until the "sacred months" was over. There could not be any war, quarrels or hostilities.

However, this time it was during the "sacred months" when Muhammad attacked the seventh caravan that also resulted in the death of a member of that hapless caravan. In order to justify what Muhammad had done, another divine revelation absolving him from killing anyone during the "sacred months" was needed from Allah. Allah did not disappoint Muhammad:

They question you (O Muhammad) with regard to warfare in the sacred month. Say: "Warfare therein is a great (transgression), but to turn (men) from the way of Allah, and to disbelieve in Him and in the Inviolable Place of Worship, and to expel His people thence, is a greater sin with Allah; for persecution is worse than killing" (Sûrah 2:217a).

Thanks be to Allah, Muhammad was vindicated of his hostile actions during the sacred month. As his child bride, Aisha once told the Prophet, "I feel that your Lord [Allah] hastens in fulfilling your wishes and desires" (Sahih al-Bukhari, Vol. 6, Book 60, No. 311, bracketed clarification mine).

Because the Meccans needed to conduct peaceful, unobstructed trade for the sake of making a living and feeding their families, something had to be done. While they made every effort to avoid war, it was decided that the next caravan would need to be protected; however, the armed forces the Meccans sent to protect the eight caravans from an unprovoked attack by Muslims, resulted in their defeat by Muhammad at the Battle of Badr; thus the first war between Muslim and non-Muslim armies was an unprovoked attack by the Muslims against people whose only crime was that they wanted to protect themselves from Muslim terrorists. The Battle of Badr set the course for Islamic history for millennia to come.

These violent and unprovoked actions on the part of Muhammad did not go unnoticed by the three Jewish host tribes of Yathrib, but they would soon realize that once they became involved with Muhammad, there was no turning back. It wasn't long before Muhammad was able to create justifiable reasons to turn on his Jewish allies, just as he did with the people of Mecca. During Stage Two of the defensive jihad, any satirical poets who poked fun at Muhammad—as well as anyone who criticized the Prophet of Islam—were expected to be killed, a tradition that continues to this very day.

Stage Three: "I'm Over You and I Want Revenge"

Now we enter Stage Three, or the aggressive jihad stage, when Muslims have ascended to power—due partially to their high birth rate which allows their ever increasing population to create a shift in power—through ownership of businesses, supplementing the laws of the host country with Shari Law, infiltrating the government through political appointments and through elected offices. With the openly offensive stage, we now have the uncompromising revelations from Allah, which abrogates the conciliatory language found in Stage One when Muhammad was in the courting stage:

O Prophet! Strive against the disbelievers and the hypocrites! Be harsh with them. Their ultimate abode is hell, a hapless journey's end (Sûrah 9:73).

Fight those who believe not in Allah nor the Last Day, nor hold that forbidden which hath been forbidden by Allah and His Messenger, nor acknowledge the religion of Truth, (even if they are) of the People of the Book, until they pay the Jizya with willing submission, and feel themselves subdued (Sûrah 9:29, Abdullah Yusuf Ali).

O ye who believe! Fight those of the disbelievers who are near to you [neighbors], and let them find harshness in you, and know that Allah is with those who keep their duty (unto Him) (Sûrah 9:123, bracketed clarifi8cation mine).

Once Islam takes hold, there cannot be any tolerance. One of many examples can be found in modern Saudi Arabia where churches and synagogues are discouraged. U.S. Military Chaplains are not even allowed to wear their chaplain pin (Cross) on their lapel:

Sahih Muslim Volume 19, Number 4366: "'The Book of Jihad and Expedition" (Kitab Al-Jihad wal-Siyar):

It has been narrated by 'Umar b. al-Khattib that he heard the Messenger of Allah (may peace be upon him) say: "I will expel the Jews and Christians from the Arabian Peninsula and will not leave any but Muslim."

Based on the Qur'an there is no room for loopholes. Islam declares an eternal (never-ending) war against all other religions. In Islam there can never be any closure or end to hostilities against the Jews and Christians. Because of Muhammad's last words, Islam can never be tolerant toward Christians and Jews:

Allah's Apostle, in his fatal illness said, "Allah cursed the Jews and the Christians, for they built the places of worship at the graves of their prophets." And if that had not been the case, then the Prophet's grave would have been made prominent before the people. So (the Prophet) was afraid, or the people were afraid that his grave might be taken as a place for worship (Sahih Al-Bukhari, Vol. 2, Book 23, No, 472).

Therefore, of all the religions in the world today, Islam is the only socio-political-legal-religion that only allows for Allah and world denomination—if not through peace and subterfuge—then through the force of arms. There is no wiggle room in the Qur'an or Hadiths for tolerance. How can there be when its founder's last words were "...Allah curse the Christians and Jews!" Consequently, Islam (submission) is not only incompatible with democracy, but based solely on its core teachings of absolute dominance, it cannot fall under the protection of our First Amendment because the overthrow of our Constitution lies at Islam's very core and is necessary for Islam to be fully realized.

Dr. J.P. Sloane has researched various religions, sects and cults in order to understand how they interact, and influence each other. Dr. Sloane graduated from: Purdue University, The Institute of Charismatic Studies at Oral Roberts University, The Moody Bible Institute, and The Institute of Jewish-Christian Studies. He earned a B.A., Summa Cum Laude, from The Masters College where he studied at their IBEX campus in Israel and earned an M.A. in Counseling. At the Trinity Theological Seminary he earned two doctorates one of which is a Ph.D. with Distinction, in Religious Studies (World Religions).

7
Benghazi: A Tale of Two Reports

by Michael Ingmire

September 12, 2012, is a date that changed the purpose of my existence. I was a Blues/Roots musician rehearsing, playing gigs, writing songs and I would use my music history background and writing ability to write music articles. However, on September 12, 2012 everything changed when my wife and I found out that our nephew by marriage, Sean Smith, had been murdered in the September 11/12th terrorist attack in Benghazi, Libya. Sean's murder devastated our family. It led me to question why he had been deployed to this area without adequate security. He had worked for the State Department for several years, under Rice and Powell, without incident. Sean's mother Pat has never been told why her son was not protected.

Sean's murder led me to justifiable anger and hundreds of hours of research on exactly what happened on that terrible night in Benghazi. This also led me to being the first family member to support Congressman Frank Wolf's 28 efforts to establish a House Select Committee to investigate the attack. I then placed hundreds of phone calls to Congressional and Senatorial representatives asking them to support and sponsor the Select Committee process. That effort has resulted in over 50 print, radio, and television interviews on a variety of Benghazi subjects. I am still a Blues musician and it was not my aspiration to be an activist. But considering the before, during, and aftermath of Benghazi, it is my responsibility as a citizen to do so. Considering the state of our country, it is important for all citizens to embrace that responsibility. I was taught to always speak out against injustice.

Now there is a movement among the mainstream press corps to consider the subject of Benghazi to be over. Considering that they never reported honestly on Benghazi how could it be over for them? That is also the frame of reference for some politicians, on both sides of the aisle, who deny that any sense of accountability should be applied to the Obama Administration.

Because the media refused to cover the Benghazi terrorist attack it was a under reported issue on the 2012 presidential campaign trail and Obama was not held accountable for his failed foreign policy and won re-election. Now the media again is for the most part ignoring the findings of both the House Select Committee Report and the Citizen's Commission on Benghazi report.

It has been three years and ten months and there is still no accountability for the four ghosts of Benghazi.

The House Select Committee on Benghazi released their final report on June 28th, 2016. 29 On June 29th, 2016 just as important, but grossly underreported by all members of the press, was the release of the Citizen's Commission on Benghazi report: "Betrayal in Benghazi: A Dereliction of Duty." 30

I will first examine the House Select Committee's Final Report on Benghazi. When I attended the first hearing of the House Select Committee on Benghazi in September 2014, I remember the following words from House Select Committee Chairman Trey Gowdy, "I remain convinced that all our fellow citizens are entitled to all of the facts about what happened before, during, and after the attacks in Benghazi."

In my continued analysis of the recently released House Select Committee on Benghazi report I am deeply troubled by the lack of any real emphasis on the before that Gowdy mentioned in September 2014. The House Committee did address the deteriorating situation and the attacks on the British Ambassador, the State Department's Diplomatic Outpost and the Red Cross. But no mention of Libya during Gaddafi's reign and no addressing of why he was deposed. These are far too important of a fact to omit when considering the atmosphere that prompted the attacks.

For me personally, the strongest points of the House Select Committee's report and the many hearings are as follows, along with my opinions:

- There were over 600 requests for additional security by Ambassador Chris Stevens that were refused or ignored and security was actually reduced at the Benghazi Diplomatic

Outpost on the anniversary of 9/11.

- In the report there was an honest recollection of what happened in the Diplomatic Outpost by a Diplomatic security agent who was there with my nephew Sean Smith and Ambassador Stevens on September 11, 2012. Moving to my soul.

- Hillary Clinton and her staff had a 7:30 PM meeting on September 11, 2012 to determine what sort of statement she would issue regarding the attack. The House report indicates that the ruse of the video was discussed during this meeting. Note: So as Tyrone Woods was fighting for his life on the roof of the CIA Annex, Mrs. Clinton was practicing yet another attempt at a spin. She is apt with that skill. In an interview a couple years back with FOX news I stated that Mrs. Clinton and President Obama made a political decision as opposed to a security decision.

- The House reports states that both President Obama and Secretary of Defense, Leon Panetta, both ordered forces to be deployed to Benghazi. Really? Well where were they? I will ask again: Who gave the order for forces to stand down? If orders were ignored, who was dismissed from their position in the Obama administration?

- Why were Marines coming from the Marine Fleet Anti-Terrorism Team, or FAST, based in Rota, Spain made to change their uniforms four times at the Tripoli airport when in transit to aid the personnel at the Outpost and Annex?

- As determined by her e-mails referenced during her October 2015 testimony before the House Select Committee on Benghazi, Mrs. Clinton stated in her phone call to the Egyptian Prime Minister, to President el-Magariaf of Libya and in her e-mail to her daughter Chelsea blaming more than a video. In her phone calls and e-mails she blamed Ansar al Sharia or "an Al-Qaeda-like group" for the being the perpetrators behind the attack.

- It details the preparation of the talking points about the "infamous video" and the grooming of Susan Rice as a taxpayer-paid liar for the Sunday talk show circuit. President Obama and Hillary Clinton continued to promote that lie.

- It was pro-Gaddafi loyalists that came to the aid of the

CIA Contractors and personnel at the CIA Annex on September 12, 2012. The 13th of February Militia and British Blue Mountain Libya security personnel were largely ineffectual.

- Additionally, we can thank The House Select Committee, Judicial Watch and Catherine Herridge for bringing the discovery of Mrs. Clinton's various private, and illegal, e-mail servers to light. Don't blame Trump; blame Clinton for making us less safe with her carelessness in safeguarding classified information.

These are the important points as detailed by the House Select Committee's final report on Benghazi. It is a responsibility for all American citizens to read the report in its entirety. You can access the report at the following website link: http://benghazi.house.gov/NewInfo 2

Ultimately, I feel the House Select Committee's report fails, as it does not provide pre-attack information on Benghazi. Nor does it really hold anyone responsible for the events leading up to the attack, the lack of security, and the cover-up. The House Select Committee dealt with the politics of Benghazi first hand by the obfuscation of the Obama Administration for failing to provide all the pertinent documents. Additionally, the Democrats on the committee obstructed the process whenever possible. It is a grave mistake to call this the "final" report.

By contrast, the Citizens Commission on Benghazi's report, "Betrayal in Benghazi: A Dereliction of Duty," makes no declaration that this is their final report. Unlike the 800 page, unwieldy, House Report, the Citizen's Commission 76 page report describes effectively the before, during, and aftermath of the attack. The report reads clearly and was designed by the staff at Accuracy in Media. The Commission includes members such as Clare Lopez, Vice President for Research and Analysis at the Center for Security Policy in Washington D.C. Lt. Col. Dennis B. Haney, USAF (Ret.), and Former Congressman and Retired Army Lieutenant Allen West among other distinguished citizens.

Here are some of the key findings as covered in the "Betrayal in Benghazi: A Dereliction of Duty" report:
- The Obama administration actively supported the replacement of quasi-secular North African rulers in Tunisia, Libya and Egypt with Muslim Brotherhood rule. Note: In this

report, I found it particularly fascinating that Muammar Gaddafi was trying to establish a pan-African currency based on the Libyan Dinar. Gaddafi's desire to stop selling oil in U.S. dollars was alarming to French President Nicolas Sarkozy who saw it as a threat to "the financial security of the world."

- In Libya, the Obama Administration turned against Muammar Gaddafi in favor of supporting the Libyan Muslim Brotherhood and supplied material aid to known al-Qaeda linked militias to topple his regime. Note, by my assessment and understanding, President Obama and Hillary Clinton became illegal gunrunners and instituted an illegal, without Congressional approval, regime change.

- The Obama Administration deliberately withheld urgently requested security for the U.S. Mission in Benghazi. Note: This was done at least in part to buttress the false campaign narrative that "al-Qaeda was on the run."

- The Obama administration ignored multiple advance warnings about an impending attack. Hillary Clinton bore the ultimate responsibility for diplomatic security and failed to do so in Benghazi.

- Despite a failure by the Pentagon to pre-position forces in advance, various U.S. assets were available to deploy immediately, but were held back. Note: Again, I ask who gave the stand down order? Who had the authority to do so? Answer: President Obama.

- The President, former Secretary of State Hillary Clinton, former Secretary of Defense Leon Panetta and Gen. Martin Dempsey, former Chairman of the Joint Chiefs of Staff, must be required to answer for their dereliction of duty. Note: Damn straight, this is a criminal offense that smacks of treason and should be prosecuted as such.

- The Obama White House and Clinton lead a concerted two-week campaign to cover up the facts of the Benghazi attack. Note: Without a doubt, the Obama administration made a political decision to hide their gross negligence of failing to make an appropriate security decision.

I wholeheartedly support the findings of the Citizen's Commission on Benghazi report. I find it to be factually accurate and well written. Unlike the House report, they hold key members of the Obama administration guilty of dereliction of duty. I recommend that every American citizen read this report, which can be found online at the following website link: http://www.aim.org/wp-content/uploads/2016/06/AIM-Citizens-Commission-on-Benghazi-FINAL-REPORT-June-2016.pdf 3

The irresponsible behavior of President Barack Obama, 31 Hillary Clinton, 32 and various members of the Obama administration supported the United State's involvement with Libya's "Arab Spring" and supplied material support to America's enemies. It is also one of the many reasons why President Obama should be removed from office and prosecuted for war crimes and why Hillary Clinton should never be President.

President Obama and Hillary Clinton are guilty of involuntary manslaughter for deploying Ambassador Stevens and my nephew, Sean Smith to Benghazi on the anniversary of 9/11 without adequate security measures in place. They knew the risk and ignored them in order to promote a false narrative that their foreign policy was working and the war on terror was over. This partisan decision and gross dereliction of duty cost four Americans their lives.

The American media died an ignoble death in 2008. The lack of reporting on the details of the Benghazi attack by the press is shameful and, in its own way, a dereliction of duty. The rare exception is the Pulitzer Prize worthy reporting of Catherine Herridge. Catherine did the heavy lifting in her reports regarding the Benghazi attack. We found out that the gross criminal behavior of this administration surpasses that of the Nixon administration because no one died in Watergate.

The destabilization of North Africa and the Middle East by the Obama administration created the chaos that led to the formation of ISIS. President Obama and Hillary Clinton are the creators of that organization. I pray that we elect someone that will appoint a competent Attorney General that will prosecute them for their crimes.

Michael Ingmire is a musician, writer, and activist based in North Carolina. As a musician he has opened for musicians/performers as varied as Albert King, John Lee Hooker, Johnny Copeland, Allen Ginsberg, Wilson Pickett, Mac Arnold, Bob Margolin, among many. After the death of his nephew by marriage, Sean Smith, in the 2012 Benghazi attack, Michael's writing took on a political tone and in addition to being a regular contributor for PolitiChicks he has written for The Daily Caller, Fox News.com, and The Daily Signal. He is an active voice in the search for accountability about Benghazi.

PART FIVE: PARENTING

To allow teachers, social media and journalists, who are espousing an almost propaganda philosophy, to be the strongest voices in our children's life, we are abdicating our responsibility as parents. – **Tina Drake**

1

SEVEN THINGS EVERY PARENT SHOULD INSTILL IN THEIR CHILDREN ABOUT POLITICS

by Tina Drake

"When you hold your baby in your arms the first time, and you think of all the things you can say and do to influence him, it's a tremendous responsibility. What you do with him can influence not only him, but everyone he meets and not for a day or a month or a year but for time and eternity." **-- Rose Kennedy** [1]

For Rose Kennedy to share this quote would cause someone to think she had stood at the foot of every mother's bed after she had delivered each of her children. Whenever a parent is first introduced to their child, the thought of their future potential is absolutely overwhelming. At times, it is unquestionably the heaviest burden placed on the heart of a parent.

Parenting is such an enormous task. As parents, we recognize the obvious things that a child must learn to survive life. The arduous lessons in children feeding themselves, using the bathroom and dressing themselves are sometimes overwhelming. That is until it is time to teach them how to drive. One dynamic area of parental teaching is based in the essence of what we believe and what our children will grow to believe.

In previous generations, religious and political beliefs of families were passed from generation to generation, with little or no resistance. The spiritual belief of the family was passed along, based on tradition, sometimes rather than heartfelt contemplation of each person. Even if a child didn't agree with the traditional family belief, it maintained a semblance of obedience, to maintain familial harmony. This also translated to family political beliefs.

If the patriarchs of the family were conservative, so were

the offspring. The same behavior also occurred in liberal families. As society has aged, descendants have developed courage to renounce the family political beliefs. For some, this has been liberating, but for others, it has been tragic.

Politics and religion are the two topics deemed taboo by previous generations to discuss in public. As a result of that encouragement, wisdom from past generations has been denied today's youth.

There is certainly a need for all individuals to learn, develop and defend a belief system, both politically and religiously, on their own. However, with today's youth, we are allowing these belief systems to be developed in a social networking environment, sometimes based on nameless and faceless individual's beliefs and ideas. Because of our strong desire to allow young people, even our own children, to develop their own ideas and opinions, we are retracting ourselves too far from our children's sphere of influence. There is a tipping point, where our avoidance of political and religious influence in our children's life, becomes dangerous. When we require our children, whether pre-teen, teenage or young adult, to find, investigate and adopt beliefs in these areas, without our influence, we are endangering not only our child's future, but also the future of our country.

When we sit and spend time discussing current events in religion and politics, as well as the history that has lead us to this point, with our children, we are investing in everyone's future.

To allow teachers, social media and journalists, who are espousing an almost propaganda philosophy, to be the strongest voices in our children's life, we are abdicating our responsibility as parents.

Open and detailed conversations with our teenage children are a daily occurrence in our home. Our family has been blessed to have those opportunities. I know there are some families where daily conversations aren't possible, but weekly ones are probably doable.

In a recent conversation with our son, seven elements of "life participation" emerged. These elements are keys to helping our children, no matter what their age; develop a belief system, which will not only benefit their life but also the lives of those around them.

1. Study history – In doing this, a person will learn what leaders have done, that was successful and beneficial to their country. A person will also learn what was a failure and brought the demise of countries.

2. Study literature – Through the study of literature, a person will learn, understand and discuss the philosophies that have greatly influenced leaders throughout history and today. These are the concepts, good and bad, which create political and religious culture.

3. Influence – Through discussion people create and develop ideas. In most cases, when we discuss ideas, philosophies and theologies, we make decisions on major topics. Our conversations with others are always an influential opportunity.

4. Lead – Leading is different than influence. Leading is being the example of a belief or idea. It is acting out that belief or idea, in the hope of creating a positive effect.

5. Get involved in the process – Don't be afraid to write letters, read about candidates, and engage in sometimes intense and philosophical or theological developing discussions. Just because you discuss an idea, concept or belief with someone, doesn't mean you have to agree or adopt that philosophy or way of life. You will, however, be better educated in what is happening around you.

6. Be spiritual – It is obvious that a spiritual drive comes from a deeper place in our heart. Our family's spirituality is deeply rooted in the teachings of Jesus Christ and the Bible. As parents, my husband and I entertain all types of questions from our children. It would be a lie to say we aren't prayerful our children will stay in the teachings of God. We also know, for them to stay, they must be allowed to ask questions and find their beliefs on their own. When spiritual beliefs are found, there is a sense of fulfillment and wholeness that is achieved. This type of knowledge and fulfillment assures us, we are not the center of the universe.

7. Commit – Decide what you believe and commit to it. Each day do something to move your beliefs forward. If we commit to a belief and never deepen our stand in it, our roots will begin to grow weak and we will be at risk of falling prey to the turbulent winds of despair and confusion.

All good parents understand what Rose Kennedy was saying. It should be our joyful burden and responsibility to mold our children into adults. Never delegate that beautiful and rewarding opportunity!

Tina Drake is a follower of Christ, who loves helping others see God in all things. She is a wife and mother who enjoys spending time with her family and serving her community. Tina is a graduate the University of Arizona.

2

ARE WE RAISING A GENERATION OF NARCISSISTS?

by Morgan Brittany

What is it with many college students today? Actually, what is it with non-college kids as well? What is it that has given them the attitude that they are "entitled" to success without putting in years of working their way up the ladder?

I don't mean to paint with a broad brush here, there are plenty of kids today who work hard and have good values. Just look at our men and women in the military and you can see that there is hope for this country. No, I am talking about a group of young college students who were asked to take the American Freshman Survey [2]. Nine million young people have taken this survey over the last 47 years and when you analyze the results you can see that young people today are convinced of their own greatness whether they have accomplished anything or not.

They tend to believe that they are smarter, more talented, more confident and more apt to succeed than any of their predecessors. *They* may believe it, but researchers have found that there is a disconnect between the student's opinion of themselves and the actual truth of their ability. These kids actually believe that just by wanting and wishing for success, they will get it without putting in the blood, sweat and tears it takes to really succeed.

So where does this skewed since of self-worth come from? I can pinpoint the day that I realized we were in trouble with this generation. It was my son Cody's first Little League game. Three or four of the kids on the team were standout players. They practiced all the time, went to the batting cage and really worked at being good at the sport. Others either didn't have any athletic ability or just flat out didn't want to be there. They never picked up a bat until the day of the game and couldn't wait to go home and do something else.

100

The dedicated kids played their hearts out and Cody's team won. The coach put the kids all in a circle, congratulated them and then proceeded to give each of them a "game ball" for an outstanding job. As Cody and I walked to the car, he tossed the ball in his bag and asked me, "Why did everybody get a reward? I made three base hits and Casey made two RBI's. Some of those kids didn't even try."

I didn't quite know what to say to him. He continued. "Why should I try so hard? I'll get a game ball anyway." At that point, I tried to explain to a seven year old that he had to try and be the best at whatever he did. He needed to practice and hone his skills so that he could be proud of what he accomplished and not just get a reward for doing nothing. I told him that you don't appreciate anything that you don't earn and work hard for and that some day he would understand.

So here we are today. Those seven year olds are now graduating from college and expecting their "reward". Look at Occupy Wall Street [3]; there is a perfect example of privileged, coddled children who probably have wealthy families that paid for their law degrees at some liberal institution. They are so outraged that they have to actually "pay" for their student loans when they can't find a job. How dare they be asked to do that!

The future doesn't look too bright for these narcissistic young people. Studies now say that they will more than likely suffer from depression as they get older, have trouble finding meaningful relationships and have to come to grips with the fact that they are not as great as they thought they were.

Narcissism is defined as *excessive self-love and vanity, self-admiration and self-centeredness*. Remember when it was a bad thing to be full of yourself and conceited? You were looked down upon if you acted that way. Today, whether it is because of the celebrity culture, social media or parenting styles, kids aspire to be "known" and talked about. Their heroes are more than likely celebrities and reality stars than hard working business people. In one sense, how can you blame them when they see the Kardashians [4] and the Jersey Shore [5] kids pulling in millions of dollars for doing nothing? Why bother to spend years going to college when you can become a YouTube sensation? Have an affair with a famous sports star and you can take it to the bank.

Unfortunately this will end badly. We can already see where our country is headed with its runaway entitlement mentality. If this generation of young people doesn't wake up, our society really is lost.

As bad as this all sounds, I like to try to find a glimmer of hope. Perhaps all of the turmoil that we are going through in this country and with this culture is for a reason. Perhaps God has put these challenges in our way to finally make us wake up and see the light. Maybe a jolt into reality for this young generation will actually make them better people as they age.

The world didn't end on December 21, 2012, as predicted by the Mayans. Maybe it wasn't an ending that was predicted, but enlightenment instead.

3
AMERICA: LAND OF THE FEELING, HOME OF THE HIGHLY EMOTIONAL

by Ann-Marie Murrell

America could learn a few important coping skills from my Texas upbringing.

Growing up in Texas, all the boys I knew were taught to deal with their emotions privately. They were raised to either stuff it all inside or take it out on the football field— or maybe have a few beers with friends. (Yes, there was a bit of teenage drinking back then...) Crying or whining about their problems in public was never an option with any of the Texas boys I grew up with and to this day I still respect them for that.

When my best friend's father died, I don't recall seeing any signs of sorrow when he came back to school. He was very quiet for a while, maybe a little withdrawn—but soon after he was completely back to normal (although maybe hitting a little harder on the football field).

I have an image of those Texas boys as strong, independent, and exceptional. They all worked hard during the summer--bailing hay, working at the local ore mining company or at T & N Railroad, and they worked just as hard in school. Those young men are now even stronger, exceptional adults, all living a standard of life everyone should aspire to.

With all of us Texas girls, we dealt with our problems in the usual 'girly' way by talking to friends, crying on each other's shoulders, or in extreme cases (when talking wasn't an option) we suffered silently.

Of course "suffering silently" is probably an unimaginable concept with today's youth. Every tiny thought bubble of emotion that pops into their heads is immediately blasted throughout social media to be commented on, liked, and/or retweeted. Kids are told, via media and the educational system, that their problems and feelings are *everything*. They are made to believe that the entire universe revolves around their emotions. And with the new Feelings-Oriented style of parenting, *not* crying in public is now something to be ashamed of.

In this new myopic world of today, people are encouraged to look at the trees instead of the forest. They are told the Big Picture is completely irrelevant and in fact, the only thing that matters is the way the little things in life make them *feel*. They have no understanding that so many "news" items are false flags meant to distract them from seeing the real problems of the world. Instead of stopping to think, *"Hey, are these politicians using me to further some nefarious agenda?"* they fall back on that giant, slobbering monster they were raised to pay attention to above any and all else in life: their Emotions.

When it comes to virtually every issue in the world today (other than ISIS and Iran, which actually need our attention), Emotions take over. It doesn't matter if something doesn't make sense logically—it's all about how it makes you Feel. For example, this sentence alone has the ability to send many Emotions-driven folks to the brink of an all-out conniption: "Illegal aliens are here illegally."

Why would this sentence make them go insane? For one, the word "alien" bothers Emotional people. It doesn't matter that the literal meaning of the word "alien" is *"foreign"*—which they are. The other word that makes them angry is the word "illegal," implying that the foreign people broke the law to live here--which they did. But again, things like facts don't matter because the word "illegal" makes them *feeeel* bad.

As for my Texas friends and me, the way we coped with our problems as children helped pave the way towards making us the strong adults we are today. If we had an issue with something, big or small, we dealt with it the best we could and we moved on. We didn't sweat the small things because there were so many big things to actually sweat about. Speaking of sweat, here are a few things this ultra-emotional America could learn from my Texas upbringing.

We didn't call Child Protective Services if a scalding-hot Texas classroom didn't have air-conditioning, and let me tell you, an un-air-conditioned room in Texas is hot like you can't imagine. But out of all my years in Texas no one ever died from being too hot in a classroom. If an out-of-state kid moved to our town and asked, *"Why is it so hot in here?"* the answer would be, "Because we're in Texas, you _____" (insert preferred derogatory cuss word). How do you cope? You drink lots of water between classes. End of the issue.

In the summer we played outside, all day and into the night. We didn't have iPhones or cell phones to keep us busy, we found things to do on our own and didn't complain about it. We walked miles in the woods or rode horses all day without adult supervision and none of us died from snakebites (and none of our parents were worried about it because we knew how to deal with snakes). We rode our bikes on rocks and dirt without bike helmets and if we fell or got hurt, we dusted ourselves off and got back on that bike.

If we *did* get hurt, our parents didn't freak out and call an ambulance (not that we had an ambulance service back then). If you had a bleeding gash, you got a squirt of Bactine, a Band-aide, and went back out to play and you didn't sit around crying about it all day. (And if you did sit around crying, you'd be shunned and rightly so.) No one ever died or became emotionally traumatized from scrapes and scratches.

We didn't call our local news channel and threaten to burn things down if a kid got paddled, which they did, and often, myself included. When we got paddled, we knew there was a darn good reason and sometimes we'd actually weigh the odds and risk it. We chose the difference between right and wrong, and paid when we chose the latter. Our *feelings* weren't hurt, just our bottoms for a few moments. We all lived. No scars. No police involved.

In the summer we swam at Daingerfield State Park or went water skiing at Johnson's Creek from sunup to sundown largely without parental involvement. Instead of SPF 5000, we slathered our skin with baby oil and/or cooking oil to get as tan as humanly possible. As far as I know, none of us have died from skin cancer.

If we had the sniffles, our parents didn't coddle us and

keep us home from school. In my house you had to have 104 degrees fever and vomiting non-stop to miss a day, and even then you were thoroughly questioned ("Is there an important test you'll miss today?").

We were not only required to say 'yes ma'am' or 'yes sir' we were publicly reprimanded if we didn't. Even if someone was only a few years older than us, they were 'ma'am' or 'sir'. It was a matter of respect and dignity, and every child I grew up with understood the importance of this. When I first moved to California, barely 20, I was often scolded when I called someone 'sir' or 'ma'am'. Even if they were 90 years old, they were angry that I was perhaps accusing them of being old. Which they were. (By the way, I raised my son to call his California teachers 'ma'am' or 'sir' even if they asked him not to.)

Speaking of reprimands, if we acted up in public it was dealt with then and there. If we dared to act like petulant brats in the grocery store, our parents didn't wait until we got home to put us in "time out". Matter of fact, we would have PRAYED for time out back then. Worst-case scenario we were given a good swat on the bottom--or my mother would give my sister and me her most effective threat: *"You better stop it or I'm going to pinch a plug out of you!"* No one ever took videos of parents reprimanding their children to give to the police, and no once called them 'bad parents'. The only disapproving looks came from people who saw parents ignoring their screaming kids, and in many cases they'd not only say something to the kids but they'd also fuss at the parents, too.

No one called the ACLU when we sang Christmas carols at school and no one demanded we change the lyrics to accommodate atheists. Period.

We were raised to unconditionally respect our flag, our country, our American history, and the great state of Texas. (And the Dallas Cowboys, back when Tom Landry was coaching. True story.)

We didn't blame our coaches (or football field conditions or weather) if our football team didn't win. Winning football is very important in Texas but you win by being the best team. Period. Texas football players and all us cheerleaders knew this and worked hard to make it happen every season. Or not.

If we did get mad at our coaches or teachers, we'd roll their house with toilet paper (aka 'TP'). And in many cases, we TP'd the houses of the coaches and teachers we loved the most. No one ever called the police or put us in jail for this, and many times we even helped clean up after. (As the daughter of a favorite teacher, I had to clean a lot of toilet paper out of our front yard...)

During Homecoming week in high school we made huge bonfires (without any fire trucks nearby) where we held our pep rally. One year, while in the middle of our Fight Song (and yes, that's what we called it), a spark landed on my polyester cheerleader uniform and it started to catch fire. I didn't scream for help and I didn't try to sue the makers of the uniform--- I quickly patted it out, rubbed off the pain, and continued cheering. (I still have the uniform with the giant, blackened hole in it.) We were also never reported for threatening violence when we made signs like 'Kill the Lions!' because we never killed any Lions other than on the football field. Oh--and my senior year during Spirit Week we had a "Hunt the Lions" day and we carried around guns and knives all day. During school. Were they real, or toys? Good question. No one died, no one called the police, and no one was Emotionally Damaged...

As a child in Bishop, Texas, all us kids used to ride our bikes behind the trucks spraying out billowing white clouds of DDT. None of us got cancer and/or died from this, and of course none of us got malaria from the ginormous mosquitoes, either.

The national news networks never came to our school to report that every truck in the Hughes Springs High School parking lot had a gun rack and a rifle in the back window. (Unlocked trucks with possibly loaded rifles, mind you.) The reason the news never covered this is because no one ever used any of those guns for anything other than hunting and protection. And, needless to say, no guns or trucks were ever stolen from said parking lot.

Speaking of, every boy I knew in Texas learned to shoot as soon as they were old enough to hold a rifle. They were taught to respect their firearms and knew how to take care of them. No one ever questioned this, or thought of it as "violent" or dangerous, because no one I grew up with considered God-given rights "dangerous".

Yes, there were gay people (which I found out years after graduation) but there were no "gay issues" in our school. No one demanded special treatment, or preferential bathrooms, or threatened to sue anyone for not calling him or her by the correct terminology. All we knew was that some people were different; some people got teased. In fact at different times, all of us felt 'different' and we all got teased for various reasons. You either learn to cope, or you don't. If you do, you're set for life. If you don't, bless your heart.

And yes, there were both white and black racists in our school, and everyone knew who those racists were---but we never called them out about it. Most of us just prayed for them and hoped they'd someday see the light. And most of them did.

Every time I find myself going ballistic over any single topic—whether it's flags or sex-oriented issues or politicians—I remind myself to look at the overall picture, Texas-style and ask myself these three questions:

1. Is there maybe something bigger I need to focus on rather than the way this one issue makes me *feel*?

2. Is there something lurking behind that issue they're trying to prevent me from seeing?

3. Am I being manipulated by a media--and a political system-- that thrives on stirring up my emotions?

If so, I step back, take a big breath, maybe drink some Sweet Tea, and refocus. Because folks, we can't save a country as big as America if we keep watching those shiny, sparkly things the media keeps throwing at us. It's time to toughen up and start looking at the big giant forest, because those tiny little trees might distract us and make us cry.

4
MEMO TO THE MOM IN THE STORE WITH BRATS

by Jenny Kefauver

MEMO *to the mom in the store who wasn't paying attention, watch out: You just avoided a lawsuit waiting to happen.*

The scenario played out like any typical one in suburban America – a last-minute trip to a regional big-box store to shop for the usual accouterments of the family fridge. I am attempting to park my cart at one of the open cash register lines, when I am blocked by two little girls, guessing around ages 2 and 4, shoving each other around as siblings do. I did not see their parent/guardian right away as I did not realize their back was turned to them – not paying attention or even looking their way - as they too were waiting to be rung up by a cashier.

Next thing I knew, the two little girls, with wide-open eyes, looked around for their next source of amusement as shoving each other was just not cutting it. To their delight, they find one of those long, curly plastic elastic cords that are used to close off a cash register line and proceed to stretch it all the way towards the next register lane – while eying the nearby unmanned desktop computer and monitor at the nearby supervisor's desk as their next possible target – and I saw an accident waiting to happen. I could not stand by and allow for either one of them, or a passerby, to get needlessly hurt.

So I quietly walked over to the two girls, gently took the cord from their hands and put it back while saying to them, "Now, we shouldn't do that OK, someone could get hurt."

Then as I am turning my back to go back to my cart, I hear a nasty, incredulous voice – apparently the children's mother/grandmother/aunt/guardian (you just never know these days) yelling at me to mind my own business.

Wow, really? I couldn't believe she was yelling at me

because I was attempting to prevent her children from hurting themselves, or another innocent person.

NO! I was not going to mind my own business when children are putting themselves in a dangerous situation, and/or they have the potential to hurt other innocent bystanders.

NO! I was not going to stand by and not take any action so that an accident would happen, a lawsuit would/could be threatened, and someone gets hurt. NO! I was not about to take that chance.

I turned my head to glare at the woman and said, loudly, "Great parent you are."

After the nasty woman went away and out of earshot, one of the employees of the store came up to me to thank me for doing what I did. I said sure, it's not a problem – I just did not want to see anyone get hurt. I still can't believe that someone was yelling at me because I was trying to prevent a possible accident/lawsuit/Saul Goodman-type looking for a fat settlement.

No one ever said that being a parent was an easy walk in the park. But it astounds me profoundly that one would purposely ignore the risk factors that could hurt their kids. Or did it even occur to them that someone else could get affected by unsupervised actions?

As for me, I'll take my walking orders from Edmund Burke who said, *"The only thing necessary for the triumph of evil is for good men to do nothing."*

Jenny Kefauver is a longtime public relations professional and owns JK Public Relations. She works with a variety of clients including New York Times best-selling author Scott McEwen, author and investigative reporter Richard Miniter, Lt. Col. Dave Grossman/Killology Research Group, Southeastern Legal Foundation, and others. She has been writing for PolitiChicks since 2013.

5
TEN WAYS TO TEACH A CHILD OR TEEN ACCOUNTABILITY AND RESPONSIBILITY

by Margie Mars

Teaching children responsibility and accountability is a lost art. Somewhere along the way, it seems that my generation in particular (Gen X) juxtaposed spanking and discipline with accountability. Our country is suffering from millions of people who think they are owed something and that doing what's best for yourself, regardless of how it affects others, is the ideal. "If I don't love me first...." Many kids are taught this in school where they have little to no consequences and are constantly told how they're getting the short end of the stick in life.

In our country religion is made fun of, kids look up to people like Kylie Jenner and Kim Kardashian rather than real role models and the media blasts false narratives ("Hands up, don't shoot"). So how do you teach a child to be accountable for their own actions and embrace personal responsibility? Starting young is ideal but even teens who have been coddled for far too long can learn this vitally important life skill.

1. Demonstrate Personal Responsibilities
Did you ding the door of the car next to you in the parking lot? If you left a mark, leave a note! Modeling good behavior is essential in teaching kids the same. Be kind, don't talk about people behind their backs and practice The Golden Rule.

2. Offer Extra Chores
Having a list or chart of extra things children can do in order to earn money or privileges teaches them that work pays off. Some parents use chores as a way to earn extra TV or video game time or even extra school clothes. You have to determine what you expect (below) and what is an "extra."

3. Expect Things
Extras are important but make sure your kids know that some

things are just expected, like keeping their room clean, behaving at church and doing their homework. Providing rewards for every behavior will make the child expect something for everything they do in life. They get enough of that outside of the home!

4. Allow Children to Help You

Often times it's easier to just get something done rather than letting your kids "help" you. As often as you can stand it, give kids jobs they can do alongside of you, especially younger children.

5. Structure, Routine and Consequences

Children need structure and routine to thrive. Knowing what to expect helps kids make the connection between action and result. For example, they know that at 8:00, it's time to take a bath, brush teeth and get pajamas on if they want time to watch a little TV with mom and dad before bedtime. It's the same with household rules and the consequences of breaking them.

6. Allow Natural Consequences

Does you child have a project due at school but keeps putting it off? Reminders are great, especially for younger kids, but if you've bailed out your kid or teen last minute in the past, it's time to stop. Make sure they know that you won't rescue them again and let the chips fall where they may. After-school suspension? Oh well! Be sure to keep this age appropriate.

7. Have Reasonable Expectations

Be sure that you're not expecting too much from your child. While setting the bar high teaches children to strive for more, don't exceed their ability. You know them better than anyone. Just because the 6-year-old next door is polishing the silver, don't expect your distractible little guy to do the same!

8. Include Behavior

Laying out expectations for children with behavior issues can help them remember. Are you tired of repeating yourself to your preteens and teens? Sit down together and map out which things are non-negotiable. Put them on a chart, along with the consequence of breaking the rules and follow through 100%.

9. Offer Help and Praise

Remember that children thrive on praise just like adults! Don't go nutty and lay it on too thick, kids are smart. But reminding them how proud you are for their compliance and growth is essential for success. Make sure you're always available to help, too. Taking the time for a special one-on-one trip for ice cream can do wonders for a kid's attitude.

10 Don't Give Up

If you're starting this with an older child, it will take time. Don't give up! You only have your children for 18 or so years. Habits are developed very early in life and while people can change, it's far more difficult the older they get. The foundation you provide now is critical.

Margie Mars is a Conservative-Libertarian writer and parenting expert. Along with writing and designing graphics for PolitiChicks, Margie writes as an expert on Attachment Parenting, pregnancy, childbirth, breastfeeding, child rearing and autism. She holds a degree in Early Childhood Education, certification in Special Needs Education and has taken courses in Legal Assisting and Political Science. Margie and her husband Rob have eight children, seven boys and one girl (three on the autism spectrum) and three grandchildren.

PART SIX: RELIGION

We hold these truths to be self-evident, that all men are created equal, that they are endowed by their Creator with certain unalienable Rights, that among these are Life, Liberty, and the pursuit of Happiness. - **U.S. Constitution**

1

PRAYER: THE PRESCRIPTION
FOR HEALING OUR NATION

by Tina Drake

"If my people who are called by my name humble themselves, and pray and seek my face and turn from their wicked ways, then I will hear from heaven and will forgive their sin and heal their land."
-- 2 Chronicles 7:14

For those of us who believe in the Bible and trust its writings, we should all be "first in line" for America's annual National Day of Prayer. In 1775, the first Continental Congress called for a National Day of Prayer[1]. Since 1775, 1,419 state and federal calls for national prayer have been raised and counting[2]. From 1789 to 2015, 144 national calls for prayer, humiliation, fasting, and thanksgiving have been given by the President of the United States.

Healing is what our nation needs at this most critical time in our history. So many issues are plaguing our land: financial hurdles too tall to jump, social issues creating dissension and strife between citizens, arrogance in our leadership causing those in high positions to distort and destroy our Constitution for their own political gain. These are true signs of a troubled land, which none of us want to see get any worse.

In our nation's history, prayer has not been taken lightly. It has had a purposeful focus in the creation and sustaining of our country and our freedoms. Presidents George Washington and Abraham Lincoln unashamedly prayed for our country and wisdom to lead it. What will be our response be to prayer and reflection for our nation, to God?

According to Barna[3,] a research group who has tracked the prayer habits of adults since 1993, 84% of U.S. adults claim to have prayed in the past week, when surveyed. In a world where God is being excluded rather than included and those who believe in God are attacked continually, four out of five adults still pray weekly. What an amazing and encouraging number! The mainstream media would have you believe no one calls on the name of God, except to curse. They would have you believe God is dead. Obviously, He is not dead!

Imagine the strength and guidance our nation could receive from God, if we harnessed the power of the 84% who regularly pray. If God was willing to bless His people before through prayer, (2 Chronicles 7:14) why are we so hesitant sometimes to ask Him now? I believe He can heal our broken, selfish, nation.

As a person of faith who prays daily, I understand the need for asking for God's guidance and for giving thanks to God, daily. Personally, I know when I think of asking for guidance, it is for my own life and the lives of my family. Rarely do I sit in prayer, contemplating our nation's leaders and asking God to bless them with His guidance. This survey has caused me to realize how few of us actually pray for our leaders and the fate of our country. We are still a praying nation, but why have we come to a time where we no longer pray for its well-being?

When pondering my reasons for not focusing my prayers on our nation, I have realized my approval and trust of Washington is in direct correlation to my prayers for it. The less I approve and trust in what happens there, the less I pray for those in positions of leadership.

It isn't so much a commutative reaction of, "if you do well, you get prayed for", but more of a "how long do we throw pearls before swine". Is that really a legitimate choice for any of us to make? As voters, we certainly have the choice to make decisions regarding our elected officials and for those whom they appoint in other offices. However, if Christ is our example, He wasn't picky for whom He prayed or spent time with while on earth. He ate with tax collectors, the dredges of society, and spoke with and forgave adulterers. That population is certainly represented in our government today.

So why should any of us stop praying for our government and our nation? That is why the National Day of Prayer is an incredible opportunity for us to renew our faith in our country and in what God can do in our country. It isn't a renewing of our faith in those who are already in office, yet a renewing of our faith in our God given, God blessed land. Renewing our hope in the process of government is where our destiny lies. In a belief that the American way of living free, bound only by our Constitution, is where our exceptionalism once was and where it can be reborn. That rebirth can be achieved by prayerfully submitting our requests at the feet of God. Asking Him to renew and heal our land. To create a stirring of what He intends America to be from this time forward.

The National Day of Prayer is a freedom we should all hold dear and translate into each and every day of our lives. Prayer doesn't have to be a burden around our neck. It can be a small, on the go whisper to God when you hear a concerning story or event, each day. A moment where we utter our request to God to heal our nation, give wisdom and humility to our leaders and to protect our shores from our enemies.

It is obvious our struggles in America have been spawned by selfish desires and egotistical behaviors, by those who once presented themselves as humble servants and now have become authoritative elitists. Maybe those of us who believe in prayer have become selfish and egotistical also. Believing there is no hope for our country. There is hope. Hope in the power of prayer.

If you have lost faith in prayer or never had a faith in prayer, science has substantiated the power of those who pray. In a San Francisco[5] General Medical Center experiment, patients participated in a double-blind "drug" study on the "efficacy of Christian prayer on healing". The test had a randomly divided group, where Christians prayed for patients in the test group and the placebo group received no prayer. Statistically, there were no differences in the groups, before the study began. The study found those who were prayed for suffered "less congestive heart failure, required less diuretic and antibiotic therapy, had fewer episodes of pneumonia, had fewer cardiac arrests, and were less frequently intubated and ventilated." (Originally published by Rich Deem, GodandScience.org[6])

Amazing! Science has proven that prayer has a positive

effect on individuals who are sick. In the same way, prayer can heal our sick nation.

Proverbs 11:1 says, *"Where there is no guidance, a people falls..."* 93% of what Christians are praying for is guidance; let's make sure that is personal AND national guidance. Otherwise, our country may fall.

Every National Day of Prayer, let's not only pray during those specific twenty-four hours for our nation, let's pray for the desire, courage and strength to pray 365 days a year for America!

2

MY STORY OF CANCER, FAITH, AND A WOMAN NAMED RACHEL

by Shannon Grady

I met fellow cancer patient Rachel while receiving our chemotherapy at Tripler Army Hospital in Hawaii. Our encounter was brief but it was one of the most unforgettable moments of my life. Sitting there chatting about our situations and our cancer prognosis I came to learn that God constantly reminds me how blessed I am even in the midst of what I believe to be a curse.

Just moments before I sat down in a chair beside Rachel, I had been in my doctor's office receiving what I believed to be fairly dreadful news. All along the hope had been that my chemo would shrink my tumor thus allowing me to have a lumpectomy rather than a mastectomy. The previous appointments had given both myself and my doctor hope that it was working as the tumor appeared to have gotten considerably smaller.

However, weeks before I had submitted some blood work to be tested in the genetics department. It would tell me if I had one of the BRCA gene's known to signal an increased risk for certain types of cancer. Among those would be breast cancer and ovarian cancer and it was called the BRCA1 mutated gene. You may recall that Angelina Jolie, one of Hollywood's leading ladies, suffered from the same mutated gene and opted to have a double mastectomy and surgery to remove her fallopian tubes. Her decision was prompted in part, by the death of her mother who died from breast and ovarian cancer.

The results were back and I had the BRCA1 gene. As I sat there hearing that my hopes of a lumpectomy and breast conserving surgery were gone forever I felt like I had been kicked in the gut. Suddenly, I was no longer going to be able to save my breast and would be facing not a single mastectomy but a double mastectomy as well as a hysterectomy. In addition, there was concern noted by my oncology OB/GYN that I may need to have my cervix removed. I was feeling extremely sorry for myself and hardly acknowledge my two aunts sitting in the room with me as the bad news was delivered.

I somberly made my way to the chemo room to start my IV's and fought back the tears that were welling up inside me. Just once I wanted to have my doctors give me good news and not bad news about my cancer. As I sat in my chair staring at the ceiling, my aunts asked if there was anything they could do for me. I mumbled something about a drink or some chips but really I just wanted a moment to be alone. As they headed off to get me something they thought I needed or at least wanted, I noticed a young girl sitting beside me.

She had the same nearly baldhead as I did, a telltale sign of the chemo treatments that tends to be unmistakable. I noticed that she had a lot more hair than me and I thought, "She must be nearly finished and cancer free." Boy was I about to have my preconceived notions smashed. I struck up a conversation by asking what type of cancer she had as I noticed she had already undergone a double mastectomy. I knew it was breast cancer but there are many types.

Rachel told me she had been diagnosed with Stage 2 breast cancer...not unlike my own diagnosis. She had made her discovery while breast-feeding her baby girl. Her initial thought was that it was an infected milk duct, common with breast-feeding moms. However, as the weeks past and the lump grew larger she noticed her nipple inverting and decided to go see her doctor. In the midst of the cancer discovery, they also discovered Rachel was 21 weeks pregnant.

She opted not to terminate the pregnancy even though her doctors suggested it. She held off having some of the harsher chemo treatments until after the birth of her healthy baby boy. Then she finished her chemo and was scheduled for a double mastectomy. The surgery had gone well but the radiation and reconstruction surgery was problematic. It was during one of the examinations 6 months after her surgery that doctors made the discovery that Rachel's breast cancer had returned and spread to her bones and other organs. She was diagnosed as Stage 4 terminal.

As I sat there listening to this 27-year-old mother of three young children, all my earlier frustration melted away in compassion for her pain. She was finishing her last treatment at Tripler, and heading to Maryland the next day, to hopefully join a research study to give her a chance. I couldn't help but notice that she was sitting in that chair alone. I, on the other hand, was surrounded by two of my wonderful aunts who had flown all the way from South Carolina to Hawaii just to be by my side.

At that moment, I realized this was no chance meeting. God had orchestrated this meeting and I wasn't going to miss its intended mark. I spoke to Rachel about faith and the hope that only exist in a relationship with Christ. She shared with me that she had the same faith and hope and I saw a smile and a glow that told me it was true. How else could a mother of three children under the age of 4, facing such a prognosis alone...find a way to smile at a stranger? In truth, what I soon realized was that this young woman had more faith and hope than I did despite facing a much harsher prognosis.

I whispered a prayer of forgiveness for not trusting that God had my situation under control. I thanked Him for sending my aunts to be with me and to help me at home. I thanked Him for reminding me that there are always others in worse situations than our own and we should never think it's the end. He is the Alpha and Omega so if I start with Him and finish with Him there really isn't anything other than a happy ending waiting.

So now, I'd like to ask that those of you who pray to add Rachel to your prayers even though she will not know we are praying. Our Father in Heaven will know and hear. We may never know what miracles He works in her life because of our prayers...at least not while we are on Earth. Yet I have this confidence, not in the flesh but in the spirit that God will do something amazing.

I'll close with Philippians 3:7-11:

"But whatever gains to me I now consider loss for the sake of Christ. What is more, I consider everything a loss because of the surpassing worth of knowing Christ Jesus my Lord, for whose sake I have lost all things. I consider them garbage, that I may gain

Christ and be found in Him, not having a righteousness of my own that comes from the law, but that which is through faith in Christ—the righteousness that comes from God on the basis of faith. I want to know Christ-yes, to know the power of His resurrection and participation in His sufferings, becoming like Him in His death, and so, somehow, attaining to the resurrection from the dead."

Shannon Grady *is the wife of active duty Army officer LTC Matthew Grady. While assigned to NATO in Brussels, Belgium, Shannon covered events across Europe, including covering the Charlie Hedbo Islamic terrorist attack in Paris, the Memorial Day events at Flanders Field, Belgium and the 70th anniversary D-Day events in Normandy, France. Shannon has a BA in History, a Masters from Webster University, and a doctorate from Liberty University. She currently teaches online AP courses in Macro and Micro Economics and AP US history. Shannon and Matthew are the parents of one rambunctious little boy.*

3
RELIGION AND POLITICS
(AND WHY THEY DO GO TOGETHER)

by Sonya Sasser

In 2013, many God-fearing Patriots cheered as they watched the video of Class President John Hardwick [7] defy the attempts to stop traditional graduation prayer at his Kentucky high school.

For those familiar with the Book of Daniel, they remember that courageous Daniel was actually thrown into the lion's den for an act rather similar to John Hardwick's.

In recent years, we have been witnessing the bold ascension of the Post-modern (secular) movement, and its attempt to eradicate Christianity from government and the public square altogether. As a result, "separate of church and state!!" –is the cry we often hear from those who misunderstand the original intent of Thomas Jefferson's famous letter to the Danbury Baptists, and by those who have themselves been bamboozled by the Left's revision of America's Christian heritage.

Surprisingly, many of these cries are even coming from Christians.

Yet, Believers may actually be astounded to find just how many Judeo-Christian precepts influenced our government's very foundation and structure, and why it is so critical to tear down the secular misconception of Jefferson's wall between church and state before it's too late. At this point, a well-informed (and morally courageous) Christian like Class President John Hardwick can make all the difference in saving this nation...especially since our Republic is practically on her deathbed.

For a Christian, forgiveness of sins is the main essence of the Gospel. Yet, the Bible has another unique quality: a power that inspires transformation in the very individual it touches.

And through these very individuals, it also has the power to transform entire societies. If you and I are truly Bible-believing Christians, this very power is within us. This means you and I have the power to make a positive impact not just only on our families; but also on our neighborhoods, our communities, and even on Washington D.C.

Matthew 5:16 tells us, "Let your light shine before others, so that they may see your good works and give glory to your Father who is in heaven." This command can certainly be applied to doing good works when it comes to influencing our nation's laws and policies. In fact, we can look to Scripture to find God's faithful servants (such as: Joseph, Moses, Daniel, Nehemiah, Mordecai, and Esther) — actually influencing secular governments and pagan officials to advance laws and policies that are consistent with God's principles.

Daniel even counseled King Nebuchadnezzar:

"Therefore, O king, let my counsel be acceptable to you: break off your sins by practicing righteousness, and your iniquities by showing mercy to the oppressed, that there may perhaps be a lengthening of your prosperity." (Daniel 4:27)

After all, how can rulers (especially pagan ones like "King Neb") know what is right and wrong policy if they don't have a "Daniel" to give them any moral guidance on what is good and evil?

And, if Christians do not begin to speak up about moral and ethical issues currently facing our nation, then who will? Where will the American public learn right from wrong? Hollywood movies? Mainstream media? Pop culture? Rap music?

In his book: "Politics According to the Bible," [8] Wayne Grudem explains, "If we are here to glorify God, we will glorify Him by obeying His command, "You shall love your neighbor as yourself (Matt 22:39). But that means that I should seek the good of my neighbors in all parts of society."

This means we should seek good policies that include:
1. Protecting unborn children
2. Protecting marriages and families
3. Protecting citizens from criminals who want to harm them

4. Protecting children from corrupt influences (i.e. pornography and pedophiles)
5. Protecting God-given rights of law-abiding citizens
6. Rewarding hard work and success

Grudem emphasizes, "Jesus' command that "you shall love your neighbor as yourself" means that I should seek good of my neighbors in every aspect of society, including seeking to bring about good governments and good laws."

In his book: "How Christianity Changed the World," [9] historian Alvin Schmidt also points out how the spread of Christianity and Christian influence on government was primarily responsible for:

1. Outlawing infanticide, child abandonment, and abortion in the Roman Empire (AD 374).
2. Outlawing the brutal battles-to-death in which thousand of gladiators died (AD 404).
3. Instituting prison reforms such as segregating male and female prisoners (by 361 AD).
4. Stopping the practice of human sacrifice among the Irish, the Prussians, and the Lithuanians.
5. Outlawing pedophilia.
6. Granting property rights and other protections to women.
7. Prohibiting the burning alive of widows in India (1829).
8. Outlawing the painful and crippling practice of binding young women's feet in China.

In addition, Schmidt argues that several specific components of modern views of government also had a strong Christian influence in their origin and influence, including: individual human rights, individual freedom, the equality of individuals before the law, and even freedom of religion.

We can also turn to other Biblical principles to find what God actually says about civil government. Romans 13:4 teaches us that a government official is "God's servant for your good." This means that our government officials are actually designated by God to serve their fellow citizens. And because government is instituted by God to be a "servant for our good," we are also commissioned by Him to abide by our nation's laws.

In fact, as a Constitutional Republic, U.S. citizens have

often taken great comfort in that fact that we are governed by the Rule of Law ("Law is King" where the law is our compass, and everyone is subject to the same laws- including our leaders) as opposed to being governed by the Whims of Man ("Man is King" where human feelings and impulses are rulers over us- including the feeling of arrogance that drives so many (especially politicians) to act as if they ABOVE the laws of the land).

Our Rule of Law is much like our nation's moral conscience, an alarm that tells us what is right and wrong for everyone within our nation's borders. This is because many of our laws are rooted in religious and moral convictions (i.e. "thou shall not steal" and "thou shall not kill"...etc.). There is tremendous security in our Rule of Law as a U.S. citizen.

1 Peter 2:14 also teaches us that government officials are sent to punish those who do evil and praise those who do good. Therefore, we should view the activities of government (when it rewards good and punishes evil) as something that is "good," according to God's word.

But, how can officials restrain "evil" and reward "good" if they no longer have any guidance on what is "good" and what is "evil"? What happens when the government no longer sees itself as accountable to God? What happens when officials begin creating mandates that force citizens to actually disobey God? What happens when government officials start targeting law-abiding citizens (instead of actual criminals) by bombarding these "good" citizens with: excessive regulations, abusive taxation, and intimidating government agency audits? When the STATE cannot discern between what is truly "good" and what is truly "evil," it can easily become the devil.

Which brings us to the American Revolution and why our Founders declared the necessity to rebel against the British. Wayne Grudem says, "The reason that a number of early Americans thought it was justified to rebel against the British monarchy is that it is morally right for a lower government official to protect the citizens in his care from a higher official who is committing crimes against these citizens."

According to Greg Forster, [10] a scholar with expertise in the history of government theory, "One common argument among Christian writers was that a 'tyrannical' government is not really a government at all but a criminal gang masquerading as a government, and therefore not entitled to the obedience that governments (properly so called) can claim."

Therefore, our Founding Fathers thought of themselves as doing something that was morally right and even necessary, for they were protecting the citizens in their care from the evil attacks of King George III of England, who repeatedly acted as a "tyrant."

In the Declaration of Independence, the Founders declared: *"When in the Course of human events, it becomes necessary for one people to dissolve the political bands which have connected them with another, and to assume among the Powers of the earth, the separate and equal station to which the Laws of Nature and Nature's God entitle them, a descent respect to the opinions of mankind requires that they should declare the causes which impel them to the separation."*

They were proclaiming that God Himself gave our nation the right to become independent from a tyrannical government. After declaring that God gave the authorization for the very existence of the United States, they stated: *"We hold these truths to be self-evident, that all men are created equal, that they are endowed by their Creator with certain unalienable Rights, that among these are Life, Liberty, and the pursuit of Happiness. That to secure these rights, Governments are instituted among Men..."*

Here, they stated that the entire purpose of government is to protect the rights that are given to the people by God.

However, in "Politics According to the Bible," Wayne Grudem also explains, *"Independence from Britain did not come cheaply. In the War of Independence, approximately 4,500 Americans died. Later wars were even more costly....*

These hundreds of thousands of men (and many women as well) sacrificed their lives to protect their nation and preserve the freedoms we enjoy today. Is it right that we simply enjoy these freedoms while giving to our nation nothing in return?"

A significant portion of the ruling power in the U.S. is entrusted to us citizens through the ballot box. To be able to vote is to have share of ruling power. Therefore, all citizens who are old enough to vote have a responsibility to know what God expects of our government. That's why it is critical to know what kind of government God is seeking.

As we have discovered, we can learn this from the Bible. As we have learned, God instituted government to be a "servant for our good". But, how will our leaders know this if there aren't any "Daniels" to remind them?

Kentucky Class President John Hardwick was certainly a modern-day "Daniel," bold enough to pierce the secular myth of the wall between church and state. His very act of courage showed us all how to stand up for our First Amendment Right: free exercise of religion. In addition, he reminded us all that there is a God who endowed us with this very right, and that we are each accountable to Him (yes, even those in Washington).

As Christians, we do not have to be afraid to let our light shine before others, especially when it comes to influencing our nation's laws and policies. In fact, Christians should be on the politically forefront reminding government officials they are accountable to God:

- To be servants for our good
- To restrain evil doing
- To reward good behavior
- To actually know the difference between good and evil
- To protect the very rights that God has given us.

In fact, how will anyone in our nation know these basic principles if we don't "Daniel-up" and guide them?

4

THREE EPIC CHRISTIAN VICTORIES
THAT SAVED THE WESTERN WORLD,
AS WE KNOW IT

By Susan Swift

For over fifteen centuries, Christianity has been fighting for its very survival against Islam, which defenders term the "Religion of Peace." Each anniversary of the September 11, 2001 Muslim attack on our nation, it is a sobering reminder that the United States is one of the more recent victims of Islam's centuries old war on Christendom, precisely because America is a *Christian* nation.

As America faces new threats that would crush Christian faith and religious freedom, history provides proven means of defeating militant Islam's deadly plots. These three epic Christian victories saved the Western World, as we know it today:

1. The Battle of Tours [11]

In an epic defeat outside Tours, France in 732 A.D., Charles "the Hammer" Martel, grandfather of Charlemagne, [12] and his brave band of 1,500 Christian foot soldiers stopped a Muslim mounted cavalry force estimated to range between 40,000 and 600,000 riders.

Historians consider this battle to be of "macrohistorical importance" because it stopped the Muslims' northward advance and "preserved" Christianity as the controlling faith in Europe." Translation: The reason why any of you has the freedom and the ability to read these words in English is due in large part to Christian general Charles Martel. If this warrior-hero and general-extraordinaire had not epically beaten the Muslims at the Battle of Tours, all American men would be reading in Arabic; females over the age of eight wouldn't be allowed by their Muslim husbands to be reading much more than a cookbook; and I as a Christian woman would be burnt alive, beheaded, drowned or repeatedly raped for daring to write the historical truth of what happened back in the Dark Ages. So much for Islamic tolerance.

2. The Battle of Lepanto [13]
On October 7, 1571 a young and dashing John of Austria (the real life Don Juan, [14] successfully led a Catholic naval force against an undefeated Muslim fleet. The Battle of Lepanto "heralded end of Turkish supremacy in the Mediterranean." The seemingly miraculous victory at Lepanto has been described as the battle that "saved Christian West from defeat at the hands of the Ottoman Turks." [15]

The victorious Christian forces credited the intercession of Mary, the Mother of God. The defeated Muslim force also acknowledged the Christian victory as "an act of Divine Will." Muslim losses outnumbered Christian casualties by approximately 7 to 1.

3. The Battle of Vienna [16]
In July of 1683, a huge Muslim army laid siege to Vienna, Austria. After two months, with food and supplies almost exhausted and the defenders mere days away from total collapse, Jan III Sobieski, the King of Poland, successfully led a combined Christian force of German and Polish armies to relieve the city from Turkish attackers.

King Sobieski credited God with the victory, saying "Veni, vidi, Deus vicit" – "I came, I saw, God conquered". The Christian forces of 70,000-80,000 soldiers opposed a Muslim force almost twice its size in a battle that included the "largest known cavalry charge in history." King Sobieski's decisive victory at the Battle of Vienna was a turning point in the centuries old struggle between the Christian and Turkish Empires. [17]

The history of Muslim aggression down through the centuries illustrates Islam's unrelenting and ongoing jihad against Christians. The attacks on 9-11 were yet another tactical step in Muslims' ongoing holy war in Americans' homeland.

If we are to survive as a nation founded on Judeo-

Christian beliefs, it's past time to acknowledge that we are facing a religious war bent on fundamentally transforming America from the Christian faith to one of Islam. Just as Christian warriors in centuries past, to be victorious in today's battles against Islamic evil, Americans must be prepared to answer Islamic jihad with force and strong faith in Christ.

5

MAY 4, HOLOCAUST REMEMBRANCE DAY: WE MUST MAKE "NEVER AGAIN" A REALITY

by David Weissman

On Wednesday, May 4th at sundown, the people of Israel celebrate the holiday **Yom Hoshoah Ve-Hagevurah** that literally means the "Day of Remembrance of the holocaust and the heroism". It marks the anniversary of the Warsaw Ghetto uprising. [18]

Traditionally since the 1960's you hear the sound of a siren on Yom Hashoah at 11:00 a.m. Traffic everywhere in Israel will halt and people will stand in silence to pay respects. Radios or televisions will be playing something that connects with Jewish people during World War 2, including personal interviews with holocaust survivors. No public Entertainment such as theaters, cinemas, pubs, or other venues are open on Yom Hoshoah.

Quotes like "Never Forget" and "Never Again" [19] are quotes that were inspired to remind people of the Holocaust and what happened there. History is there not just for people to get a diploma but to help us not to make the same mistake. Sadly history continues to have repeated itself.

There is a new evil in our midst: Radical Islamists are the new Nazis and they have murdered over hundreds of thousands of Christians, Armenians, and Israelis. [18] North Korea is also known for its own concentration camps and its genocide of its people.

Never Forget and Never Again is supposed to have meaning, to never let genocide happen again. [20] You can only achieve so much with air strikes and sending a small amount of troops. The United Nations, along with the rest of the world, condemns the one country that truly tries to prevent genocide of its own people Israel but does nothing about genocide. But we have the training and tools to really make a difference. Sometimes it's the right thing to do is to put politics aside to help people.

What can we do to help combat genocide? Continue to teach about the holocaust as well as informing people about what is happening now. We can't keep people in the dark to continue to let the same mistake to happen not once, not twice but multiple times. It is time to truly make "Never Again" a reality.

David Weissman is the married father of 3 daughters. Originally from Queens, New York, David joined the United States Army as a Chaplain Assistant where he served 13 years with two deployments to Afghanistan. After serving honorably, David made Ailyah, the Jewish right of return, and moved to Israel where he experienced the 2014 war with Hamas while living in Ashquelon south of Israel. David and his family are currently living in Jerusalem where he works as a freelance writer and contributing foreign correspondent for PolitiChicks.

6

LIBERTY AND JUSTICE FOR ALL – EXCEPT CHRISTIANS

by Pamela Anne

American Christians are experiencing an escalation of persecution for invoking their liberty to follow their conscience of faith. Protection was guaranteed by the founders under Article VI of the Constitution and unfiltered in the First Amendment of the Bill of the Rights:

Amendment 1 – *Congress shall make no law respecting an establishment of religion, or prohibiting the free exercise thereof; or abridging the freedom of speech...*

"Congress shall make no law . . . prohibiting the free exercise [of religion]" is called the free-exercise clause of the First Amendment. It is to assure the right to freely exercise one's religion and that the government shall make no law prohibiting the free exercise of religion.

The clause is considered absolute, yet it is interpreted with limitations. The Supreme Court has held that religious freedom must be considered in the context of the general society's well being allowing reasonable restrictions to be adopted to protect the health, safety and convenience of the entire community. For example, courts would not hold that the First Amendment protects human sacrifice even if some religion required it. The Supreme Court has interpreted this clause so that the "freedom to believe is absolute, *but the ability to act on those beliefs is not."*

Herein is the problem for the Christian faith. The principle of following our faith *requires acting on our faith, not just believing.* The acting is the final expression of the faith.

James 2:17 (NIV) says, *"In the same way, faith by itself, if it is not accompanied by action, is dead."*

Being commanded *to act* on our faith includes living our lives out of the teachings and principles taught in the Bible, correctly interpreted, with the understanding that we have.

The issue is one of liberty for Christians. The cases against Christians, such as florists or bakers, who were approached to participate in the weddings of same sex marriages were not based on someone's right to marriage or perceived sin but charged against Christians who by conscience declined to participate in the event due to their religious faith.

Ward Connerly in a 1996 lecture for Heritage Foundation stated,

"When we become citizens of this nation, at birth or otherwise, we get a warranty. That warranty is supposed to [be] honored by every government franchise in every village and hamlet of this nation. It is not transferable, and it is good for the life of the vehicle.

We are guaranteed the right to vote; the right to due process; the right to be free, not to be enslaved, as long as we conduct ourselves in accordance with the laws of our nation; and the right to equal treatment under the law, regardless of our race, color, sex, religion, or national origin. These are rights which attach to us as individuals, not as members of a group."

These rights are our liberty. Liberty, by one definition in the political context states it *"consists of the social and political freedoms guaranteed to all citizens."*

The government is responsible for the protection of these rights. Yet we have a list of Christians charged for exercising their *freedom of religion* rights. They have been bullied, maligned, fined and many have lost their businesses, jobs or positions.

Another definition of liberty is freedom from arbitrary or despotic government or control.

One case in point is the Christian owners of the Oregon bakery, Sweet Cakes, Aaron and Melissa Klein, who refused in 2013 to bake a cake for same-sex marriage of Rachel Cryer's wedding to Laurel Bowman.

Their decision was not one intended to discriminate, nor to deny anyone's civil rights. The business happily served people. Declining to bake a same-sex wedding cake was an issue of religious faith not discrimination of a couple's lifestyle choice.

The gay couple had a plentiful supply of other vendors to choose from, so this is *not* a societal civil rights issue.

The Oregon judge obviously saw the case differently.

The Kleins were fined over $135,000 by the Labor Commissioner, Brad Avakian, in damages to the same-sex couple for refusing to bake their wedding cake.

GoFundMe, a crowd funding website, had an account for the Sweet Cake bakery setup by a third party to help the Klein's pay off the fine. The GoFundMe site abruptly dropped the Klein's account stating they violated their terms of service because they were convicted of *discrimination*.

Supporters of Sweet Cakes owners continued to raise over a half a million through another crowd funding site, ContinueToGive.com.

Tammy Bruce, a Fox News contributor and political commentator summarized the issue on Fox and Friends: *"They happily served people. The difference is that you are being asked to participate in an act that violates your faith. What this suggests is being true to your faith is being hateful."* She added, *"Defending your conscience, acting on faith, doesn't hurt the gay community."*

The Klein family was denied their liberty to freely exercise their freedom of religion—a right clearly defined in the Bill of Rights and the United States Constitution. And they are not the only Christians persecuted for their faith.

The growing list of persecuted Christians compiled by WND.com (2015) should be a ongoing concern to Christians in the United States. The list includes: Dieseltec owner, Brian Klawiter of Granville, Michigan; Thomas Holland and Gilbert Breedlove, two magistrates in NC, ordered to perform same-sex "weddings" or resign; Memories Pizza; Ocean Grove Camp Meeting Association; Liberty Ridge Farm; Masterpiece Cakeshop; Hitching Post Wedding Chapel; Arlene's Flowers; Benham Brothers; Elaine's Photography; Brendan Eich; Aloha Bed & Breakfast; Walders; Wildflower Inn; Just Cookies; Victoria's Cake Cottage; Fleur Cakes; All Occasion; T-shirts; Twilight Room Annex; Phil Robertson and Craig James.

Pamela Anne *is first a Christian and secondly a constitutional republic* *patriot. Pamela is a communications specialist with a background in business management, leadership, and public speaking training. She is a Distinguished Toastmaster, a keynote speaker, conference presenter and events emcee. Pamela Anne served as a judge in youth's public speaking competition and was a panelist on public speaking for a local television segment. Her PolitiChicks articles have been picked up by multiple political websites including Breitbart and DC Watchdog.*

Morgan Brittany (left) and Ann-Marie Murrell (right) after they opened for soon-to-be President Donald Trump at the NFRA Conference in Nashville, Tennessee. (2015)

Julia Seay at the 2015 Republican National Convention

2016 Texas Republican delegate, Brian Bledsoe

Lydia Goodman interviewing Center for Security Policy founder
Frank Gaffney in Washington, D.C. (2016)

Becky Noble (left) speaking at the Fair Tax Rally in Missouri and (right) Dr. Sarah Condor on Amato Talk in San Diego.

Sonya Sasser interviewing Congressman Jim Bridenstine (R-OK) at the 2014 South Carolina Tea Party Coalition Convention.

Macey France (left) talking about Common Core in Oregon and (right) Sonya Sasser speaking at a 2nd Amendment rally

Dr. Karen Siegemund, founder of Rage Against the Media (photo: Marc Langsam)

Sarah Palin with Susan Swift in Hollywood, CA.

Morgan Brittany and Ann-Marie Murrell covering the CNN GOP Presidential debate at the Reagan Library

Ann-Marie Murrell and Morgan Brittany appearing on *Nieuwsuur*, the '60 Minutes of the Netherlands' in New York. (Election night 2016.)

The Glazov Gang (left to right): Morgan Brittany, James Patrick Riley, and Ann-Marie Murrell with host, Dr. Jamie Glazov.

TOP: Kimberly Klacik on One America News Network

MIDDLE: Proud Texan, Patti Terrell

Jin Ah Jin with former Governor Rick Perry (R-TX)

TOP (right) Morgan Brittany speaking at the U.S. Senate and (right) Dr. Sarah Condor on One America News Network

Susan Swift celebrating her 2nd Amendment rights

Ann-Marie Murrell on Hannity (with Geraldo Rivera)

Lainie Sloane after interviewing former Sen. Rick Santorum

Michael Ingmire (right) on Hannity

Ann-Marie Murrell, Morgan Brittany, and Sonya Sasser panellists at the 2016 Bakersfield Business Conference and with Dr. Ben Carson

Morgan Brittany on FOX News

MIDDLE: Ann-Marie Murrell on MSNBC
BOTTOM: (left) Monty Morton with Dr. Jamie Glazov on The
Glazov Gang and (right) Lydia Goodman w/the late Phyllis Schlafly

Ann-Marie Murrell and Morgan Brittany with Sen. Ted Cruz

Sonya Sasser, LTC Allen West, and Ann-Marie Murrell
speaking at the Bakersfield Business Conference

PART SEVEN: HEALTH/ HEALTHCARE

My staff did not get a raise in 2015 or 2016. They won't in 2017, either. Their raise will be eaten up by the cost of health insurance. I can't fund my retirement like I should. I had to fire someone that I didn't want to lose.

Math is an exact and inflexible science. Numbers do not lie.

And the math is telling me that I can't afford the Affordable Care Act. **– Dr. Bill Simpson**

1

WHAT DOCTORS REALLY THINK ABOUT OBAMACARE

by Sonya Sasser

When I first met my husband, Paul, I remember him distinctly explaining to me why he chose to become a surgeon. First, he absolutely loves helping sick people feel better. Because he is a compassionate person, he absolutely loves being a doctor and helping people heal. With each patient Paul cares for, he always asks himself this critical question: "What if this person was my own wife, mother, or child, etc.; how would I want them to be treated?" Paul sees each patient as an individual who has value. And that's what he's supposed to do –since he took that Hippocratic oath in medical school (which basically acknowledges the intrinsic value of every human being). The second reason why Paul chose the medical profession is because he loves the independence that comes with being a small business owner. "I just love being my own boss," he tells me all the time.

Yet, Paul is certainly not the only physician who has chosen the medical profession for the art of healing and the love of independence. Many other of our nation's brightest have also chosen to become doctors for these two very same reasons. So, it is no wonder many physicians are concerned about the Affordable Care Act ("Obamacare")— their two main incentives for practicing medicine are now at stake.

While the mainstream pundits may be focusing on those "evil" insurance companies, or which Republican or Democrat to blame this week, or what kind of legacy the healthcare law will leave our sitting president, I can't help but to ask, "What about the two people this healthcare law impacts the most—the doctor and patient?"

Like my husband, most physicians just want to take care of their patients and not have to deal with more regulations and more government bureaucracy. Dr. Tim Shepherd, [1] a family practice physician in Texas, explains:

"Every person is a unique individual, and you can't cookie-cutter medical care; it's individualized. I am concerned about health care under the new law, and my patients are very concerned...In the past three decades, I have seen health care become more and more regulated by government. Of the 15 employees I hire, five of their jobs are completely devoted to filling out insurance forms and government paperwork. All that administrative work can detract from time spent on patient care...It makes it difficult to take care of the whole person— body, mind, and spirit—if you don't have an environment where you are free to do that. The biggest problem with Obamacare is that there are going to be layers and layers of government bureaucracy that will try to tell me how to treat patients I've helped for over 25 years. More federal control is the foundation of it. These new boards and commissions to be established under Obamacare will tell doctors: 'These are the procedures you will do, and these are the ones you will not do.' Treatment will be restricted, reimbursement will be further decreased, and more doctors will retire early, as I have already seen with many colleagues."

Dr. Shepherd also addresses another major concern for many physicians—that they can no longer even afford to practice medicine under these new Obamacare conditions. Many doctors have invested an enormous amount of time and money toward their medical education to now struggle to pay their practice overhead. As Dr. C.L. Gray, [2] Founder of Physicians for Reform, and a hospital-based physician in North Carolina, also explains:

"Half of the people who gain insurance through Affordable Care Act ("Obamacare") do so by enrolling into Medicaid. For many states this means the size of Medicaid under the Affordable Care Act ("Obamacare") will exacerbate both federal and state budget shortfalls and force states to cut Medicaid reimbursements to physicians even further.

In many states, Medicaid already reimburses less than the cost of delivering care. This means that even though these "newly insured" patients have healthcare coverage, they will have a difficult time finding a physician who will provide care for them. Remember that many physicians are small business owners. When their expenses exceed revenue (as in the case of Medicaid), their businesses cannot survive—no matter how well intentioned."

All the new burdensome Obamacare regulations are already beginning to drive up physicians' overhead costs. With its increasing bureaucracy, private-practice doctors say they will also need to hire more employees just to keep up with the "red tape".

As my husband says, "One way the government can cut its costs is by decreasing the number of patients that doctors can see each day. This is achieved by increasing the amount of time-consuming paperwork they have to complete on each patient."

Not to mention the fact that as Washington D.C.-area orthopedic surgeon, Dr. Robert Nirschl [3] argues, "Doctors must comply with a morass of paperwork requirements that adds no value to the doctor-patient relationship."

Between the decreased reimbursements rates, increased regulations, and high malpractice premiums, many doctors question whether or not they will be able to keep their doors open once Obamacare is fully implemented. Dr. Nirschl also states, "Many physicians are talking about quick retirement, or cutting back or not participating in the practice of medicine."

Obamacare may very likely result in doctor shortages in the very near future –which will also lead to problems with Americans being able to access medical care they need. So President Obama's promise that, "If you like your doctor, you can keep your doctor" is about as likely as being able to keep your current healthcare plan. As Dr. Nirschl says, "The problem is now they (patients) are stuck with either losing their health insurance, and of course, that affects a doctor's practice because the patient comes in and says, 'Well, I don't have insurance anymore.'"

In fact, a medical doctor and cancer patient himself, Shaun Carpenter, is a board certified emergency physician in the New Orleans area who has first-hand experience of what it is like losing his own health insurance. PJ media [4] reports:

"Add to hemochromatosis, which is now under control, Dr. Carpenter has been stricken with cancer twice. He suffered and beat both lymphoma and melanoma, in 2003 and 2005, respectively.

Obamacare, aka the Affordable Care Act, came packaged with lofty promises. President Obama said his law was supposed to make denials of insurance based on pre-existing conditions a thing of the past. President Obama specifically promised that Americans would no longer be denied coverage based on pre-existing conditions, along with promising that if we like our doctors and current health care plans, we can keep them. So imagine Dr. Carpenter's shock when he received the news that he and his family were losing their health insurance at the end of this year."

Of course, the president has now decided that Americans can keep their current health plan for another year (until conveniently after next year's midterm elections).

Doctor Carpenter describes his own perspective of Obamacare, *"As a physician I've been opposed to Obamacare from the get-go. It doesn't begin to fix the real problems with our health care system, and creates new problems. I see it from both the private practice side and the ER side. In fact, we knew that when patients came into the ER without insurance they would actually get better care because we knew we had to run every test imaginable on them or risk getting sued."*

The problem isn't lack of health insurance, he says, but lack of health care. Just because you have insurance doesn't mean you'll get health care. Just ask anyone who has Medicaid how hard it is to get an appointment with a specialist. The wait can be several months, if you ever get in at all.' That's what Obamacare promised to make more accessible and more affordable."

President Obama's own cousin, Dr. Milton Wolf, shockingly, also called Obamacare, "a lie". Dr. Wolf [5] states, "They call it the Affordable Care Act? But not a word of that is true. It's not affordable and it does not provide care." Dr. Wolf says that his cousin is wrong about his signature piece of legislation, "He's wrong to think the government should step between a doctor and their patient."

Many physicians also see Obamacare as an open door to socialism. In fact, retired Johns Hopkins University neurosurgeon, Dr. Ben Carson, [6] reminds us of what Vladimir Lenin once said: [7] *"Socialized medicine is the keystone to the establishment of a socialist state."*

Of course, many will argue that Obamacare isn't socialized medicine; single-payer is. However, as Dr. Nirschl says,

"Obamacare and single-payer are essentially the same...The facts of the matter are that now physicians are now beholden to the policy of the government on the basis of Obamacare. Also, the insurance industry is beholden to the government. Whether or not the government merely becomes the insurance broker versus the government is the controller of a subsidiary insurance broker (which is private insurance companies). The facts of the matter are that the process is exactly the same."

So, it is, in fact, socialized medicine.

The other issue is, of course, is that this is a huge transference of wealth. In other words, what is happening is that the Obamacare system (as it has now evolved and as the law states), what is occurring is that the productive folks who basically have their own private insurance are losing that insurance and in the process when they go back to the exchanges to get insurance, the prices are high because they are substituting their insurance and paying for those who basically pay nothing.

That is a mandatory contribution. All of that transfer from productive citizens, the transfer of wealth is socialism."

That's why doctors will argue that Obamacare has little to do with health care and everything to do with control. As Dr. Ben Carson [8] boldly claims,

"Obamacare is the worst thing to happen in this country since slavery...In a way it is slavery because it is making all of us subservient to the government. And, It was never about health care– It was about control. That's why when this administration took office, it didn't matter that this country was going off the cliff

economically. All forces were directed toward getting this legislation passed."

For doctors, this means that Obamacare has now certainly fundamentally transformed the way the treat their own patients. In fact, they are now being forced to do what's best for the government as opposed to doing what is actually best for the patient. Under Obamacare, doctors essentially become slaves of the State.

Of course, not all doctors oppose Obamacare. In fact, top Harvard doctors claim [9] that "supporting Obamacare makes moral and medical sense."

Forbes [10] also reported in July 2013 that, "Major physician groups, including the American Medical Association and the American Academy of Family Physicians say they continue to support the individual mandate."

Also, in 2013, the American Academy of Family Physicians, in a statement from its President, Dr. Jeffrey Cain, [11] said, "The Affordable Care Act's requirement that individuals have health insurance is the foundation of improving access to care and vital to ensuring everyone has health care coverage."

However, Mayo Clinic Chief Dr. John Noseworthy [12] still claims, "Obamacare is Not Focused on Improving Quality of Care."

It's no secret that our pre-Obamacare health care system certainly had some serious problems. According to Physicians for Reform, [13] TWO of the biggest issues include:

1. The bureaucracy of the current system that drives inefficiency and increased spending. This leads to massive overuse and waste.

2. The third-party payer system (whether Medicare, Medicaid or private insurance) blinds both patient and physician from the real cost of care. This disconnect removes the breaks that normally constrains spending in a free-market system.

In many cases, Obamacare is actually making these issues much worse. Dr. John Noseworthy also says about the Affordable Care Act:

"It doesn't modernize how we drive to higher quality care. What's missing is a link between quality of care and reimbursement. Correcting that could lower costs...Right now, we're in a system where we're reimbursing volume of care, not quality and outcomes of care — safety, efficiency and so on. And that's where most of the costs are."

It is very questionable whether or not Obamacare will ever be fully repealed. However, doctors at Physicians for Reform [14] have proposed patient-centered solutions in place of Obamacare:

* Stabilize Medicare for seniors. The Medicare cuts to physician reimbursement will severely compromise access for seniors unless a budget solution is found. Severe cuts can be prevented and paid for by fundamentally restructuring Medicaid. Converting Medicaid's current system into a system of limited state block grants will save the federal government tens of billions of dollars annually. This savings can offset the massive Medicare cuts.

* Let individuals purchase insurance with pre-tax dollars regardless of where they purchase insurance. This increases the portability and lets individuals customize their policies.

* Encourage low cost, high deductible plans combined with a Healthcare Savings Account (HAS) for patients who are best served by this model. This model encourages preventative medicine while reducing the cost of healthcare.

* Let individuals and businesses purchase insurance across state lines to escape burdensome state regulations and mandates.

* Create small business pools to spread risk and decrease health insurance costs.

* Incentivize states to pass patient-centered medical malpractice reform.

* Create state-run, high-risk pools for patients with chronic disease.

* Put the Medicaid program on a budget and develop a sliding scale, premium support system to assist those who cannot afford health insurance. This accomplished three things:

1. It enables states to create fixed Medicaid budgets.
2. It empowers individuals in this system to purchase private coverage that best suits their needs.

3. It creates opportunity for individuals on Medicaid to exit the system by gradually increasing their income.

* Put Medicare on a budget and restructure Medicare with a premium support system where seniors can choose from a variety of competing plans. The system is structured so that those who have fewer financial resources or more medical need receive more support. This reform empowers individuals to purchase the private coverage that best suits their needs. It would also dramatically reduce the tens of billions of Medicare fraud by giving seniors an incentive to get the best value for their healthcare dollar.

2
UNDERSTANDING WIDOWHOOD

by Carolyn Elkins

These days there are so many different groups clamoring for attention, special rights or demanding justice. While I'm not out to occupy or demand anything at all, I'd like to share a bit on widowhood. There are some misconceptions and no real understanding of what it is like to be a widow in today's society.

Sometimes helping others who are dealing with similar situations, or bringing awareness helps us work through our own fears and heartaches. For me, writing has often been my best way of communicating and working through what's on my mind. Maybe because there's more going on in this world and things seem so out of control, that things which I usually write about are overwhelming, I've had a hard time writing much. So maybe by writing something more personal, it will help others as it helps me find my voice again.

It wasn't until I was in my 40's that I realized that not all widows are old. When I was a kid, the only widows I knew were so much older. My Nana was old; my mom's oldest sister was in her late 60's. My mother in law was in her 70's and one of the neighbor ladies down the road was in her 70's as well. But then a couple of the ladies in our home school group lost their husbands; one was in her 40's and the other, her mid 50's. Another neighbor lady lost her husband in her mid-30s while her daughter was a toddler. I can't comprehend how many young widows there are who were married to men in the military.

The point is that widows are not necessarily old.

Some widows are left with a safety net through theirs or their husband's pensions and social security, or a lifetime of savings and they own their own home. Some however, don't have much in savings and they have no support from the government. I found this out by checking through social security and finding out I'm too young to be a widow.

While some of us are too young, many of us are also deemed too old compared to those coming into the work force and have a hard time trying to find decent work to support ourselves. Especially if we've been out the work force to raise families.

We've got life degrees, but not the kind that hangs on the wall- the kind that most employers are interested in.

Where divorce, diverse families and feminism is acceptable and glorified, it's more difficult for those of us who struggle with unexpected loss of spouse, income loss and becoming single mothers through widowhood. For decades feminists have been declaring that single moms are free, can have 'weekends off' from the kids when they go to their dads', can get child support, alimony and/or government benefits, they can have it all. No, we can't have it all. Most widows have an immense struggle through the first few years just to get by, and forget about even getting ahead.

Most people see us without a husband and assume we're divorced or are single and raising kids by choice. Many people don't seem to consider things or even care when we have no one to turn to for help with employment or help for our kids.

Not all kids from divorced families have a loving or caring mom and dad. Many though are fortunate enough to have two parents so they are able to have even some interaction with their dads. Kids of widows don't have that chance, and I don't care who says otherwise, young kids and teens need a dad or at least a strong male role model or mentor. Especially for boys, to help with things that only men can provide.

Often times I've found ways in which God has used my painful past to help others through similar circumstances. Even still, I never would have expected to comfort another so soon after losing my own husband, but I did. Exactly one month to the day after my loss, my sister lost hers to complications from cancer. Two months later, a good friend lost her husband, and again, I tried to help her through the initial shock and legal/financial preparations that she was facing.

Not all widows have legal/government and financial expertise to navigate the incredible amount of paperwork, forms, taxes and financial bureaucracies we have to deal with at the most vulnerable time in our lives. We often have to blindly navigate the system alone. If we make any mistakes, those can come back and hurt us more later.

When my brother in law died, my sister had been battling her own cancer, and wanted to downsize. She was fortunate that her husband owned his home and had her name put on the deed. She had some good family friends help her with the legalities of selling the house. Due to circumstances beyond my control, I had to leave my home months after losing my husband. After losing my husband, losing the only home our son had known his whole life, and the place I knew as home through our marriage was almost as painful as losing him.

Not all widows are secure in their homes, and can feel easily manipulated at a time when they are not in the right frame of mind to make instant, yet life changing decisions.

Through many hard and heart breaking experiences in my life, I was always considered "the strong one". There's nothing wrong with that, but there are times when we are not strong, we need help, but being considered strong, people don't think we need help, or we would ask for it. But we don't always know who to ask, or even what to ask.

The past year and a half can only be described as being like a deer caught in the headlights. Some days I feel paralyzed in my mind, not having a clue of what to do, where to go or what to think. Simple things that I used to take for granted... Simple things like filing income tax, dealing with a power outage from storms, or car problems are real struggles when you used to work on things together or your husband used to do the car repairs.

And then there are days when I do find my backbone, and think- *OK today you're going to get your butt in gear and get over it. Move forward...* only to get frustrated with mood swings and find I've accomplished nothing by the end of the day.

Depression is real. We don't need Obamacare to tell us that. We don't need sympathy, but understanding goes a long way. I've been blessed to have friends help through some real hard and tight times this past year, which I never could have gone through alone. I am grateful. But it's not easy to ask. As far as moods go, not all widows have a set time for moving on. It helps when I know people are praying for my son and I. They might not know what exactly we're struggling with at any given time, and again, it's not easy to describe sometimes, but prayer does help.

I've been told that some widows move on quickly, while others take years. None of us are programmed to all have the same grieving and adjustment time. When my husband died, for days I was in autopilot but I remember every detail. The days after, I spent as much time as I could to try to "do" normal things. I needed time to process it in my own way, but I also had to "be strong" for my son and others. When I found out I had to look for another place to live a couple of months later, I was devastated all over again. Having to move quickly, having to go through all of his things, years of things, and years of mine and my sons things, sorting, donating, trading and packing, setting other things aside for his family, looking for a place to live that I could somehow afford, kept my mind busy. I was knocked down, but still having to be strong.

But once we were resettled... reality of life alone and in a strange place set in. People tell me I'm in a better spot, not so much to worry about and to enjoy it. Get used to it. It takes time. While I'm grateful for having a roof over our heads, some days it's hard sitting out on the stoop watching the interstate traffic go by, remembering chickens in the yard, helping plant the veggie garden every year, seeing the place in my mind. A little boy running next door to his Grandma's house... a pre-teen boy's face lighting up every time his dad's truck pulled in the yard, scratching out another year's growth on that old kitchen door post. So many memories... It's going to take some time for me to find my way.

I lost my husband 4 days before Thanksgiving 2014. My sister lost hers 3 days before Christmas. My friend lost hers 2 days after New Year's Day. Holidays are hard. Valentine's Day, Birthdays, wedding and death anniversaries, Memorial Day, Father's Day...

Sometimes widows seem strong. Oftentimes we are strong, because we have to be, but some days the strength just isn't there. We don't ask for sympathy, but understanding and patience, and maybe a prayer every now and then.

MULTIPLE SCLEROSIS: FOR MY FAMILY AND ME, IT'S PERSONAL

by Ann-Marie Murrell

Throughout my life I was the healthiest, most physically fit person I knew. In high school I was the cheerleader who could out-run, out-do almost anyone, and it was the same in college and my early actress years in California--always working, always very physically active. Other than the usual colds and flu, I was rarely sick (with the exception of a bout of pneumonia, the result of trying to learn how to smoke Clove cigarettes, unfiltered. Less than a pack later, I was in the hospital. Moral of that story, smoking is NOT as cool as it looks...) In the late 1990's I worked at 20th Century Fox Studios and after working 8-10 hours I sometimes co-taught an advanced aerobics class on the lot. I don't drink, smoke (see above), don't do any drugs, and other than one cup of coffee in the morning I only drink water throughout the day. No sodas, no aspartame. Healthy as can be.

But all that changed when I suddenly began having a series of health problems around 1999. It started with my vision, then major stomach problems, then muscle and joint pain that I'd never experienced before. Soon after, everything snowballed into an all-out assault on my body. It got to the point where I couldn't sit up straight in a desk chair and could barely hold my head up, much less exercise anymore. Someone suggested I see a rheumatologist so after a barrage of doctor's appointments and testing (including trips to Scripps's in San Diego), I was ultimately diagnosed with Fibromyalgia and Ulcerative Colitis.

For almost a decade I obediently took all the pain and sleeping meds prescribed to me, but nothing helped. I still hurt and rarely slept. The most difficult part for me was not being physically able to work anymore, so to stay busy (and stave off depression) I did charity work for the LA Children's Hospital and worked part-time as a Children's Director at a church. In 2009 I began my political work, writing for various websites from home and doing on-camera interviews from political events, all which ultimately morphed into PolitiChicks. Around the same time I stopped taking all the prescription medicines my Rheumatologist had prescribed; they weren't helping anyway and mostly made me groggy. So I took lots of Extra Strength Tylenol; very rough on colitis but it was a choice I felt I had to make in order to remain active.

Other than a few Facebook posts I've never publicly discussed my health issues so it's always funny when I'm asked how I have so much energy to do what I do, going all over the U.S. to speak at events. The reality is that after those events I'm usually in bed wrapped in heating pads, sometimes for a week or more. Only one dear friend, my former PolitiChicks producer Beverly Zaslow, could always tell when I'd "hit my wall" and needed to rest during those events. Bev has diabetes and says she can always 'see it in my eyes' when I've had enough.

Despite my joint and muscular pain, everything was manageable--until January 2016.

I had just finished speaking at the 2016 South Carolina Tea Party Coalition Convention and was on my way home to California. As always after a big event, I was tired but nothing out of the ordinary. Then, while changing planes in the North Carolina, my vision went out. It was as if a thick veil of fog suddenly covered my eyes, just enough that I could still see but bad enough that I knew something was terribly wrong. I sat down a few minutes until the "fog" lifted but after that none of my eyeglasses worked anymore--not the bifocals I had recently gotten, nor my reading glasses. I'd been tested for cataracts just a few months earlier so I knew it wasn't that.

Once home I mentioned the incident to my husband, Mark, but we both brushed it off as just being overly tired. I bought several different pairs of reading glasses in various strengths; none of them worked.

Then an avalanche of strange symptoms began. It was as if my body was being attacked, beginning with a numb, 'tingling' sensation in my left hand and forearm. It felt like my hand and arm were trying to fall asleep but couldn't quite make it--but it was constant, never went away. I also had bladder problems for the first time in my life, and my usual "fibromyalgia" pain was now almost unbearable. All of it was like nothing I had experienced before.

Interestingly most of the more serious symptoms occurred in April 2016 during the 5K MS Walkathon at the Rose Bowl in Pasadena. This was the second MS Walkathon my family and I had participated in. Our first was in 1996 when Jason was 10 years old---but this time we were walking because in 2015 Jason, now 31, was diagnosed with MS.

While walking that day I became extremely dizzy, as if someone had spun me around in circles. I was staggering and unsteady so I had to hang on to my husband's arm for balance. Next came an intense migraine that seemed to be spreading into my eyes. I told Jason about this and all the symptoms I'd been experiencing the last month or so, convinced I might have early onset Alzheimer's or maybe a stroke.

Jason said, *"Mom, I hate to say this but it sounds like you have MS."* He suggested I see a neurologist.

Long story short, after a barrage of doctor's appointments, multiple MRIs, a 3-day hospital stay with IV steroids, and a spinal tap, I heard the same words the doctors had told my son the year before--things like "lesions" and "elevated white blood cells" and "optic neuritis". And ultimately my diagnosis was the same as my son's: Multiple Sclerosis.

Each day the past few months I'm never sure what will happen next, or which new symptoms will pop up. Some days it's dizziness/vertigo, which leads to balance issues and trouble walking. Sometimes I have difficulty talking because my throat muscles tighten up, constrict. I have cognitive problems, sometimes forgetting what I'm doing or where I'm going. The numbness that was only in my left hand has now spread all over the place at different times, sometimes causing a maddening burning/itching feeling that is only relieved by putting cold towels all over me.

Other symptoms are flat-out frustrating. A few days ago during a manicure I was asked to relax my hand but when I tried to un-stiffen my fingers, I realized I couldn't. I stared at that hand, trying (but failing) to "will" those fingers to relax, to move. I remember trying to be strong when Jason first told me the same type thing had happened to him, which summarizes the most difficult part of all of this--experiencing firsthand the same type of pain and suffering my son has been going through the past year.

Had I been diagnosed correctly over a decade ago, would I be in less pain, have less extreme symptoms and damage to my spinal cord now? I've since learned that if I had initially gone to a Neurologist instead of Rheumatologists I may have had a "fairer fight". But eh, that's neither here nor there and not something I can dwell on. You can't go backwards. Now I know, and now I can deal with it correctly.

So here I am today, learning how to live in this "new normal". My son has had huge success with Dr. Terry Wahls' diet book, **The Wahls Protocol**, [15] so since the day I got out of the hospital I've been drinking tons of cold-pressed green juices loaded with kale, spinach, beets, and zero sugar, and I'm eating more fish and root vegetables than ever before. I'm also giving up dairy and am now drinking almond milk, which is something my friend AlfonZo Rachel has been trying to push on me for many years (thanks Zo, and yes, you were right, it's a great alternative!). I'm also currently using a cane to walk, mainly for balance issues, and have resigned to the fact that I may never see as clearly as I did before--but at least I can still see, and that's all that counts.

And since Multiple Sclerosis is officially a family thing, I'm going to do what I've done all my life and I'll fight to bring awareness to this disease and hopefully help find a cure. May is **World MS Day** [16] so I hope you'll visit the **National MS Society** [17] website for more information about this disease and what you can do to help fight it, too.

I will be fighting to stay out of a wheelchair and I'll do that by following Jason's dietary lead and my doctors' orders. Thankfully there have been major advances in MS research over the years and the meds my son and I are taking should keep more brain and spinal cord lesions from forming.

As far as my political career goes, I've been forced to take it easy. I've turned down numerous television and radio interviews because of vocal or cognitive problems, or flat-out pain. I'm continuing to fulfill speaking obligations but am trying to pace myself, and not to allow the stress of politics affect me. (Not an easy feat...)

The support I've received from my family and friends has been awe-inspiring. My PolitiChicks family--especially my writers and social media prayer warriors-- stepped up in major ways. I received cards, flowers, and lovely gifts in the mail from many people who are going through difficult times of their own. Most of my 'real life' friends either called or texted me every day, but unfortunately a few all but disappeared from my life. Over the years (with my misdiagnosis of Fibromyalgia and colitis) I learned that's to be expected; some people have enough "drama" of their own and don't want to deal with anyone else's. But the friends who've been there for my family and me through all of this will never be forgotten as long as I live. They are making me want to be a better person, a better friend.

All in all, life is good. I continue to be blessed beyond all reason. My family's story remains a good one, and with God's grace is to happily be continued.

4

OBAMACARE: FURTHERING THE MORAL DECLINE OF AMERICA

by Michele Holt

For twelve years prior to Obamacare closing our private practice, our office and staff worked with Georgia and South Carolina Human Resource agencies. The Department of Family and Children Services (DFCS) and Department of Social Services-SC (DSS) were government agencies that would contract services out for families who were at risk or their children were in foster care. I served as the CFO of both our for-profit and our non-profit agency under the umbrella of our regional agency.

During those years I wondered if anything could top what I witnessed on a daily basis in terms of tragic decay of family values, but as soon as I would wonder a case would be handed to us by a caseworker or court system and the circumstances were worse than the others we worked.

Our agency hired 1,099 contractors who had Master's degrees in either social work or counseling. Several of our team members including my husband had extra credentials in substance abuse counseling as well. On top of my fiscal responsibilities I also garnered a degree in criminal justice and took certification training to handle domestic violence. My degree concentration was in family violence. For over 3 years every Saturday I handled a group of domestic violence offenders. That's right – offenders, not the victims. I had to handle to attitudes, the twisted outlook of acceptable behaviors and the common threads of such violent behaviors every person in the group shared. There were women as well as men charged with violent behavior so for 26 weeks not only did they have to show up they also had to participate in order to get a satisfactory completion from me on top of paying their fees.

Excuses in this line of work were frequent and consistent. It was never the adult's fault if their children were taken away, it was never the fault of the abuser that they lost control of their temper and unfortunately it was few and far between that we would see a successful outcome in any of the cases we worked or were involved in.

Sadly, the most consistency we saw was the continued outcome for many of the children and adults in these situations. You see, for the families that were in crisis and the children were in foster care consistent situations were generational welfare and generational abuse (whether physical, emotional, or substance). In my training I learned about theories that would explain why people became what they are today. I watched potential in children to be successful and be the one out of the family who would make their outcome better diminish because of what I saw as an addiction to their normal surroundings. Yes, addiction. These families for the most part were duplicating behaviors and outcomes that they were raised with. Many of the families we tried to help were single mothers with multiple children by multiple fathers. Those fathers were either incarcerated or dead. In half of the cases we worked a grandparent or an aunt was raising the children. Very seldom did we have cases where a father figure or uncle was involved. So the pattern of behavior continued.

Unfortunately many of the teenagers in foster care were involved in gang activity or they already had criminal records. My husband and I saw many of the people we dealt with on the evening news, being arrested for armed robbery or murder. Their lives seemed to have no chance of success. It was heartbreaking and tragic.

The government spending on entitlements was at an all-time high throughout those years [18] as they are today and many budgets were squeezed and often providers who worked hard for these families never got paid for the services they billed. One state alone owed our agency over $50,000 for services provided [19] and used in the court systems, but we were told there was no money in the budget. That created a whole new crisis of shortages of providers to offer services and this was back in 2008. It is worse today.

There is definitely a moral crisis in our country today. It has become the "new normal" to push for single parent

170

households because our Government will reward you with monthly checks if the father figure is not in the house. For many of these single mothers the thought of obtaining an education or a job skill is unlikely because they are either too concerned with where their next check will come from or where their next "high" will be bought. We saw the abuse of the system first hand. We witnessed the state write a check for some families for furniture for the house at the tune of $10,000 before knowing that taxpayers are footing the bill. Society today glorifies teen pregnancies, thug life in music videos and rap music glorifies criminal behavior and domestic violence while touting youth today can be a success without hard work or education just like the thug rappers they idolized.

The Democrat Party has waged a war on accountability, moral values and faith because for the most part this party has been successful in doing so. They have provided continued cradle to grave financial assistance if people keep them in power despite how it impacts the country as a whole. We have a stark reality we are facing today, as soon those of us who believe in moral values, accountability, hard work, and faith will be outnumbered by those who want the Nanny State. It is incumbent for us as conservative women especially to band together and make a change. We must voice our beliefs and not allow the socialist progressives on the democratic side to speak for women as a whole.

I have seen the worst case scenarios play out in person. I have watched the faces of the abused children as they came through our doors. I have witnessed the potential of a child be snuffed out by the promises of a gangster life. Ladies and gentlemen, this is a war we must fight to win.

Michele Holt served as producer and co-host of a popular Fox News affiliate station WNRR1380. Michele interviewed such guests as Ambassador John Bolton, Newt Gingrich, Economist Peter Schift, and many more. Currently Michele works as a social media political strategist for various state and local political campaigns as well as a small business owner with her husband Dr. Joe Holt. Michele's PolitiChicks articles have been shared on the Daily Caller and several other conservative media sites.

5

"AFFORDABLE" CARE? NOT FOR THIS DOCTOR.

by Dr. Bill Simpson

It was a first for me.

After thirty years of practice as the only dentist in a small town in rural Mississippi, I fired an employee. I've had employees retire, employees move on to other jobs, and have had some employees who, by mutual agreement, decide that a dental office wasn't a good fit for them, but I've never had to fire one. I didn't want to terminate someone that I needed and valued but I really didn't feel that I had another option.

I hated the experience.

First, a little background. Furniture manufacturing was once the linchpin of the economy in this area. The majority of those jobs are now in China. Then the recession hit. In 2011, the unemployment rate here was 13.5%. In the next county it was 20.1%.

Over the years unemployment decreased slightly but most are still waiting on the recovery. Folks around here don't talk about income equality; they talk about income, period.

My practice serves lower and middle-income patients. I don't have a high-end, high-fee practice like some dentists in more affluent areas. That is by choice. I grew up in a small town; I love the people in a small town, the sense of familiarity and community. I guess I'll die in a small town but it is not an easy way of life. Years ago, my cousin, a Harvard-educated architect, spent the summer here in order to design and build my dental office. As the building neared completion he turned to me and said, "People say that if you can make it in New York City, you can make it anywhere. They're wrong." He pointed to the ground. "If you can make it HERE, you can make it anywhere." So true.

My point is this – I have to run my practice as a business. I have to watch my pennies, compare prices on supplies to find the best deals, run my practice as efficiently as possible. I constantly monitor and manage all aspects of my business so that I can provide a bright, clean, affordable, and safe professional environment for my patients and employees. In spite of all my efforts there are some things I can't control.

The one expense that has skyrocketed over the last five years is the cost of my employees' health insurance. Prior to 2009, health insurance premiums grew at a rate comparable to other expenses. Since the Senate passed the Affordable Care Act in 2009, the premiums have increased by almost 65%, this in spite of switching to a plan with a higher deductible. In 2015 I received notice that they will rise again on January 1st, an increase of 90% since 2009.

This kind of inflation wrecks the balance sheet in a small business. It was painful, but the math told me I would have to fire someone. If I could have kept just half of the premium increase, I could have found a way to keep my employee.

In addition to health insurance, I provide my employees with a retirement plan. Last year I fully funded the plan for my staff. I can't say the same for myself. I'm 57 years old and I need to sock away as much for retirement as I can but last year I didn't make enough to fully fund my own retirement plan.

I have raised my fees slightly to compensate but in an area hit hard by the economy, the more I raise fees the harder it is for struggling families to get the care they need.

My staff did not get a raise in 2015 or 2016. They won't next year, either. Their raise will be eaten up by the cost of health insurance. I can't fund my retirement like I should. I had to fire someone that I didn't want to lose.

Math is an exact and inflexible science. Numbers do not lie.

And the math is telling me that I can't afford the Affordable Care Act.

Dr. Bill Simpson practices dentistry in rural Mississippi. Raised on a small farm, he has worked in road construction, roofing, a mobile-home factory, pharmacology research, and as a clinical instructor at a dental school.

6

I LIKED MY HEALTHCARE PLAN – AND NOW IT'S BEEN CUT (THANKS, OBAMACARE)

by Sean O'Reilly

It was coming up on my Independence Day holiday weekend, and I should have never gotten the mail...

It was innocent enough; my new normal 'workout' walking a few laps around the cul-de-sac on a sunny morning in Minnesota. With the dog park in the middle, and cabins and houses all around the outside-it really is a beautiful stroll to start the day. Slap on the ear buds, dial up some IHeartRadio country station and I'm off!

I finished my third lap, and saw that the flag was down on the mailbox. Knowing I had sent off some bills the day before, I thought I'd check.

Gun Magazine; another bill...'Blue Cross Blue Shield'. Hmm...

I walked into the foyer, already tugging at the folded flap of the envelope. Chewie was barking insults at me (she didn't get to walk with this morning), and Nancy was in the kitchen putting away some groceries.

"I got a letter from Blue Cross", I told her. "The first line says: 'We regret to inform you'."

That's when I headed for the couch. I sat down, unfolded the rest of the letter, and took a breath.

"Dear Sean..." Then, I read it aloud:

"We regret to inform you that at the end of this year, Blue Cross and Blue Shield of Minnesota will be discontinuing all individual and family insurance plans..."

That's when I heard Nancy say, "Oh no."

I could tell she had stopped putting groceries away. In fact, she wasn't even making a sound.

"As Minnesota's largest health plan with more than 80

years of history in this state, we did not make this decision lightly..."

I heard Nancy, almost in a whisper, say: "I'm done, too."

"Blue Cross was hoping that recent premium increases could generate some level of market stability for the future. Unfortunately, the situation has only become more unstable, with health costs to our individual and family plans continuing to accelerate beyond the pricing of our plans and what many member can afford..."

I put the letter down. There wasn't much more I really needed to read at that point. I looked up, as Nancy slowly walked past me and down the hallway to the bedroom. I looked at her, hoping to catch a glimpse of her face - or at least her eyes.

She just closed the door behind her.

It's pretty sad, actually. "If you like your health plan, you can keep your plan," they told us, over and over again. Yep. As a matter of fact, I DID like my health plan. Even though my deductible had doubled and my premiums had tripled in 6 years, I was working with it.

I liked my plan...and now it's been cut.

Sean O'Reilly *says his conservatarian roots grew from being a small business owner in the liberal land of Minnesota. You can find him daily, managing, moderating and leading political debate on the popular Fox News Fans Facebook page. His passions include photography and fishing. Sean also enjoys countryside living with Nancy, his partner of 20+ years.*

PART EIGHT: SOCIAL ISSUES

Republicans are often told not to talk about social issues. But if we don't express our beliefs, who will? The same people who've been defining who we are for decades: Democrats. If we don't learn to properly explain who we are as Republicans and what we stand for, the Left will happily continue doing it for us. – **Ann-Marie Murrell**

1

MICROAGGRESSIONS: ACADEMIC CENSORSHIP FOR PERCEIVED OFFENSES

by Pamela Anne

So how do you destroy the First Amendment of the United States Constitution?

You make human frailty an offense, get academia involved by giving university seminars to other academics that propagate the error leading to punishing the students for perceived offenses. The mind-set taught in the seminar trickles down to the college students, who then become voters.

Leading the pack of degreed censurers is Janet Napolitano, president of the University of California. The former secretary of Homeland Security and former governor of Arizona is partnering with Wisconsin University.

Seminars were adapted from Derald Wing Sue's book, *Microaggression in Everyday Life: Race, Gender and Sexual Orientation* (Wiley & Sons, 2010) specifically for training on microaggression. Napolitano sent out letters to UC deans and department chairs *"inviting"* their presence at the seminars, *"to foster informed conversation about the best way to build and nurture a productive academic climate".*

The First Amendment of the United States Constitution is once again usurped by assigning infringements for a "noble reason".

Just what is a "microaggression"? According to UCLA Diversity and Faculty Development, (2014) PDF (p.10): *"Microaggressions are the everyday verbal, nonverbal, and environmental slights, snubs, or insults, whether intentional or unintentional, that communicates hostile, derogatory, or negative messages to target persons based solely upon their marginalized group membership."*

The Tool: Recognizing Microaggressions and the Messages They Send, (2014) PDF (p. 1) adds: *"The first step in addressing microaggressions is to recognize when a microaggression has occurred and what message it may be sending."*

Social scientists Sue, Bucceri, Lin, Nadal, and Torino (2007) describe microaggressions as *"the new face of racism"* adding, *"saying that the nature of racism has shifted over time from overt expressions of racial hatred and hate crimes, towards expressions of aversive racism, such as microaggressions, that are more subtle, ambiguous and often unintentional. Researchers say this has led some Americans to wrongly believe that racism is no longer a problem for non-white Americans."*

Simply, it's the *perceived* bias, implicit or otherwise, in any communication by the recipient, (or a progressive onlooker), regardless of conscious or unconscious intention by the speaker. However, it should be noted that none of us are without bias.

Our brain filters the data we encounter through our perceptions that are initially structured by our family of origin, the significant influences of others, institutions attended, our exposure to media and our personal learning experiences. We select certain data, then sort to retain or delete it pertinent to our values or needs. All processing involves our beliefs, which are basically notions we infer or assume to be true. The brain makes generalizations from specific experiences for future judgments. Biases are a normal part of intellectual processing. They can be modified to a certain extent, but they are part of our humanity.

Secondly, have any of these extensively "lettered" faculty ever considered *assertiveness training* to manage offenses? Are none of these academics familiar with Suzette Haden Elgin's, Ph.D. or Deborah Tannen's, Ph.D. work? Their expertise is in "verbal defense". Both have taught extensively different skill sets to capture belittling or offensive communication and to respond assertively—not aggressively. But then such a reasonable solution would support America's First Amendment, recognizing that the individual should take personal responsibility for offenses rather than academia or the government censuring free speech.

Such a practice of reprogramming students compromises the right and freedom of personal thought and judgment. This is a form of fascism through social engineering.

The PDF handout dispersed during the nine of the ten UC campuses throughout the school year can be downloaded online: "Recognizing Microaggressions and the Messages They Send" (2014). Here are a few examples:

[Theme:] Color Blindness[:] Statements that indicate that a White person does not want to or need to acknowledge race.

[Microaggression Examples:]

"There is only one race, the human race."

"America is a melting pot."

"I don't believe in race." ...

[Theme:] Denial of Individual Racism/Sexism/Heterosexism[:] A statement made when bias is denied....

[Microaggression Examples:] ... To a person of color: "Are you sure you were being followed in the store? I can't believe it."

[Theme:] Myth of Meritocracy[:] Statements which assert that race or gender does not play a role in life successes, for example in issues like faculty demographics.

(Author's Note: Notice the *biased* labeling of meritocracy as a "myth".)

[Microaggression Examples:] "I believe the most qualified person should get the job."

"Of course he'll get tenure, even though he hasn't published much—he's Black!"

"Men and women have equal opportunities for achievement."

"Gender plays no part in who we hire."

"America is the land of opportunity."

"Everyone can succeed in this society, if they work hard enough."

"Affirmative action is racist."

The handout is so nuanced with meta-messages implied by the author that if nationally implemented we couldn't talk to one another without taking offense. Ironically, bias is evident in the framing and statements used as examples.

U.S. Supreme Court Justice Louis Brandles' (1856 -1941) quote is more germane today than ever before: *"If there be time to expose through discussion the falsehood and fallacies, to avert the evil by the processes of education, the remedy to be applied is more speech, not enforced silence."*

2

"LEGAL KIDNAPPING" BY CPS – IT IS DOMESTIC TERRORISM

by Terri LaPoint

How did we get to this place as a nation? Michelle Rider [8] had it right. She referred to the actions of Child Protective Services as "domestic terrorism." The mother of medically kidnapped teenager Isaiah Rider nailed it. [9]

There is nothing more terrifying for a parent than the thought of someone taking their child. When a child, whether infant, preschooler, or teenager, is kidnapped, the parents are in an acute state of terror, not knowing whether or not they will ever see their child again, not knowing whether their child will live or die, and not knowing what horrors their precious baby will face while in captivity, alone, without mom or dad to help them through.

If ISIS terrorists were coming down their street, executing everyone in their path, could it possibly be more terrifying? After all, it would all be over soon. Not so with kidnapping. It is hours, days, weeks, and months. Years of uncertainty, of constantly living in a heightened state of fight or flight, while being utterly, and completely, helpless to save that person in their life that means more to them than life itself. Yet, this terror is the state of existence facing, not just a few, but thousands of parents – our friends and neighbors - in every single state in America, some more than others. And the enemy is within, paid for by our tax dollars, in the form of Child Protective Services (CPS). [10]

These are parents who know that they have committed no crime, so they aren't like the bank robber or the drug dealer afraid that the law is going to justly come after them and punish them for their crimes. They committed no crimes. Nor are they like the abusers and molesters who inflict torment and pain on their victims, knowing somewhere inside that there will come a day of reckoning and justice for their evil deeds.

No. These are parents - like you; like me. Parents who are trying to put food on the table and make ends meet, dealing with the exhaustion of parenting toddlers or the emotional roller coaster of parenting teenagers, or the heartache of parenting a very sick child. Parents who know they aren't perfect, who know they make mistakes, and who beat themselves up for not being enough or for losing patience and yelling. Parents who don't know all the answers, or thought they did and tried their very best.

Imperfect perhaps, but nevertheless they are parents full of love for the most amazing little people they have ever encountered.

And they are looking over their shoulders.

If Child Protective Services knocks on the door of a loving parent, or comes into the hospital room when their child is sick or injured, there is little on this earth that is more terrifying. It is because they have the power to literally take away a child without any real proof, without any real evidence. It is happening all over the country.

It isn't supposed to be that way. It hasn't always been that way. They are supposed to only take children away who are truly in imminent danger. But there are more children taken unjustly from good homes than there are from abusive homes. The reality is that there are "medical kidnappings" and "legal kidnappings" of loved children from innocent parents on a regular basis.

Most of America has no idea. I didn't. When I heard about the Justina Pelletier [11] case, I thought it was an isolated case. Surely parents getting a second medical opinion and having their child taken away by the government *had* to be extremely rare. This is America! This couldn't be happening. It's unconstitutional. It's corrupt, and it's wrong. Children belong with their parents, unless they are truly being abused.

But I was wrong.

I once wrote a piece asking if there was a growing trend in these types of cases. Someone commented, "Where has THIS author been? It's been going on for twenty years." I didn't know. I would be willing to bet that most of you didn't know that either.

They were right. It just hasn't been made public. Parents were bullied and intimidated into silence.

The media hardly pays the slightest bit of attention to the greatest threat to families in America today. While they are playing the ratings about gay rights and abortion and measles, a much greater threat to the American family lurks right under our noses.

Because of federal programs like CAPTA, ASFA (Adoption and Safe Families Act), [12] and Title IV-E funding, children have dollar signs on their heads. Because states get federal money, to the tune of billions of dollars, for children in foster care and for children who are adopted, children have become commodities to be bought and sold, with no regard to the destruction of their very souls. Corrupt agencies and lawyers and judges get a piece of the pie, and what is legal or right and wrong gets thrown out the window.

I have seen more laws broken that you can imagine, not by the parents, but by the agencies and legal system that are supposed to protect the children.

Doctors needing human medical lab rats for their research studies have blood on their hands as well, because, as the nation learned with Justina Pelletier, children who are wards of the state may be entered into medical research studies and drug trials without their parents' knowledge or consent.

An extremely high percentage of foster children, [13] even very young ones, are forced to consume a cocktail of experimental and psychotropic drugs. A child with a rare medical condition can literally represent millions of dollars to medical researchers.

Earlier today, I came to a place of being very overwhelmed by all the injustice I see with this "domestic terrorism," and I posted my heart's cry on my own Facebook page. People all around us are hurting. They are facing giants far bigger than they can handle by themselves. Those of you who care about liberty, who care about families, we need you in this fight. These families cannot do it alone.

"Can the world just please STOP being wicked and horrible to families? The cruelty, by people in our own government, blows my mind. And it never stops. Every. Single. Day. I hear about new stories. I want to help everybody. But I can't. I don't understand why local media doesn't seem to care unless someone else writes the story first. I don't understand why conservative talk show hosts aren't talking about this on a regular basis.

I don't understand how anybody can think it is ok to undermine families and rip them apart. I don't understand how people can abuse and destroy an innocent child. I don't understand how anyone can tell a loving mother that the government knows better than she does how to take care of her kids, and can rip those babies right out of her arms.

Were all those tyrannical regimes in world history any worse than this? Tell me how. Ripping families apart is the cruelest form of tyranny and abuse. There is no escape from the pain.

And yet I have to find a way each day to try to encourage families to stand strong and have hope. I pray with the mamas for God to put angels around their babies and hold them close. I cry with them, and I die inside a little more. I can't do this alone. I am just one person.

Please, friends, help share the burden. Encourage these parents. Fight with them. Call and write legislators. Individually, the parents are picked off, one by one. But together, we can stand united against this tyranny.

It may not be you today, but it might be tomorrow. We need each other.

Terri LaPoint is an advocate for families and for pro-life issues. In addition PolitiChicks, Terri writes for Medical Kidnap and is a contributing author to the book, Medical Kidnapping: A Threat to Every Family in America. Terri is a regular guest on blog talk radio programs and speaks at events that advocate for families. Terri holds a B.S. in Cultural Anthropology/World Missions, with minors in Bible/Theology and Behavioral Science. She is a Christian mom with four children, and has been married for over 25 years.

3
HOW PLANNED PARENTHOOD MADE ME PRO-LIFE

by Beth Baumann

"**A**re you pro-life or pro-choice?" It was a question I would frequently get when a political discussion would erupt.

"Both?" I would say, semi-reluctantly. This was the one question I hated answering. I had to explain myself, which caused a greater discussion. It wasn't a simple answer. It was more complicated than a one-word answer.

I would get looks of confusion, and in some cases, amazement. No one understood me. I had to explain myself.

"I'm pro-choice for everyone but pro-life for myself. I don't think I could ever go through with an abortion but who am I to tell someone else what they can and cannot do?"

Most of the time, my response shocked people. I've been told that most people haven't heard of this stance before. Abortion is such a divisive issue that it's always assumed that a hardline stance has to be taken. You're either fully in favor of abortions, with no exceptions or you're fully against abortions.

In 2015, I had to reevaluate how I felt about abortion. I've seen the graphic posters and pictures that depict an aborted baby. Different groups held protests on my college campus. And most of the time, I would stand back and watch. I wanted to take in both sides' argument and understand why the felt so passionate about the issue. I was curious.

Yes, the pictures grossed me out. Yes, it made me think, but more than anything, those pictures made me angry. I felt like those things were being shoved in my face and here I was being forced to take a stance on an issue that I didn't feel impacted me. I can honestly say that I've never thought, "I need to protect abortion rights in case I need an abortion down the road."

The Left frequently uses the argument that women who are victims of rape should have the decision to have an abortion.

As someone who has been the victim of sexual assault, I can say that making a decision to have an abortion would add additional emotional trauma to an already traumatic experience. You're already full of shame and guilt. The last thing you need is to know that you killed an innocent life.

The undercover videos about Planned Parenthood [14] were more graphic to me than any of the pictures I had seen of aborted babies. Knowing that Planned Parenthood is not only aborting babies, but selling their organs and tissue for profit, upset me. Hearing the graphic detail about how baby's skulls are crushed during an abortion sent chills down my spine. Hearing about baby's legs being broken to protect vital organs caused my jaw to drop. How could a doctor – someone who took the Hippocratic oath – kill an innocent child and make money off that killing? If any non-medical specialist did this, it would be considered murder, but in our society, it's looked at as another day at the office.

These chilling stories made me come to a conclusion: innocent life needs to be protected. Even though I believe in limited government, we have a duty to protect those who can't protect themselves. That's why I'm now a member of the pro-life community.

Beth Baumann is a California native who attended Northern Arizona University where she founded the NAU chapter of Young Americans for Liberty. Beth received national attention when she defended Freedom of Speech on campus. Although she faced misconduct charges, she stood by her Constitutional rights and was eventually exonerated of all charges. During her tenure, she was copy editor for the newspaper, marketing director and film festival director for the campus TV station, and news correspondent for political talk radio. Beth works for a public relations firm.

4
MAN-HATING FEMINISM IS ILLOGICAL

by Katie Zehnder

In 2015, comediennes Sarah Silverman and Chelsea Handler were featured in a commercial for T-Mobile, [15] which resulted in the hashtag #SorryItsABoy [16] trending on Twitter. Although they probably thought it was hilarious, it was not. I found it appalling because I absolutely despise this brand of "feminism". Originally feminism was about equality between the sexes, including giving women the right to vote. Now feminism has evolved into a man-hating monster that has completely reversed the roles of the sexes and it is not about equality, but instead superiority of the female sex.

Not only do feminists seek to elevate the female sex as being better than men, but they also do everything they can to emasculate men and undermine their ego.

Feminism has greatly contributed to the death of chivalry as well. Women complain that men no longer treat them with respect but the reason is because many times if a man tries to open the door for you, in your superior "femininess", you verbally assault him, assure him that you were perfectly capable of opening the door for yourself. In fact, *how dare he open the door for you* simply because you're a woman...

Men tend to have sensitive egos to begin with and it doesn't take much of this man-hating behavior to utterly emasculate them.

The irony in this new feminist, man-bashing movement is that they are now endorsing the very thing it fought against: Superiority of one sex over another. Or perhaps they think they are getting their revenge for all those years of "female oppression."

The lunacy of these gender wars is that there would be no women without men, and vice-versa. How can you feel such disgust for someone so crucial to your very existence? So not only is this man-hating feminism appalling and disgusting, it's illogical.

Men are not better than women, and women are not better than men. However, as a general rule, women are better than men at some things and men are better than women at some things. For example, men are generally physically stronger than men. Are there women who are physical stronger than some men? Yes.

Our value is not based on our gender or what we do best. We are valuable because we are human beings created in the image of God.

I honestly wonder what all these man-hating women would do if they found themselves in physical danger and "Prince Charming" came to their rescue. Would they turn on him and say, "How dare you try to rescue me? I can take care of myself!" I don't think so. I believe I speak for all of us PolitiChicks in saying that we refuse to be man-hating women – and please, gentlemen, don't be afraid to open our doors for us. Sure, we can do it ourselves, but every now and then it's nice to be reminded of the difference between ladies and gentlemen.

Katie Zehnder is a PolitiChick, assistant editor for Red Millennial and Political commentator for The Federalist Papers.

5

WAKING TO THE REALITY: HUMAN AND SEX TRAFFICKING IN THE U.S.

by Lee Bagdasarian Rech

In a 2015 Politico article, "The Truth About Sex Trafficking," [17] human trafficking is cited as the second fastest-growing criminal industry in the world, generating over $32 billion annually.

I live in the U.S. and my 4th of July was spent celebrating with my family and friends. I hold the classic viewpoint of praising the nation's heritage, laws, history, society, and people. I think of independence and freedom as opposed to coercion, abduction, fraud, deception, abuse of power, suppression, exploitation, and vulnerability.

Yet, as we gather this year, a very real and complex crime is proliferating; human trafficking is happening right here in the U.S.

With more than 20.9 million worldwide victims, [18] mostly women, and 5.5 million children, according to one projection by the Polaris Project, this despicable crime trend is modern slavery on a worldwide scale.

According to the same Polaris Project source, traffickers use a combination of criminal tactics to control other people for the purpose of engaging in commercial sex or forcing them to provide labor services against their will. All trafficking victims share one essential experience—the loss of freedom.

In 2014, Utah Attorney General Sean Reyes had a personal experience with the trafficking of children, which became game changing for him and a priority focus for his administration. In March 2014, the Utah AG's office filed 34 felony charges [19] against human trafficking criminal Victor Rax, who later killed himself in jail. With eyes, mind, and heart wide open, AG Reyes gained international acclaim when news broke of his travel to a dangerous area of South America last year with Operation Underground Railroad (OUR). [20] During the covert operation, AG Reyes posed as a bodyguard and translator to help liberate more than 100 children from a sex trafficking ring that spanned multiple locations. The sting had the support of both the U.S. and Colombian governments; two U.S. Department of Homeland Security investigators were also present.

OUR jump team including Tim Ballard [21] and AG Reyes [22] celebrates a successful undercover bust that resulted in saving over 100 girls from Colombian sex trafficking cartel.

"Protecting children and women from exploitation by providing advance notice of intended travel by registered child-sex offenders to the government of the country of destination is another powerful step toward stopping this all too true crime trend," said Reyes. "I can tell you this deplorable multibillion dollar industry continues to flourish and must be stopped. By advancing International Megan's Law, I am hopeful we can significantly reduce sex tourism and human and child sex trafficking on a nationwide and global scale."

In July 2016, in cooperation with local and national law enforcement agencies, the Utah Attorney General's Office announced a multi-month investigation that resulted in 70 arrests of a number of individuals on human trafficking and child sex exploitation charges. The arrests were related to cases where victims of human trafficking were trafficked inside Utah, yes Utah. Some cases involved minors and some crossed state lines; and several of the Utah child sexual exploitation arrests were related to a nationwide operation known as Operation Broken Heart III, which involved the 61 ICAC Task Forces across the nation.

There isn't an Attorney General in the United States more involved in tackling human and child sex trafficking than Reyes, who in May 2015 testified before Congress in support of H.R. 515 International Megan's Law, sponsored by Congressman Chris Smith (R-NJ), a bill that if passed into law would do the following (Source: H.R. 515): [23]

Directs the Secretary of Homeland Security to establish within the Child Exploitation Investigations Unit of the U.S. Immigration and Customs Enforcement the Angel Watch Center, which shall:

- Receive information on travel by child-sex offenders;
- Establish a system to maintain and archive all relevant information, including decisions not to transmit notification abroad and responses of destination countries to notifications;
- Establish an annual review process to ensure that the Angel Watch Center is consistent in procedures regarding providing notification to destination countries;
- Establish a mechanism to receive complaints from child-sex offenders affected by notifications of destination countries.

And, also requires the Center to engage in ongoing consultations with:

- Nongovernmental organizations (NGOs) that have experience in identifying and preventing child sex tourism and rescuing and rehabilitating minor victims of international sexual exploitation and trafficking;
- The governments of countries interested in cooperating in the creation of an international sex offender travel notification system or that are primary destination or source countries for international sex tourism, and;
- Internet service and software providers regarding technology to facilitate the implementation of an international sex offender travel notification system in the United States and in other countries.

According to the Congressional subcommittee that oversees human trafficking, [24] our government runs sting operations abroad to catch U.S. pedophile sex tourists and rescue victims. However, the U.S. often has to look to others to conduct rescue operations or run investigations that fall outside its jurisdiction. For this reason, NGOs with expertise are leading out in an effort to bust traffickers on the worldwide stage.

One such NGO is former CIA agent and Homeland Security undercover operative and special agent Tim Ballard. [25] He spent

11 years investigating child trafficking and pedophile rings in the U.S. By December 2013, he was so upset by what he witnessed and so frustrated by governmental restrictions, that he quit and founded his own not-for-profit rescue team called Operation Underground Railroad (OUR).

According to Reyes, [26] an advocate of OUR, "Operation Underground Railroad is an amazing organization. They set up operations worldwide to liberate children from the clutches of traffickers and then provide them with the care, counseling and recovery resources needed for survival. OUR deals directly with law enforcement and child services in each of the countries they operate with the invitation and blessing of the ambassadors, heads of state, or other top government officials, and they do so with the support of American federal agencies."

Reyes added, "Most of the OUR leaders came from U.S. federal agencies, including the CIA, FBI, and Homeland Security. OUR also has Navy Seals and Army Special Forces members comprising their elite operations teams."

Ballard and his team of mostly volunteers—who call themselves the Abolitionists [27] because of parallels to the movement to end slavery—have completed missions with the cooperation of foreign governments and police departments in Haiti, Columbia, Nicaragua, Dominican Republic, Mexico and other locations. Ballard also testified with AG Reyes before Congress in support of pending sex trafficking legislation.

Early on, an investor offered to fund a film on OUR's operations. The process started with a feature-length documentary, "The Abolitionists," [28] produced by FletChet Entertainment, which chronicled the launch of OUR and its first two missions. To date, the documentary has had private screenings and is yet to be released theatrically.

"No project has ever moved me in my career the way 'The Abolitionists' did," said Mazza, [29] former president of Sony and Paramount TV, in a recent Deadline.com interview. "These are true heroes, Tim Ballard is today's Chris Kyle. To see the show was quite remarkable—it's a mission for me as much as it's a business."

To learn more about human and child sex trafficking,

Operation Underground Railroad and how to get involved as part of a jump team or donor, go to: ourrescue.org.

Lee Bagdasarian Rech founded LBR Communications Inc., an independent marketing/public relations and professional writing agency in 1996, placing numerous editorial broadcast segments including: Forbes.com, The Wall Street Journal, New York Times, Bloomberg, among others. In July 2016, Lee was invited to join the Trafficking In America Task Force advisory board. She received her master's degree in literature from King's College, University of London, and a bachelor's degree from Denison University. Lee can be found spending time with her husband and two children.

6

DO BLACK LIVES MATTER
ONLY AFTER DEATH?

by Kimberly Klacik

Black lives, Hispanic lives, and White lives matter, but I personally tend to care about everyone. It's like this curse passed down from my parents. With so many specific crimes taking precedence these days, I decided to reach out for some clarification.

According to the BlackLivesMatter.com website, BLM is "not a moment, but a movement". It continues,

"When we say black lives matter, we are broadening the conversation around state violence to include all of the ways in which Black people are intentionally left powerless at the hands of the state."

Completely powerless? I am most certain that a criminal case acquittal does not protect anyone from a civil case, which is actually not a bad idea to consider before marching.

Their website states, *"Black Lives Matter is a unique contribution that goes beyond extrajudicial killings of Black people by police and vigilantes."* So, naturally, I thought I would ask for a little evidence to support that statement.

In 2016 I tried to directly contact Black Lives Matter with the intention of finding out what it is they do *before* these tragedies occur. I wrote, *"Please provide any evidence that you actually care about these black lives before being riddled with bullets. I would appreciate the information."*

I believe they intentionally ignored my inquiries. Mainly I wanted to know what it is they are doing to encourage others to make positive impacts in the communities in the recent media frenzies.

After waiting 7 days for a response, I decided to chalk it up as a loss. I believe if you truly care about young black lives, you would be doing a bit more than marching down the street without their knowledge.

Black lives absolutely matter, and they mattered long before someone like Michael Brown held up a convenience store. Where was this organization *before* Brown made the decision to forego being a positive role model or a contributing member to society? Is Black Lives Matter able to fund black people dealing with mental health problems? Does Black Lives Matter provide opportunities for continuing education, after young Black Lives graduate from high school? Are there recreation centers erected by Black Lives Matter in communities to provide safe environments for young Black Lives?

Unfortunately I wasn't able to communicate with anyone involved – which perhaps answers all my questions...

__Kimberly Klacik__ is the Founder/Executive Director of the nonprofit, 'Potential Me', which supports women going into the workforce, college, trade school, or the military. She is a volunteer on Capitol Hill, conversing daily with both members of Congress and their staff in hopes of gaining some insight on what makes them tick. Kimberly is a frequent guest on One America News Network as a political commentator.

PART 9: MILITARY

Thousands of men and women have lain down their lives for the cause of America and the protection of it. That "shining city" reflects the courage and sacrifice of these men and women. – **Sheri Sharp**

1

A SEASON FOR FLAGS

By Dr. Bill Simpson

My father's hands always trembled and his head always shook. Once, as a child, I asked him why. He said, with a sly grin, "Must be those bad Simpson genes." He was totally deaf in his left ear. Again, if asked, he gave the same response.

I learned at an early age to gauge my father's state of mind by the degree of his tremors, sort of an emotional Richter's Scale. Quick to laugh but also quick-tempered, he almost never erupted at his family. Instead, if upset or angered, he would step out onto the porch and smoke a cigarette.

One day I found a samurai sword in the back of a closet in our small farmhouse. When I asked him about it he didn't answer. When pressed, his tremors increased and I knew to back off. The same thing happened later when I found an old shaving kit full of black & white photographs of my father and other young men, all dressed in military uniforms. Over the years I accepted the fact that my father would never talk about his war so I quit asking.

I was born into a house without a telephone, television or air conditioning. In the Deep South, the AC is what you miss the most. My father struggled to make ends meet for his family on our small farm in the hill country of Mississippi, in spite of the fact he worked from can 'til can't. I remember him coming home at dusk after working all day as hired labor on another farm to eat a quick meal before heading to our barn. Late at night I would watch the headlights of our small tractor as it crossed the fields.

One year he made a deal to plow and plant some land that a local physician owned. He miscalculated the cost and wound up losing money, money we could ill afford to lose, but he kept his word and finished the job. To make up for the loss, he just worked harder.

Another time my mother wanted to buy a set of

encyclopedias for my sister and me. My parents knew we couldn't afford them, they both said so frequently as they discussed the matter. This was a major expenditure for our household and after they talked I knew we wouldn't be getting the books, but a few weeks later a heavy box arrived. You know what it contained.

Something changed when I was about ten years old. I found out later that the doctor had prescribed a new medicine for my father, a drug called Valium. My father took a job with an insurance company. We sold the farm (Hallelujah!). We built a new house – it was HUGE, almost 2000 square feet, and, best of all, it had central air and heat. Very quickly my father worked the family up into the lower middle class.

But on weekends, when he intentionally refused to take his medication, the shakes would return, sometimes to the degree that he couldn't sign his name legibly.

While packing up after college I found an American flag lying on a trash heap at the curb. It was old and tattered but clean, so I used it to wrap some of my things. Later, my father helped me move to the small house I rented when I started dental school. As I unpacked, I threw the old wrappings and empty boxes into a pile. When I got to the flag I did the same thing.

Then my father walked into the room. He asked about the flag. I told him how I had found it and, honestly, I didn't think much about it. I was a child of the 60's and 70's, I had seen flags burning on the nightly news for years, seen National Guard troops shoot students at Kent State, seen our president resign because he was a bone-deep liar and a crook.

"You shouldn't treat the flag that way," he said in a quiet voice.

"I found it in the trash," I repeated.

"You shouldn't do that. I've seen too many good men die for that flag."

He turned and walked out. I watched him through the window as he walked around the back yard, his tremors subsiding as he smoked. I took the flag, folded it, and set it on a bookcase.

Years later I was sitting with him on his patio at home. In spite of the August heat, he was fully dressed with a robe for extra warmth. His hair was sparse due to the chemo and he struggled to breathe even with the oxygen tube clipped to his nose.

He talked about many things – how he wanted his estate handled, things he wanted me to do for my mother and my disabled sister, things he wanted me to tell my young children.

"I've had a good life. I've been blessed," he said.

Then he said something that surprised me.

"The sea off the shore of Iwo Jima was filled with more ships than I thought was possible."

He proceeded to tell me about his war. It was an unvarnished, unflinching narrative.

He hit the beach early in the afternoon of the first day of the invasion. He had originally been slated to go in on the third day but there had been more casualties than expected. He was a naval radio operator assigned to the command center on Yellow Beach, the center of the beachhead.

He told of chaos, of the dying and the dead, the screams of agony, the rain of bullets, mortar shells the size of small cars exploding, the sound a dead body makes when it is run over by a tank, the sound a live soldier makes when he is run over by a tank, the scraps of human flesh and body parts flying, the sprays of blood, the smell of eviscerated bowel and burning flesh, but the overlying smell was the sulfurous stench of the volcanic island itself. For some reason his mind flashed back to an old country preacher he had heard who pounded the pulpit while warning of fire and brimstone.

"And I knew I had arrived in Hell," he said.

Around midnight the command post took a direct hit from the shelling. A lot of the officers were killed. My father was lucky, by some miracle he only had his eardrum blown out by the concussion of the blast that lifted him up and threw him down the beach. When he stumbled back to the command post, he located a working radio and informed his superiors out at sea of the situation. Because of the chaos Yellow Beach was shut down until daylight. My father's orders: Dig in and stand by the radio.

So he dug in as the shells kept falling...and falling...and falling. But he couldn't just burrow and hide. Enemy soldiers were entering the sea above the beachhead. They would float with the current until they reached the American line, then sneak out of the surf and attack from behind. My father spent the night burrowing into his foxhole, digging himself out after artillery fire buried him under the choking sand, then popping up to check the shoreline for the enemy.

"I've never been more surprised in my life," he said.

"By what?"

"That I was still alive when the sun came up."

My father paused to catch his breath. I sat in silence as I watched his tremors kick up another notch.

"I couldn't understand all the ropes," he said. "It was the ropes that got me."

"The ropes?" I asked, thinking I had misunderstood him.

"Yea, the ropes. They had shut Yellow Beach down. There hadn't been transports unloading supplies but the ropes that lashed the boxes and crates together were everywhere, as if the unloading had continued all night. They were everywhere. I thought they were ropes."

Until he stepped on one. The ropes were human intestines.

Days later, when the American flag went up on Mt. Suribachi, the beach erupted in celebration. The ships offshore joined in by ringing the ship's bells and blowing their horns.

"And that was the first time since I had set foot on the island that I thought I had a chance to one day go home."

He talked for a while longer about Iwo, about the Kamikaze blooms off of Okinawa, how he got busted down to third class for taking a jeep without authorization to visit the gravesite of a close friend, about the end of the war.

After the war the service tried to give him disability for his shell shock. He refused. The argument with the doctor grew heated. My father was adamant. He could look around the hospital and see the disabled, men in worse shape than himself. He still had both eyes, he still had one good ear, he could walk, he could work. It didn't seem right.

"Well, you can't argue about the deafness," the doctor replied and gave him a partial disability over my father's objections. So my father finally got to return home.

"I had a lot of trouble adjusting," was all he said before he asked me to help him back into the house.

Three weeks later he died. His coffin was draped with the flag of the United States.

Years later my uncle told me that my father tried to go to college on the G.I. bill but at night, in his dorm, the younger students would shoot off fireworks and he would roll out of his bunk and hit the floor. He left college before the end of his first semester, leaving the youngsters to wonder why the "Old Man" was so upset about a little harmless fun. I think that missed opportunity was the reason he always stressed the importance of education. He backed his words with financial support to help me earn two degrees, both with honors.

I did not add that last point to brag, only to emphasize a point. I learned a lot in the classroom; I learned a lot more from my father.

My father wasn't perfect; far from it- but most of my success resulted from the seeds he sowed, most of my failures because I strayed from his example. He instilled in me a good work ethic. He taught me about sacrifice, self-reliance, and perseverance. He taught me the importance of a good attitude, the power of gratitude, and the futility of complaint, that it is better to grin than to grimace. That laughter is like sunlight in its ability to banish the shadows that try to creep into our lives. That each day is a gift.

And he taught me about flags.

Flag Season is the time from Memorial Day through Flag Day and on to the Fourth of July. Flags pop up like daffodils in the spring - one day they are scarce, the next they are everywhere. Some will see Old Glory and be filled with pride, some will see the Red, White, and Blue and grumble about all that is wrong with our country, and some will simply overlook them. Some will think of loved ones that gave the last full measure of devotion for their country, or perhaps think of those that survived their service but also made sacrifices, sacrifices of many and varied degrees with scars visible or unseen. Some will think of loved ones overseas and some overseas will, like my father, think of home. I know what I will think: Thanks, Dad.

2

FOR LOVE OF COUNTRY
THEY ACCEPTED DEATH

by Sheri Sharp

John Winthrop [1], a Pilgrim and advocate for freedom, wrote about the "shining city on a hill" when describing what he imagined about America. President Ronald Reagan used that quote in his Farewell Address, [2] regularly referring to America as a special place with a special promise. He was right.

America's Constitution was created upon the *timeless* principles of freedom, life, liberty, and unalienable rights. Those who fought for these principles did so at great risk and with a devout love for their country. As the Bible states in John 15:13, "Greater love hath no man than this, that a man lay down his life for his friends." Thousands of men and women have laid down their lives for the cause of America and the protection of it. That "shining city" reflects the courage and sacrifice of these men and women.

Memorial Day first began as "Decoration Day" in 1868. At the time, James Garfield, who served in the Union Army during the Civil War, commemorated [3] the first Decoration Day:

"I am oppressed with a sense of the impropriety of uttering words on this occasion. If silence is ever golden, it must be here beside the graves of fifteen thousand men, whose lives were more significant than speech, and whose death was a poem, the music of which can never be sung....For love of country they accepted death, and thus resolved all doubts, and made immortal their patriotism and their virtue."

"*For love of country they accepted death*". Think about those words. Because of great men (and women) who died, America has been a beacon in the timeline of history where natural rights, freedom, life and liberty are all protected.

However, in today's America, our principles seem to be unraveling. Do we even love our country anymore? We are a divided nation. Some believe the principles of our founding are outdated. Others are simply ignorant. Collectively, we are uneducated about our Constitutional roots and the meaning of our history.

As Reagan also noted in his Farewell Address in 1989: [4] *".... are we doing a good enough job teaching our children what America is and what she represents in the long history of the world? ...[We] grew up in a different America. We were taught, very directly, what it means to be an American. And we absorbed, almost in the air, a love of country and an appreciation of its institutions. ...But now...some things have changed. Younger parents aren't sure that an...appreciation of America is the right thing to teach modern children. And ...for those who create the popular culture, well-grounded patriotism is no longer the style. We've got to do a better job of getting across that America is freedom — freedom of speech, freedom of religion, freedom of enterprise. And freedom is special and rare. It's fragile; it needs protection."*

Reagan was prescient in his words. While many continue to die protecting this nation, we have not properly taught our children the values, principles, and traditions of America. Hollywood despises those principles. The "progressives" in both parties want God, freedom, individualism and borders eradicated. Our leaders who wish to "change" America and suppress freedom take full advantage of our Constitutional and historical ignorance as a nation.

America has grown complacent about its traditions of freedom, God, family and truth. The servicemen and women who have died promising [5] to "defend the Constitution of the United States against all enemies, foreign and domestic" were not complacent. They believed in freedom and God-given rights so much that they *died* to preserve them.

They didn't die in the Revolutionary War so that Americans–many in places of government power–can now refer to American ideals as outdated.

They didn't die in the Civil War so that, 150 years later, some Americans could ignore those sacrifices and purposefully divide Americans by race.

They didn't die so that our government can redefine marriage, biology, families, and humanity [6] and use the force of law to attack our conscience and religious freedom.

They didn't die to save Europe only to see the cowardly ignore the dangers of radical Islam in Europe and America by embracing corrupt and misguided refugee policies.

They didn't die for open borders where millions come to America who never intended to assimilate, but rather to change America and it's values.

They didn't die in Iraq and Afghanistan so that our President could then "end" those wars, not win them, allowing our enemies to flourish in the created vacuum.

They didn't die so that a monstrous federal government could control our lives–our healthcare, homes, finances, religion, and even our privacy.

They died for the Constitution, for freedom, and to defend the United State of America. They stood against tyranny. Will we?

Samuel Adams was relentless in his battle against tyranny. In 1771, he wrote the following in the Boston Gazette [7]:

"The liberties of our country, the freedoms of our civil Constitution are worth defending at all hazards... We have received them as a fair inheritance from our worthy ancestors. They purchased them for us with toil and danger and expense of treasure and blood. It will bring a mark of everlasting infamy on the present generation – enlightened as it is – if we should suffer them to be wrested from us by violence without a struggle, or to be cheated out of them by the artifices of designing men."

Every Memorial Day, in addition to honoring and remembering those who gave us the "shining city on a hill", it is my sincere hope that we will reflect upon saving America and assuring that we do not lose that shining light that these men and women died to preserve.

3
JUST ANOTHER SOLDIER

a Poem by Carolyn Elkins

He looks around and sees barren, nothing but rocks and sand,
many times the same thoughts cuts through his mind like a knife.
Will this forsaken place be his final stand,
will this be the time, for others, that he lay down his life?
As he watches, he doesn't think of those
his loved ones back home and so far away.
Won't allow his mind to go there, those whose hearts to his are
close
but now of the others his thoughts cannot stray.
The others are close, watchful as he
they move carefully, all a part of each other.
Having each other's backs, part of the pack, their creed
he only thinks of them now, each one his brother.
***
She misses him and thinks of her soldier always
while she at home has a life, busy and on the run.
No matter what she's doing, she's counting down the days
and in darkness alone she prays until the night is done.
Time passes, she smiles and laughs, and tries
not to think about all what he must be going through.
Once in a while, even when busy she sighs
tries not to show fear, from him she took her cue.
Not letting others know how much her heart aches
missing him more with every passing of time.
She smiles and keeps on keeping for her soldier's sake
but alone she worries as thoughts of him fill her mind.
****
Traffic jams, shopping and things needing done
work goes on, living for weekends and a time of ease.
Many only thinking for the next time for a little fun
to kick back, the TV and what's on it is all they want to see.
Politics go on, complain then pat each other on the back

they bicker on pretending to be enemies of one another.
Talk about money, Veterans too, but not about what they lack
just more lip service for heroes and their still serving brothers.
News for many people is which movie star is getting married
or scandals among neighbors, and last night's ball game.
They lament at a story of a soldier being buried
sad for a moment, then back to the same old same.

*****

The blasts come intense one after another
turning desert into a new version of hell.
His body motionless, his thoughts still on his brothers
where and how they are he can no longer tell.
She senses suddenly and shivers as cold
creeps deep into her soul, something is wrong.
She thinks of him, her arms longing just to hold
she awaits word, doing as he's told her, staying strong.
Another day goes on as the world turns still
politicians and others, living for the weekend long.
Talking heads on the tube, news of war suddenly fills
they give thirty seconds to tell of just another soldier gone.

4
I DON'T KNOW YOU BUT I OWE YOU

by Lou Ellen Brown

I saw you again today, and I rolled down the side window to ask to shake your hand. You were nice, though puzzled, and you extended your hand. I said that I just wanted to say thanks, and you looked surprised. I took your hand and you looked at me with questioning eyes. You said, "Who are you? Have we met before?"

Still hand in hand, I shook my head, no. Then I said, "I don't know you, but I owe you. I look for You, everywhere I go, and when I see You, I only want to pay my debt." You were puzzled. "What debt? I don't understand."

"Sir, I said. I saw your cap, and I knew you. You are one of the best, a stranger, yet my friend and my guardian angel. Didn't You know that?"

And then he knew, and a tear, then two, wet his cheek and he tried hard to smile.

"Ma'am , I used to think that, when what I did was going to make things safe for homes like mine. I grew up Red, White and Blue and did what was the right thing for me. I saw my khaki uniform just like a cape of strength and safety, and I wore it like that. I would do it again, if I could."

Then the tears were mine, as I had not noticed sooner that the hand I still held was the only hand he had. I did not know him, but I owed him, a debt neither I nor any other caring person's handshake could repay.

You said, "It's okay lady. You live in peace and happiness because I owed you, too. Let's call it even."

Letting go was hard, that time, and as You stepped away, You gave a sharp salute, and turned to go your way.

I will see You again tomorrow, or the next day, because I look for You so that I can, handshake by handshake, pay down a debt that I will always owe.

5
TRIBUTE TO A WORLD WAR II VETERAN: A LIFE WELL LIVED

by Abigail Adams

He was born in South Georgia in December 1922, the seventh of ten living children. His father was a well known and highly sought after dog trainer; before marriage, his mother had been a teacher. He was seven years old when his mother died at the age of 36. As the older of only two sons, of necessity he quickly assumed the responsibilities of a man helping his father and siblings. Times were hard, they were poor, and all of them stepped up and helped each other, an attribute that became a way of life for them that extended well into the next generation.

He was called into World War II where he served in the European Theatre. Among his many accomplishments, he was awarded a Bronze Star with Oak Leaf Cluster for valor, participated in defense of the Siegfried Line, awarded a combat infantry badge, Sharpshooter, received the Armed Forces Expeditionary Medal, and good conduct medal, expert driver badge and stayed on for sustainment in post-War Europe. He saw real combat time on the Siegfried Line. His decorations were hard earned and not handed out merely for promotion or pomp. These men dealt with meager supplies and were often made to hold in place because of lack of food, fuel, and ammunition. He was in one of the final battles of the War, crossing the Rhine, that lead to the end of the War. His favorite rifle was the 30 carbine, and my son (Army retired) laid him to rest with a round in his pocket.

After the War, he married, became successful and even affluent. Sadly, his wife left him and took his young children hundreds of miles away. When he learned that his children were neglected and in great peril, he sold his assets so to hire detectives and attorneys to gather evidence. He pursued the matter tenaciously until he successfully gained full custody of his children. This was in the 1950s-- a time when it was unheard of for a father to be the custodial parent. But this man was. With the help of his sisters, he reared his children, and he rebuilt his career.

He was the patriarch of his family, highly regarded by children, grand and great grandchildren, siblings, nieces, nephews, and friends, and his advice and wisdom were sought after and cherished. He was a man of great character and integrity, of pride and passion.

He was my father.

As the years passed, he managed for himself and maintained his independence amazingly, as one would expect. Eventually the day came when he agreed to come and live with me. *Oh happy day!* We were so glad to have him; an answer to many prayers. After living with us for one wonderful year, he suffered a massive stroke, after which I brought him home from the hospital with me. During the months following his stroke, we made his bedroom the center of our activity; we watched ball games with him, and everyday his great grandchildren did their schoolwork and played in his room. We have priceless memories of the 4 generations of us together every day.

We loved and cared for him until God sent His Angel for my Daddy. During the night of his breath became shallow. By the time the nurse arrived on the morning of May 24, 2016, the rapid decline had begun. I lowered the rail and climbed in bed with him. He lifted his head so that I could put my arms around him. I lay my head next to his and watched as the pulse in his neck slowed and finally stopped. There was no distress, no pain, and no anguish.

God is good, and He answered my prayer exactly as I had prayed it; I was with my Daddy when he went home. I laid him to rest in Georgia National Cemetery with the honors he deserved. He is waiting in heaven for me, and the next time I see him, it will be forever.

Abigail Adams is the proud daughter of a WWII foot soldier who served on the front lines in France and Germany. Abigail is active in the home schooling of her two grandsons and works with conservative candidates on their campaigns.

6

A LIFE WELL-EARNED:
RETIRED NAVY CPO GENE BROWN

by Ann-Marie Murrell

My father, Gene Paul Brown, had a childhood most of us cannot even begin to fathom. Born in 1935 in rural Indiana, Gene was the oldest of three boys. When his parents divorced in the 40's (rare in those days) he had to help raise his brothers while his mother worked cleaning houses. Gene never had what you'd call a "carefree childhood" with toys and games to play with. He also rarely had new clothes or shoes. For his eighth grade graduation he had to wear an old, oversized suit that his father had left behind; when the kids laughed at him and ridiculed his clothing, Gene says he left right after the graduation program and never went back to school again.

Unfortunately Gene didn't have much time to attend school anyway. In addition to taking care of his 6 year old baby brother, the 14-year old worked dozens of odd jobs including setting pins in a bowling alley, bagging and restocking in a grocery store, and "pitching tents" for a carnival. After struggling several years to survive, at age 16 Gene followed in his beloved uncle's footsteps and enlisted in the Navy. (His mother had to sign for him because he was underage.)

Gene says he was "always fascinated with airplanes" so he tested high enough to enroll in Naval Aviation school in Hutchison, Kansas, studying Airplane Mechanics. From there he went to **Miramar Naval Air Station** in San Diego, California, serving on Naval ships **The Bon Homme Richard** and **The Ranger**. He was then stationed in Whidbey Island, Washington working on Early Warning Bombers.

Throughout his twenty years of service, Gene says he was mostly onboard ships but sometimes on land. "It was always about keeping those planes in the air," he says. During the Korean and Vietnam wars, he did two tours of sea duty to Japan, and Shore Patrol in the Philippines. He says it was exciting being onboard Naval ships, sometimes up to 6 months at a time. "They kept us busy and we had three meals a day. The only thing is you had to be really careful on the flight deck when those planes were taking off. Those suckers can get you if you're not paying attention," Gene says with a chuckle.

Because many of his twenty years were aboard ships, he did not experience armed combat but says he was "always making sure that the planes were ready to go."

Gene's final station was in Corpus Christi, Texas where he worked on attack aircraft aboard the Naval ship **The Boxer.** It was in Texas where he finally earned his GED and became a Chief Petty Officer—and Texas is also where Gene Brown met and married my mother, a widow with two young girls. All our lives changed for the better that day.

My father has little patience with the entitlement mentality of the world today and how young people are being raised to believe things should be handed to them without earning it.

"There's no way around it, you just have to work," he says. "You can't sit around and wait for someone else to take care of you. It makes you lazy."

I ask how he escaped being angry or bitter about his difficult childhood--being raised by a single mom and having to leave home at such an early age. Typical of my father, he just laughs and again says, "Why would I? No matter how bad things were, I always knew I was loved by my family." He adds, "That's just life. We were never promised it would be easy or fair and you just do what you have to do and get on with it."

My father says he is exceptionally honored to have served his country. "I believe America is a place to fight for, and it has never let me down. As I retired after twenty years, I am proud of my service," he says.

Navy Chief Petty Officer Gene Brown is the very definition of an "American hero." Despite all the obstacles and challenges thrown his way, he has made the very best out of every situation. He is a master mechanic and can fix everything from cars to airplanes. He taught himself how to build houses and was one of the first in America to design and build an underground home almost entirely by himself--from digging out the hillside, pouring the concrete, and installing the plumbing and electrical work. If something ever broke in our house—from can openers to washing machines—my Dad knew how to fix it. And when the economy tanked during the Carter administration and my dad lost his chain saw/lawn mower repair shop, he immediately created another business by tricking out old motor homes and selling ice cream and funnel cakes at state fairs and car racing events.

Basically, my father has had a successful life in every way possible.

My parents are the reasons I have discipline, strong principles, and a deep love and respect for my country. Thank you to all our American veterans, retired and active; thank you for your service to this country and for your undying love for God, country and family. No matter what happens to America, because of your examples of true sacrifice I will never complain about defending my country in every way I possibly can here on the home front.

7

MY FATHER'S DAUGHTER: IN HONOR OF ARMY VETERAN, HALBERT BARNETT

by Patti Barnett Terrell

Pop didn't believe me when I told him that I had nothing to do with "making it all happen." But truly all I did was ask a simple question in honor of an Army veteran –Halbert Barnett, my Dad.

In the fall of 2004 my family took a trip to D.C. At the time we didn't know that it would be one of our last family vacations. Dad has Parkinson's and it was shortly after that when he became unable to handle the long trips.

We had been the perfect tourists. We jumped on a trolley at Union Station and went on a night tour of the monuments (highly recommend this, by the way). We went to the recently opened WWII monument and looked up the name of my mom's brother, L.V. Hammack, who was killed fighting for this country on Iwo Jima. We visited the Air and Space Museum, the Museum of Natural History and the Museum of American History. We visited the National Gallery of Art (well, they all did – I could not find a parking place anywhere within three miles of the Washington Mall that day so I drove for hours and then picked everyone up at the door).

We visited Georgetown and we ate at some wonderful restaurants and drank some good wine. We went to the Capitol and the Russell Senate office building and the Canon House office building. We had a car but rode the Metro once simply because I wanted them all to have the complete D.C. experience. We cried at the memorials and laughed at the joy of just being a family.

But nothing topped our visit to Arlington Cemetery. We reached the cemetery in early afternoon and took our time visiting the gravesites of President Kennedy and his family members who are buried near him as well as paying respects to his brother, Bobby. We reflected over the 1000's of men and women buried there and their service to this country. We stood quietly in respect as a horse drawn carriage carried the body of one of this country's fallen heroes.

We reached the Tomb of the Unknown and the Changing of the Guard just as the ceremony was completing. Because the guards were operating on the winter schedule it was another hour until the next ceremony. Having come this far we decided to wait. But, Pop was just plain tired. I walked over to a man in uniform, not a soldier but maybe a park service employee, and asked if there was any way I could get a wheel chair for my Dad. He did not hesitate but said, "Wait here". He returned within minutes not only with a wheelchair but also with a young soldier. I am sorry to say that I do not remember his name; he was from Oregon and he took charge of my dad from that moment until the next changing of the guard was complete along with a wreath laying ceremony that we were fortunate enough to be able to see. As I said earlier, my Dad, SFC Barnett, is an Army veteran. He was enlisted from 1953-1955 and he served in the Army reserves for 6 years after that.

When the ceremony began, Pop and another veteran (WWII I believe) were rolled into a place of honor at the end of the ceremonial site so they had a perfect view. As family we were allowed to stand with them. The actual Changing of the Guard was heartwarming as always but the moment that brought tears to my eyes and to those of many of the spectators was at the wreath laying. Pop and the other gentleman had been seated throughout the event but when the wreath was laid, these two proud Army Veterans slowly and with some difficulty stood and placed their hands over their hearts in honor of those who have died for our freedom. It was a moment where time stopped for me. *I will never forget the feeling I had at that moment and how proud I felt to be an American citizen ----- but mostly how proud I felt to be my father's daughter.*

Patti Barnett Terrell earned a degree in Computer Science and Mathematics & recently retired from her position as the civilian director of a large Army Information Technology organization. Patti is a huge advocate of the 2nd amendment and is rarely unarmed. Patti and her husband, Larry, live in Texarkana, TX.

PART 10: MEDIA

The media should be the inoculant against totalitarianism, not its delivery system. Fight back. **– Dr. Karen Siegemund**

1

RAGING AGAINST THE MEDIA
(AND WHY WE MUST FIGHT BACK)

by Dr. Karen Siegemund

I'm not sure which exhibit it was at the Checkpoint Charlie Museum in Berlin that brought me up short, but it was during my visit there last November that it dawned on me why I do what I do. Was it the photo montage of Jutta Gallus, the East German mother who was forcibly separated from her two young daughters for several years and who protested at Checkpoint Charlie every single day during that time, finally being reunited when she won their freedom? Or maybe it was the exhibit of the two windsurfing boards mounted back to back atop a car in such a way that a person could lie between them invisibly in order to escape from East Berlin? Maybe it was the photos of Peter Fechter, the 18-year-old man who was shot going over the Wall and died over the next hour, lying there, screaming for those nearby to help, nobody able to do anything as they, too, would be shot.

Or perhaps it was the exhibit honoring Ronald Reagan, whose steadfast pressure on the East and his "Mr. Gorbachev, tear down this wall" speech did, in fact, help to bring that wall down as well as the Evil Empire itself, that nightmare of an experiment in the ultimate "let's make it all fair" ideology under which millions upon millions of human beings suffered, and to get away from which inspired those heroic efforts documented in the museum.

Perhaps it was the general sense from walking through the museum – and this was my third time there – and realizing that these walls, these tyrannical and inhuman constructs happen slowly over time, and can only happen when people do not speak up. (Would they have dared to erect the wall under a Reagan presidency? I doubt that.)

Whichever exhibit it was, at one point I was

thunderstruck. "This is why I do what I do," I thought. "The way to ensure that tyranny doesn't take over is by fighting it at every step; we must never stop speaking out, we must never submit, we must do all we can to ensure the liberties that we are guaranteed under the Constitution and not take our freedom for granted.

Of course, Berlin is not only the home of this museum, one of the most complete and poignant memorials to the horrors of the Cold War and Communism and to the heroics of those escaping to freedom. It is, of course, Ground Zero of Hitler's Nazi regime, a tyranny so horrific that the realities of it are virtually impossible to grasp. But even more than the Cold War and the wall, this incomprehensible totalitarianism did not occur overnight. Not in the slightest. Chipping away at freedoms, sometimes with a sledgehammer, sometimes with a pick, can be an all-too-effective way of taming citizens into a regime of fear; in the case of Germany, of course, this applied to all citizens, but infinitely more so in the case of those whom the regime demonized: The Jews most especially, but others as well, to a much smaller degree.

One of the biggest sledgehammers taken to destroy freedom was the seizure of the press. This, combined with the really rather genius propagandizing stifled all alternative views and reporting, while advancing a single narrative towards a single agenda: the Aryanization of as much of the world as possible, the increasing of the power and reach of the Third Reich.

Even before the recent revelations of the mind-bogging overreach of our current administration here in the United States, it has been clear that our mainstream media had an equivalent single-mindedness in their "reporting" and that is the furthering of the leftist/progressive agenda. While indeed, even from the earliest days of our nation various individual news sources have generally had political tendencies towards one side or another, two things were different historically. First, there were news sources that voiced both political sides; and perhaps more importantly, that they even had a bias was understood and a given.

In recent decades, however, and even more so in recent years, there has been a nearly monolithic voice from our dominant media sources. The "Alphabet Stations:" ABC, CBS, NBC, CNN all provide nearly identical perspectives on all the main topics of the day, all choose to cover essentially the same items while ignoring others, and most importantly, all make every effort to give the impression of impartiality. Each of these networks considers itself "unbiased," offering "The News" in such a way as to give the average American the sense – illusory as it is – that he or she now is informed about the world he or she lives in. It is this illusion of being informed that is, in fact, deeply pernicious. We don't even realize we are being lied to; at least in Nazi Germany as well as Soviet-occupied Germany, that much was clear.

And in a way, what we have here with our own press, which operates under the First Amendment-guaranteed right to its independence – the First Amendment, the very first one – is a voluntary ceding of this very right, this very independence, in favor of a unanimous advocacy of an agenda. That it is voluntary, in this, the Land of Liberty, is difficult to fathom.

So what do we have? A "free" press that opts, day after day, story after story, to not exercise that freedom and would rather be the mouthpiece of one political agenda, even under the guise of impartiality. A press in the form of all the main media sites - with the single exception of Fox - with their attendant TV stations, websites, Facebook pages, phone apps and so on, creates a sense of the world that is inaccurate, and as we are now learning, dangerously so.

When there is only one exception to this unanimity, and this exception is deliberately, constantly, consistently vilified by the party in power as well as the monolith itself, what we are forced to admit is that our press cannot tolerate diversity of opinion to the exact extent that the party it protects also cannot. The lock-step alignment both in narrative and focus on silencing alternative views is chilling and dangerous. That it is a voluntary alignment is even more so. Journalists who, in the past, saw their charter as informing the public to empower us now seem to have as their primary responsibility the assisting of this president in his too-successful efforts to "transform this nation" and who have learned since grade school that the important thing is to "change the world" regardless of what that change might be. Their lack of knowledge about the past and America's uniquely beneficial role globally –in fact, their ingrained conviction that America has been a force for evil rather than good, and that we as a nation have more to apologize for than to be proud of – clearly taints their judgment regarding their politics and their role as journalists, and between them and those (equally ignorant) who run our schools, we have a near-perfect feedback-loop of anti-American misinformation and personal missions by young, energetic starry-eyed ignorami to change the world by hand-picking the narrative and denying the validity of any other point of view. That it is those who crow loudest about diversity who are the quickest to shut down other opinions is ironic, yes, but it is also inevitable. Only by silencing dissent can the voices of leftist policies ever win over those who espouse freedom.

In fact, what we have is a press that pretends to support the underdog, yet silences it; that pretends to empower the people, yet only advocates for and protects those in power; that pretends to tell the truth, yet lies, obfuscates, omits and distorts in order to advance a single agenda that has nothing to do with the truth but everything to do with their own personal view of the world. In addition, our news media's liberal mindset is also evident in their confidence that they ought to be – have the right to be! - the arbiters of what we should know rather than assuming that we the people have a right to decide for ourselves. The disdain that liberals have for the individual, for the individuals' right to choose, is reflected in their policies as well as the press.

Ironically, while the Nazi press, and Pravda, and the press of other totalitarian regimes, worked in concert with the government's agenda of enhancing the power of the nation and increasing its stance globally, the American press, also in concert with our government's agenda, is working instead to diminish our stature globally and to cast, wherever possible, a negative light on America, American achievement, American traditional values and mores. How ironic that one way in which our current regime is worse than that of Hitler's is that Hitler, at least, saw his country as great and in some twisted way wanted to strengthen his country, whereas our president sees nothing about our country as great, and believes that a weaker America is better for us and the world at large. It is astonishing that a Head of State could even consider as a good thing the diminishing the power of the very nation he was elected to lead. It is beyond comprehension that our Commander in Chief actually believes that a weak America is a good thing globally. For a totalitarian leader to consolidate power in order to weaken the nation he leads defies comprehension, until you realize that his view of governance has nothing to do with individual nations such as this one, but everything to do with totalitarian global governance. And our press, our popular culture and our schools all have made this possible, and continue to advance this "We are the Evil Empire" anti-patriotic worldview, with the same ends in mind as our President.

So why do I do what I do? Because a press that supports the agenda that aims to weaken the very nation that gives it its lifeblood is a press that must be fought against. A self-governing nation can't survive without a press that informs the people of the truth, and we are seeing, every day, examples of how we are less and less a self-governing nation. For our constitutionally protected Fourth Estate to be willing propagandists for policies that are suicidal is something that must be fought at every turn.

So again, why do I do this? Why do I spend my days either directly fighting against the lies and false narratives of our dominant media or else devising new ways of engaging in the battle? Why do I do what I can to build an effective "army of citizen activists" to evangelize with the truth against the dishonest, depraved, destructive efforts of the media whose goal is to advance the cause of totalitarianism? Because as long as they are allowed to propagate these lies unchecked, they will win. As long as their monopoly in information is unchallenged, they learn the lesson that they have carte blanche to lie to us as they wish. And until the American people have objective information about the world they live in, tyranny has a foothold that becomes increasingly difficult to cast off.

The lessons from the Checkpoint Charlie Museum and from Berlin generally are these: totalitarianism starts with baby steps, and with a monopoly of the message. We think we are immune; so did they. Only by fighting back will the next steps be prevented. The media should be the inoculant against totalitarianism, not its delivery system.

Fight back.

*Dr. **Karen Siegemund** founded the organization Rage Against the Media after the slaughter in Benghazi on September of 2012. She did so in order to battle against the press for the reasons described in this article. Since 2016 Dr. Siegemund has been the Chairman of the American Freedom Alliance, a Los Angeles-based non-profit organization whose goal is to protect Western Civilization from a number of specific threats, one of which is this same news media. She lives in Los Angeles.*

2

CITIZEN JOURNALISTS, THE NEW REBELS (AND AMERICA LOVES AN UNDERDOG)

by Leslie Deinhammer

Relentless in their obsession to crush the voices that challenge their birthright to authority or at least hold authority accountable, the advocates of change and tolerance are once again pushing forth legislation to silence dissent and reclaim their domain. The Feinsteins and Durbins of the legislative world have declared a turf war. [8]

While the Dan Rathers and Fareed Zakarias [9] of the media empire are given Peabodys and passes for journalistic lapses, citizen journalists are threatened with the Free Flow of Information Act.

Dick Durbin's (D-Ill.) Free Flow of Information Act places the federal government as arbiter of who is a journalist and who is not. Once again only the state has the exclusive right to define who is "covered". [10]

Legislation often follows when late night mockery and the Holder/Lerner tandem of intimidation no longer warrant the elicited response of complete submission. In the case of citizen journalism, ruling class regulations and reprisals have elicited an unwarranted response – they have made it a badge of honor to be targeted.

By attacking the EIB network, Fox, and now citizen journalists, the Left has given the new media much coveted legitimacy. [10] They have made the Andrew Breitbarts "David" to their Goliath. [11] And America loves an underdog.

In 2013, Alexa, a leading web analytics firm, [12] ranked Breitbart News as the 239th most popular website in America. By comparison, the New York Post, Politico, and Daily Beast websites come in at 276, 315, and 335 respectively. By commercial comparisons, Breitbart News also ranks higher than Delta Airlines, Overstock.com, and Disney.

Even though the old guard insistently esteem themselves as pillars of journalistic integrity, their record says otherwise. No longer do they avoid misleading re-enactments or staged news events; no longer do they distinguish between advocacy and news reporting, nor are they "vigilant and courageous" about holding those with power accountable.

Audiences, rejecting Dateline NBC, CBS and New York Times' numerous apologies for journalistic oversight, are trending towards fresh perspectives devoid of kowtowing coverage and cronyism.

"Critics," according to William Zinsser, [13] formerly of Yale and Columbia University Graduate School of Journalism, "should always be among the first to notify us when the truths we hold to be self-evident cease to be true."

The self-evident truths that all men are created equal (unless you are a member of Congress, then you get an exemption from 'equal'); the unalienable right of life (another endowment usurped by convicted abortionist/serial killer Dr. Kermit Gosnell [14] or an executive stand down order); the right of liberty (though not at liberty to choose your school of choice if you happen to live on the corner of 65th and MLK in Chicago); and the pursuit of happiness (no happier pursuit than putting the Christmas trim up to anger the atheists and green activists simultaneously).

When the press abdicates their responsibility to "be among the first to notify us when the truths we hold to be self-evident cease to be true", new critics rise to fill the void. Of course when new critics, like James Rosen, [14] Pamela Geller, [15] and Michael Hastings, [16] are critical of those who hold power, they are criminally investigated, issued fatwas or silenced.

So pay attention to those who are targeted by the Goliaths on the Left, for they are the ones brave enough–and capable enough–to topple the haughty. Better yet, join them.

3
SAVE THE CULTURE – SAVE THE WORLD

by Morgan Brittany

There is no way to sugarcoat it: our culture is in decline and circling the drain at a rapid pace. Everyday there is an assault of some sort on traditional values and beliefs, a constant mantra from the media that repeats like a skipping record. This is not something that has just suddenly emerged; oh no, this has been in the works for about 100 years.

Our country has had its brushes with decadence and moral decline. Just look at the Roaring 20's with the rise of the "Flappers" who threw out the Victorian ways of the past century. Uninhibited drinking, smoking and sex were everywhere, behind speakeasy doors and underground drug dens. If you check out history books you can see the era of excess, easy money and a "devil may care" attitude.

Sound familiar? They say that history repeats itself and that seems to be true. In 1929, the great Depression hit with the fall of the stock market and the crash of the economy. It was a sober wake-up call to all Americans and suddenly the fun and games were over. The 30's were a difficult time for people trying to survive, trying to feed their families or get a job. There was little money so the only thing they had was their family, their faith and their honor.

When the country hit bottom the American people woke up, gathered their strength, worked hard and made things right again. Films were full of images of success and heroes, and a little girl named Shirley Temple gave people optimism. Goodness and morality were applauded. Hard work was rewarded and people knew that their children would have a better life than what they had.

Then look at 2008. We crashed but we didn't burn. We didn't hit bottom with the economic collapse because the government stepped in and manipulated the fall. Yes, things were bad, but they weren't bad enough for people to have a "come to Jesus" moment when they realized where we were heading morally, economically and culturally. It wasn't quite bad enough to open their eyes.

Why is that? I think it is because over the years we have been like the proverbial frog in the pot of water, slowly boiling to death.

Little by little the progressives have infiltrated our culture like a cancer. It has taken generations but they have now taken over our schools and universities, the film and television industry, the print media and the hearts and minds of many of our children.

The moral and traditional among us are demonized on a daily basis as "old-fashioned", bigoted or intolerant. We are looked at as racists, homophobes or as hating the environment if we even speak up in opposition to anything that the left has programmed into the minds of the populace.

Christmas has now become something to feel guilty about. Trees must be called "Holiday trees", nativity scenes must be taken down and even employees are cautioned to say "Happy Holidays" instead of "Merry Christmas". When does this madness stop? How is it that minorities of brainwashing leftists have seized control of our culture in such a destructive way?

I think we have reached the tipping point in our society and we will either go over the edge into the abyss or we will take a stand and fight back. There are no boundaries anymore. Anything and everything can be done or seen on television, in films or in music. As long as there is money to be made you can find someone to humiliate or degrade themselves.

There is no shame anymore. Just a few decades ago it was a scandal to be an unwed mother or a hopeless drug addict. Now it is celebrated. Celebrities are gracing the covers of magazines with their new babies with no father in sight. Drug use is nothing anymore, just go to a doctor having a bad day and I guarantee you the answer will be a prescription for Prozac or Zoloft. Or you can get your Marijuana legally in a few states.

We know the end is near when the kids from the "Jersey Shore" and "Honey Boo-Boo" are elevated to celebrity status.

They make millions of dollars for doing nothing except being a train wreck.

I don't have an answer as to where this all ends. Right now it seems to be spiraling downward with success and hard work being demonized and values and morals being sent to the trash heap.

Maybe this is like the 1920's and we will crash and burn when the out of control deficit bubble finally bursts. Maybe then our eyes will open and we can rise up from the ashes.

4

BLOGGERS: MODERN DAY THOMAS PAINES' (BUT MANY WITH NO COMMON SENSE)

by Shannon Grady

When Thomas Paine [17] famously penned his pamphlets *Common Sense, Rights of Man, The Age of Reason,* and *The Crisis,* he took little heed of today's advice from wanna-be writing professionals. In fact, writers and readers of today would hardly refer to any of his writings as "Pamphlets", being that we envision something like a nice 11 by 8.5 inch tri-fold with pictures and just a few actual words when we hear the word. No, I'm afraid many would call Mr. Paine's writings something more akin to a novel or a lengthy book.

Thomas Paine has famous quotes that we Patriotic Americans love to post on our social media sites, such as the following from his *Common Sense. (Please note this is all one sentence...or as some would call it, a compound sentence, still others, a run-on)*

Society in every state is a blessing, but government even in its best state is but a necessary evil; in its worst state an intolerable one; for when we suffer, or are exposed to the same miseries by a government, which we might expect in a country without government, our calamity is heightened by reflecting that we furnish the means by which we suffer.

It is no secret to those in the field of education that the average reading level, of the average newspaper sold today, is somewhere at or below 8th grade level. In a few cases, it is even argued that the writing is at a 4th grade level. So, I guess that speaks volumes about the literacy rate of Americans today and our education system. Let me give you a sample of a kindergarten through 2nd grade sentence and paragraph:

Next, Mickey visited Minnie. "We are having a picnic," he told her. Minnie was excited. She could not wait to share her favorite foods! This is a paragraph with four sentences from

Disney's Mickey & Friends: A Perfect Picnic. [18]

Now, recently I read a nice "How To" article on increasing traffic to your blog site. [19] One of the recommendations was that we write only 500-600 words (so as to not bore our readers, I suppose). Poor Thomas would certainly have had very few followers if this were the standard when our nation was founded. Though I do not have an exact word count, his *Common Sense* comes to around 65 pages in the paperback version I own. *Rights of Man* had approximately 232 pages and was written in two parts and five chapters. *The Crisis* comes in at around 56 pages, and is credited with helping to turn the tide of the downward spiraling morale of the Continental Army. (It's a legendary pep talk, in simpler terms.)

George Washington thought the work was so important that he read it to his soldiers and commanded that his officers read it to each unit. Again, you may recall some of the more famous lines of this revolutionary piece. (It is also worth noting that men who were illiterate would stand for hours while someone else read these pamphlets aloud.)

These are the times that try men's souls: The summer soldier and the sunshine patriot will, in this crisis, shrink from the service of his country; but he that stands it NOW, deserves the love and thanks of man and woman. Tyranny like hell, is not easily conquered; yet we have this consolation with us, that the harder the conflict, the more glorious the triumph. What we obtain too cheap, we esteem too lightly: 'Tis dearness only that gives every thing its value. Heaven knows how to put a proper price upon its goods; and it would be strange indeed, if so celestial an article as FREEDOM should not be highly rated.

Now, lest you think I am being too hard on the helpful blogging tipster...let me assure you that I understand his purpose. He was simply suggesting methods that would increase the number (quantity) of viewers or readers to your blog. He based this from his own experience having implemented four steps and one of them being to write shorter blogs, with only three to four sentence paragraphs, and as few compound sentences as possible. He noted that this step, along with others, had brought in 80% more readers. That is great, if you are concerned with quantity over quality.

Frankly, I do not want to bother with people who are either too lazy or intellectually inept to read a compound sentence or a paragraph with five or more sentences. Nor do I have time to waste on people who do not have five minutes to read something that is a mere three pages in length. We have enough idiots in Congress who refuse to read the Bills they vote on...I refuse to accept this behavior as OK. The cold hard truth is that you do not even have a paragraph if it does not contain a minimum of four sentences. You need one for the topic, two for the main body, and one for the conclusion. If you can write your information that relates to your topic sentence in one sentence...your topic is likely too simple.

When we complain about the dumbing down of America, it amazes me that no one seems to see how this occurs. When we agree to write shorter, simpler pieces, we are agreeing that people have shorter attention spans and simpler brains. I refuse to accept that self-discipline and genuine concern for our nation, our children, and our future is dead. The evidence that such attributes still exist are found in the small but loyal following of readers who still think a good story is not better when read in cliff note form. If we had more men and women who took the time to read Thomas Paine with all his compound sentences and enormous paragraphs...our nation would not be in such pitiful shape.

Perhaps it is the teacher in me who refuses to give in to the quick thrill of more traffic to my blog. Again, I care less about the quantity of readers than I do about the quality. I am not advocating that we attempt to be Charles Dickens, but I refuse to write stories that would pass for first grade material or could have been in a *Dick and Jane* book!

History can attest that simple people did not found our nation, nor will it be saved by simple people today. So, write with clarity and purpose and ignore the temptation to fit your points into neat little sound bites. We should seek to sound more like Thomas Paine and less like Dr. Seuss!

5

A MEETING OF THE MINDS WITH HUXLEY, WELLS, VERNE, AND ORWELL

by Lou Ellen Brown

Aldous Huxley, H.G. Wells, Jules Verne and George Orwell are gathered in their eternal resting place, and are settling in for their daily roundtable concerning the state of the world as they see it.

Gabriel, God's chosen ethereal attendant for various of the transitory and recalcitrant dissenters of the God who created them, has seated them for their extraterrestrial privilege, and drawn back the curtain that opens a special window wherein they observe and discuss the doings of current earthlings' behavior. They are allowed such a privilege based on their near conversions to actual belief that God exists.

Verne [20] *opens*: Greetings, and hail hearty, gentlemen. Shall we resume the current issue of a world without America, or is there something more pressing?

Orwell, [21] *the youngster at the table, speaks*: I find that we need to begin with the issue we have all been addressing for decades, the idea of a free and self governing nation that has no controllers making rules that only they are exempt from; i.e. the way of the world in **Animal Farm**, when I first tried to warn the citizenry of fascism taking charge of their lives. You know, when the smartest animals take over the farm and....

Huxley [22] *interrupts:* George that is all you want to talk about! We have spent an eon on that already and I really want to go on to something more vital: mind control. **Brave New World** told the story there, with test tube babies and building the human body, as it should be, the mind directed, as it should be. What better way to control the willful ones who want to do everything their way?

Wells, [23] *inserting his superior age and wisdom into the discussion:* Wait a minute, Aldous. Have you forgotten how poorly that turned out, when the mixture of drugs and mental health went awry? You even borrowed from Shakespeare for that catchy title, quoting Miranda on seeing her first man, "O brave new world that has such creatures in it". Her father, after all, had isolated her from seeing any man other than himself until she was full grown.

You are both misguided on the most important issue. Have you all failed to check the today view of the universe? Just look past your own thinking and see what is going on from a different viewpoint. Open the Earth Viewer Window that we need to use now, and let us observe the results of the most recent turmoil. Focus on Great Britain first, please.

Verne: Yes, thanks, Gabriel, for allowing the curtain to be drawn. We here have finally learned the way of the world was not ours to direct, and thank God again for allowing us this Semi-space to see what has been wrought. We all tried to warn them, after all.

Gentlemen, look again at the way of things. Turmoil, strife, religion versus social status. They have lost the common core, so to speak, and are worshipping the wrong idol, Humans. They learned nothing from the most vicious of all villains, Captain Nemo and his submarine invasions of any and all places he wished to conquer or dominate from afar. It was fear that won, and he had introduced a weapon that no living person outside his sycophants and indentured slaves could even understand.

Orwell *again*: True, Jules, but you were way before your time. Your vision was at least a century before the world was even near ready for your work to be believed. Who could accept the notion of men living under the sea in a machine never even dreamed of by normal people? Nemo was a genius on the wrong side of humanity, but his creation surely was copied later for others to use, for both good and bad. Very serious war machine, the submarine.

Verne: Ah, George, you were also far ahead of the field. You were labeled 'science fiction' or 'realism' by people who saw no further than the windowsill, not able to grasp what was far outside the window.

Orwell: *(a bit defensive)* Well, yes. But not everyone got that right away. I wrote **1984** in 1949 when I was just beginning to see what I wrote as fiction turning into truth. We all tried to tell the story, how mankind was trying to create itself. Yes, mind control is real, and we can look down on the British Empire as the birthing place of most of our futuristic visions. We were before our time, and I was not yet 50 when I came here. All of us saw the world with different eyes.

Verne: Yes, that is absolutely true George. I wrote **From the Earth to the Moon** in 1865. Oddly, another story title told that the first moon shot was launched from only a few miles from Cape Canaveral, many years before the NASA trip.

I find it marvelous that we who spoke so much earlier were so often used for those who came much later and proved us to have been correct.

Wells *had been quietly taking in the remarks and now cleared his throat and began*: I have listened quietly and nodded now and again either for or against what I was hearing. Man is in nature prepared for two things, those being the most caring of all creatures in protection of his family, and the most vicious of all creatures in protection of his family. That was something similar to the doublespeak of mind control in the Orwell story. But I noticed a youngster a decade ago had a saying that we must adopt. In **Brave New World** the test tube babies were divided into categories and called by that title, such as Alpha, Beta, and so forth to divide and control. In **The War of the Worlds** mind control was nothing when fear could be instilled by creatures from another entire system.... the machine.

In essence, we have spent our visions and wisdom, such as it were, all directed to the same theme: mind control. When a person is convinced that red is better than blue, it is impossible to reverse that conviction, and perhaps a bit of persuasion is needed. Hence, depriving, isolating, changing rules, all devices available are applied. Oddly, Soma, the mind control drug of choice, is now a label on a ladies' undergarment. **Soylent Green**, which is not mentioned among us, is a solution for world hunger.

And since we here are all armed with the same weapons in effort to warn our fellow humankind, I will quote the youngster I heard, albeit in improper English: *Ah toad ya so*, he said, and I translated to better speech, but absolutely correct: I told you so. Science fiction, realism, whatever we are labeled, can be a warning for things to come, and we may rue the day when such is proven true.

Gabriel *has now closed the curtain, but the story is not over.*

To be continued...

PART ELEVEN:
2nd AMENDMENT

Women, like never before, are refusing to be victims, empowering themselves and make use of their 2nd Amendment rights. – **Katherine Daigle**

1
IS CONCEALED CARRY RIGHT FOR YOU?

by Patti Barnett Terrell

Coming home from our cabin a couple of nights ago my husband, Larry, and I were discussing speed limits on the road we travel. They vary greatly and while it can be 70 in one place, it is 55 or less just a few miles down the road. In the midst of our conversation he looked in the rear view mirror and saw red and blue lights.

Busted!

We pulled over and I immediately said, "Remember the rules when you have a CHL!" I knew Larry was armed. The proper way to handle a traffic stop in Texas when you do have a CHL (Concealed Handgun License) is:

- Have your driver's license, proof of insurance and CHL ready when the officer reaches your vehicle.
- Give them to him as he approaches your vehicle and then place your hands at the 10 and 2 position on the steering wheel.
- Wait for the officer to question you.

Once we were free to proceed on our way home we began to discuss good reasons to have a CHL. I believe a CHL is important and the decision to carry concealed is personal and not to be taken lightly. However, criminals will always have guns and that in itself is a reason for law-abiding citizens to be armed. My recommendations are:

- **Know the Law.** The class required in Texas for a CHL is VERY informative an in fact is more stringent than many other states. Eight hours of intense training including a trip to the firing range. You are educated on the intricacies of Texas law concerning the justifiable use of deadly force. Even if you choose NOT to carry, you always have the option to do so should circumstances change.

- **Gun Safety**. I do not know about all CHL instructors but the gentleman I took my class from (a Baptist preacher by the way) taught a lot about gun safety and self-defense in general. He used me as an example and showed the class the proper way to hold your gun if you suspect an intruder is in your home. Trust me on this, you do not need to learn your stance from reruns of "Charlie's Angels".
- **Reciprocity**. 35 states honor a Texas CHL.
- **Purchasing a Gun**. A Texas CHL exempts you from the NICS check when purchasing a gun from a retailer.
- **Good Citizenship**. If you are going to carry, having a CHL sets a good example to your friends and family. Please do not carry without a license.
- **Makes it safer to go to Wal-Mart at night (or in the day time)**. Enough said about that one.
- **Safety in Numbers.** A large number of people having CHLs become a major influence on politicians and their voting records relating to 2nd amendment rights. Remember, we voted them into office to work for us. We can vote them out if they do not represent us well.
- **Timing.** Remember – when seconds count the police are only minutes away.
- **Officer Safety.** A CHL identifies you as someone who has not been convicted of a crime in the past 5 years. In an encounter with law enforcement, this reduces perception of threat to officer safety.

So like Paul Harvey, I will now give you "the rest of the story" pertaining to Larry's conversation with the Texas State Trooper. The officer approached our vehicle and Larry presented him with the proper documents. The conversation then went something like this:

Officer: Mr. Terrell, I stopped you tonight because you were speeding. I am just going to give you a warning but I need to know if you are armed.

Larry: Yes sir, I am.

Officer: Is it loaded?

Larry: Yes sir, it is.

Officer: Wouldn't be much good if it wasn't, would it?

Larry: No sir, it would not.

Officer: Wait here please while I print your warning ticket and then you can proceed on your way.

The officer came back with the printed warning and bid us a good evening. As we drove away, I said, "No where but Texas!"

Thank God I live in a state where our 2nd amendment rights are revered and concealed carry is encouraged for law-abiding citizens: *"A well regulated Militia, being necessary to the security of a free State, the right of the people to keep and bear Arms, shall not be infringed."* Period.

(Author's note: This was originally written prior to January 1, 2016 when the House Bill 910 went into effect. The new terminology in Texas is Handgun Licensing Program or HLP and "open carry" is now legal. Concealed permits are still valid and no further licensing is required to open carry. As a matter of personal choice, I carry concealed.)

2

LEFTIST MOUSETRAPS
AND OUR 2ND AMENDMENT

by Dr. Sarah Condor

Guns do not kill people. People kill people. Obviously, Democrats don't like westerns but the gun is as American as turkey and Coke and hamburgers. Do you remember the movie **Shane**? [5]

The Leftist rationale is that guns are inherently unsafe, thus: fewer guns equal fewer deaths. Do fewer mousetraps equal fewer rats or more rats? Would I rather have two rats in the house or two mousetraps? Then again, not every mousetrap catches a rat. Even Hamlet was not sure when he sprung his... Shakespearean references aside, to say that every mousetrap catches a rat is to generalize. [6]

A generalization is only true when the two related concepts are "instances" of each other, which means every gun causes death and every death is caused by a gun. However, even if we limit ourselves only to guns (which is grossly misleading – ISIS, for instance, use primarily knives and bombs), [7] it is not a true statement, because one instance of the latter is not always the instance of the former: a gun saves lives in as many instances, if not more, as when it causes death. I have seen robbers run out of a store at the first sight of a real gun in the hands of the storeowner...

Leftists would have to ascertain instances in which a gun saved lives vs. instances in which it caused deaths in order to limit his generalization. An unlimited generalization is necessarily an **unverified** generalization. In this instance, it is more than that: it is an unverifiable generalization, because the numbers of the two instances fluctuate and remain indeterminate. Sometimes, a gun does both: saves lives as well as kills (soldiers at war), on other occasions, it merely kills (a Chicago gang shootout).

Clearly, "make no mistake," this is an instance of reverse logic, often applied by communists and other dictators: "It works because I say it works." [8] Of course, the ultimate goal here is to disarm population and make us totally dependent on the government. It may not seem like this is what the administration is after, and it may not be readily achievable (thanks to our system of checks-and-balances and our Supreme Court), but every chip off the block makes us weaker. All it takes is a 5-4 decision, a new Democrat appointee, Congress being unable to overrule a veto, and we are there. Beware! An executive state is a police state! Of course, in a police state, you need not be afraid primarily of a foreign invasion! BLM protest against a "police state?" Spoiled babies! They have no idea what a police state is!

As we know, the right to own a firearm is anchored the Second Amendment. It is the second most important right we enjoy. The first most important rights are in the First Amendment: the right to establish and exercise religious belief of our choice, the right to speak freely, free press, assembly, and the right to petition our government. Political correctness is a ruse to persuade us that we do not need or care for these rights, because the government will do it for us.

The 2nd Amendment is based on William Blackstone's *Commentaries on the Laws of England* (Chapter 1 "On the Absolute Rights of Individuals"). [9] The right to keep and bear arms was anchored in the English Bill of Rights (1689). [10] People have always had poor (realistic) experience with absolute monarchs and demagogues usurping powers. Sir William Blackstone described the right to bear arms as "necessary to self-defense, resistance to oppression, and the civic duty to act in concert in defense of the state."

If we start giving up our rights, the Fourth Amendment on searches and seizures will follow suit. Before long, we would have to "quarter" Muslims in our homes (3rd Amendment), and our 5th Amendment right not to incriminate ourselves would also fall – NSA and other federal (executive!) branches are growing like the arms of an octopus around the Plymouth rock even as we speak... It does not take that long once you let up, resign yourself to indifference, say: "I am not going to vote for XY because I don't like his ego/face/wife..." You are voting for the preservation of your country and your rights – all of them!

Our rights have a long history and many people fought, struggled and died for them. None of them should be taken for granted or given up without a fight. Have you ever thought how amazing it is that we tolerate other religions? Before our Founding Fathers wrote the Constitution and the Bill of Rights, there had been no other country in the world that tolerated all religions and faiths. Countries were torn apart, neighbor against neighbor, they fought till death and total demise to preserve their faith – torture, murder, and genocide were common all over Europe.

The privileged left-wing propaganda babies of today, who grew up in the best country in the world enjoying all the rights and freedoms of capitalism, use words like "torture" and "genocide" and "war on women" without any meanings attached: they speak in order to "belong" and make themselves feel good and important. Why? They are not taught our history and literature in school! The Common Core masters bowdlerize and maim our literary canon by erasing n-words and phrases that do not chime in with their ideology, creating soulless slaves! Read the last page of Huck Finn: his "sivilze" means the crooked civilization of the past, subjugation of free spirit and our American souls. Read Huck Finn again; after all, as Ernest Hemingway said, all modern American literature comes from that book. [11]

Perhaps we should trade in some of our freedoms for security...? That is what left-wing cohorts continually suggest. They actually believe their own propaganda. Why? Because of their narrow-mindedness, lack of faith and courage. Education? They are reasonably well educated, yes; but: can you teach character? No. Character comes from within. It is courage and determination, responsibility and admission of truth no matter what the consequences. We are Americans; we do not cave in and give up our ground just because someone omnipotent "from above" tells us to.

Trading in any of our freedoms would necessarily mean

surrendering our rights with it. There is no absolute safety and there is no absolute freedom, true. My freedom ends where yours begins. But there are also freedoms that we have in common. Those are the freedoms anchored in our Bill of Rights. We must not trade any of them under any pretense, no matter how much good will or how many "guarantees" are offered to us in exchange.

3

FORGET GUNS - LET'S BAN EVERYTHING!

by Barbara Cook

Ban guns? Yes indeed, guns are weapons that, when used improperly, can kill and maim people. Even people who have gun permits with registered guns are not exempt from guns being used improperly. Everyday in the news, there are acts of violence with people using guns to cause havoc on others, so let's ban the guns therefore we will be free from devastation and destruction in our daily lives.

But wait - while we're at it, let's look at all of the other items to ban to keep folks safe. After all, it *is* the job of the government to prevent further calamity in our daily lives, right?

Years ago I recall a teenage boy using a fork to stab his brother in his arm, puncturing the arm severe enough to draw blood and leave holes in the arm. So let's ban forks.

Since I'm a middle school teacher, it seems we should ban pencils, too, as they are the root of many evils that have taken place. In the classroom children have been known to stab other children with pencils in the arm or leg leaving quite severe puncture marks. And let's make sure to ban fake fingernails. I read somewhere that a female student dug her nails deep into another student's arm deep enough to draw blood.

Glass containers, when broken by a student and/or thrown at an administrator in their office, should definitely be banned.

For that matter, perhaps we should ban unruly students! That one is quite tempting, as I have been kicked, spat upon, and punched by unruly students. And while we're at it, we should ban furniture, too. I have seen students throw desks - and books, too. Books have been propelled across the room aiming for and meeting said target.

Irons not only injure people, but also leave lifelong scars on human skin, so we'll just have to live with wrinkled clothes.

Coat hangers can be immensely dangerous to mankind.

The risks include stabbing and strangling the target.

Many other items can be used as a weapon—cars, knives, chemicals if used incorrectly, water (people drowning) and of course crazy people, but what defines crazy? Crazy people produce bombs made from chemicals at home – so what do we ban first, the chemicals, the home, or the crazy people?

Poison of all types definitely need to be banned, along with anything aerosol. Hairspray, perfume, it's all got to go.

Flour and powered coffee creamer have also been used to destroy buildings – good reason to drink black coffee right there. The flour particles build up, oxygen, and the right temperature can cause the flour to explode.

And of course, the government should ban all violent movies, games, and music. Better yet, let's just ban the main culprit of all violent-inducing propaganda, Hollywood.

Am I being satirical? Well, sort of. The above items are somewhat controlled with regulations in place to keep people safe, as are guns.

Can a hammer build a building by itself? Can a pair of scissors cut by themselves? Of course not. It takes a person using these items for the end result.

And of course guns should **not** be banned, any more than forks and pencils. In every instance, it is people who use items to kill and maim, not the other way around.

The government does not have the right to make decisions for us and banning guns is never the answer. The government is there to help maintain order - *not* to control its citizens - and that is precisely what our 2nd Amendment is all about.

Barbara J. Cook (Cookie) lives in the panhandle of Florida educating special needs children in a middle school. Growing up in Europe as a child and spending several years as a military wife, Barbara learned to appreciate and respect diversity in people choosing to live by the phrase, agree to disagree. Barbara says she got involved in PolitiChicks and political activism because, 'if we don't, who will?'

4

ISLAMIC TERRORISM IN AMERICA?
KEEP CALM AND CARRY!

by Laura Rambeau Lee

It was only a matter of where and when the next attack would occur. In the aftermath of the 2015 massacre in San Bernardino, CA by radical Islamic terrorists, we discovered the two killers were named as **Syed Rizwan Farook** and **Tashfeen Malik**. [12] The media appeared shocked to learn a woman was involved in the murders. It took awhile for them to report the killers' names although early on many of us were learning their identities via Twitter and Facebook. As the relationship between the two was revealed it occurred to me the K-1 visa bride more than likely radicalized her American born husband.

With gun stores reporting record sales [13] it appears the majority of Americans now understand, if they had not before, we are at war with radical Islamists. And it is not just America these terrorists have declared war against; it is all of Western culture and non-fundamentalist Muslims. They have been waging a war on "infidels" for centuries, so anyone who says that we brought it upon ourselves must acknowledge this fight has been going on long before America was discovered.

Americans have been preparing for this war and I pray more people will arm themselves and be able to stop or at least minimize any damage visited upon us by Islamic, or any domestic, terrorists. I have faith in our resolve and our courage.

We know the potential threat of terrorists whether they are Islamic or any other fanatical individual or group. What is more concerning is a government consistently shifting the narrative away from speaking the name of our enemy and instead focusing on gun violence or climate change as urgent issues that need to be addressed.

Speaking about the San Bernardino massacre and other

attacks, Leftists seemed more concerned with not offending the Muslim community than recognizing and conveying the truth to the American people or taking measures to protect us. Attorney General Loretta Lynch even went so far as to say she would prosecute anyone guilty of what she considered violence-inspiring speech. [14] So now we have the head of the Justice Department threatening to deprive the American people of their constitutional right to free speech if they speak out against radical Islam. Can we say "shari'ah?" Interesting we never heard her say the same about the #BlackLivesMatter group [15] that called for the killing of law enforcement officers – and later did so.

Americans will not tolerate any gun control measures. We are born out of revolution and hold our God given rights sacred. Conservatives should be conveying to the American people that the Bill of Rights is a list of our human rights. These are not rights given to us by government; they predate any laws of man. The right to speak freely and the right to protect ourselves, our families, loved ones, and co-workers should never be the subject of political debate.

This is our reality and will be for the future. We must realize electing a Republican will not immediately make this threat go away. The threat is in our country and in our cities. Learn how to protect yourself and your loved ones. Take firearms classes and learn how to use a firearm safely and properly. Get your concealed license permit. Refuse to be a victim.

Stealing from the British World Word II poster, all I can say is KEEP CALM AND CARRY! [16]

Laura Rambeau Lee graduated with high honors from Eckerd College in St. Petersburg, Florida, receiving a Bachelor's Degree in American Studies with a concentration on Communication. In addition to PolitiChicks, Laura contributes to various websites and has been a guest conservative radio shows. Laura is married to a retired Army officer and is the mother of one daughter and grandmother of three.

5

EVIL MEN KILL, GUNS DON'T: THE STORY OF REUBEN SAMUEL COLLINS

by Brenda Collins Morris

On August 4, 1911, Reuben Samuel Collins and his 13-year-old son Orea Collins (also known as "E" Collins) were constructing a fence on the elder Collins' property. He had been having a problem with the cattle from a neighboring farm coming onto his property and eating his crops so in an attempt to encourage the neighbor to confine his cattle, Reuben Samuel gave his neighbor a milk cow.

Some say August 1911 was particularly hot and of course farmers in those days had little or no means of escaping the cruel temperatures—often causing people's tempers to flare. The **Old Farmers Almanac** lists the traditional period called the "Dog Days of Summer" as 40 days beginning on July 3rd and ending on August 11th and some believe this period to be an evil time.

On this August day, while Reuben Samuel and his son "E" worked on his fence, the neighbor and his son came into the field and shot at Reuben Samuel with his rifle. He missed, and when his next shot jammed the neighbor yelled for his son to shoot, which the young man did. Reuben Samuel was shot in the neck and as he lay bleeding on the ground, his son held his father in his arms until he passed. Both of the neighbors were sentenced to prison, which was of little consolation to E, the son of Reuben Samuel.

E Collins became an orphan on that hot summer day. Two August's prior he had watched his mother, Annie Collins, burn to death. She was washing clothes in a kettle over a fire that had nearly gone out when she took a container that she believed to contain kerosene and poured it onto the coals. The can exploded and set her on fire. She was running around the yard screaming and E, her son, told her to run to the creek. At 11 years old, E didn't know he should direct his mother to "stop, drop and roll". He ran to the creek with his mother and saw her flesh floating to the surface of the water. The pain was so great and her screams were so loud and horrific that 11-year-old E left the house that night; he held his hands over his ears trying to block out her painful screams. She lived just 12 hours.

E grew up and married and got a farm of his own. He had livestock, horses, an old mule, and various other animals. He grew vegetables, tobacco, soybeans and other crops. His farmhouse didn't have hot water or a bathroom until he was nearly 70 and, by that time, both he and the house were too "old and broken down" to care. But one thing that E always kept stocked in that old house—and in his truck--were guns. Plenty of them. There was always a shotgun sitting in the corner of the living room and others in his bedroom. His wife, Hazie, knew how to shoot and did so on a number of occasions, usually to kill a snake. But don't think for a minute Hazie would have feared using a gun to protect herself or her family against any predator. There were children in the house always--their children, neighborhood children, and later grandchildren. Every one of those children knew not to ever touch a gun without permission from an adult family member, and none of the children ever did.

E fathered two sons and one daughter but yet another August—this time in 1955--once again brought tragedy to his life. His eldest son Delbert was killed in a single vehicle accident in rural Kentucky. Fortunately E's other son and daughter, Joe and Audrey are still alive today and they still reside in Kentucky, not too far from the old farm. They, too, always have a few guns around and seldom leave home without one.

Did E live with fear? No, he was determined to be able to defend himself and his family. Perhaps he always wondered had he or his father had a gun on August 4, 1911, if the outcome may have been very different and perhaps he could have saved his father's life.

In addition to farming E was also a prison guard at the Kentucky State Reformatory, but his real love was working on the old farm place. One month shy of his 80th birthday he and his son Joe were driving back near the old farm to look at a house E wanted to rent for the summer. He had long given up farming but was looking forward to renting a little house on Eagle Creek just down the road.. It was a rainy May morning and his son Joe was driving E's new pick-up truck when two young men in a van lost control and hit Joe and E head-on. Joe survived with minor injuries but E only lived about 16 hours. Yet another tragedy: E was killed by a drunk driver.

I've heard the story of Reuben Samuel, Annie, and E Collins many times over the years. You see, Reuben Samuel and Annie were my great -grandparents, and E was my grandfather. I remember squirrel hunting with him and helping him hoe the fields with his old mule. At ten years old I was riding a tobacco setter. I remember bathing in galvanized tubs at the farm because there was no running water, only a cistern. I remember the trips to the outhouse. In the winter we carried buckets of coal to the house every evening to fire up the old coal stove to help us stay warm through the night. I also remember the shotgun in the corner, the one I was taught to respect as well as the pistol he kept in his truck. When I was told the story of how my great-grandfather Reuben Samuel was murdered it was never about a gun--it was always about the evil men who used guns to kill him. It would have been the same had they used a knife, machete, a hammer or some other instrument often found on a farm. The truth, as all Conservatives know, is that guns don't kill people--*people* kill people. We can't allow any President or our government to take away our right to own a gun. It is first and foremost our greatest defense against a tyrannical government and evil men who seek to do us harm.

Statistics prove that where the strictest gun regulations and laws exist, there is the most crime. As the saying goes, "When you outlaw guns, only outlaws will have guns." Let's stop this gun control nonsense and instead get to the root of the real problem. Jeremiah 17:9 says, "The heart is deceitful above all things, and desperately wicked: who can know it?" Let's start putting the blame where it belongs: on people. Let's start making people accountable for their evil actions. Let's start teaching our children to respect life and God's Guidebook for how to live our lives. Only then will evil men's hearts be changed to think twice about taking a human life.

Collins, Reuben Samuel

Kentucky #20668

Male, White, Widowed

Born: December 9, 1854, Kentucky

Died: August 4, 1911, Grant County, Kentucky

Age at Death: 56 years, 7 months, 26 days

Cause of Death: Bullet Wound in Neck - Murdered

Attending Physician: J. L. Vallandingham, Mt. Zion, Kentucky

Father: F. R. Collins, born Kentucky

Mother: Sarah Webster, born Kentucky

Informant: W. S. Collins, Elliston, Kentucky

Buried: Vine Run Cemetery, Grant County, Kentucky, August 6, 1911

Undertaker: J. B. Sanders, Dry Ridge, Kentucky.

Brenda Collins Morris is a military wife, mom, conservative, and has campaigned for conservative candidates. She served on a Critical Incident Response Team assisting people in the aftermath of tragedies such as 9/11. Brenda's father is a WWII Veteran.

6
WOMEN AND OUR 2ND AMENDMENT

by Katherine Daigle

When most people think of the Second Amendment and gun rights, the image conjured up usually involves burly men wearing camo as they hunt in the woods, or perhaps husbands tiptoeing downstairs in the middle of the night to protect their families from intruders. Certainly, these people are important parts of those protected by the Constitution and its indelible decree that "the right of the people to keep and bear arms shall not be infringed". But what many people forget, tragically, are the many great things our Second Amendment provides for women. Women, like never before, are refusing to be victims, empowering themselves and make use of their 2nd Amendment rights.

We've all heard the stories. A workingwoman walking to her car at night is followed by a strange man, and saved from a terrible violation by brandishing the handgun in her purse. Once a young wife was on the phone with her husband, who listened in terror as she hid in their bedroom from a burglar who has broken in. Clutching a gun in her hands, she repeatedly warned the burglar to back off as he ignored her and encroached upon her. She is alive today only because she emptied her clip into the malevolent man.

So, instead of the unwritten rule of run, hide, and wait to be rescued, for your sake, protect yourself!

These are the stories that need to be told more often, and fortunately, of late they are. The National Rifle Association (NRA) has recently launched commercials featuring women talking about the safety afforded them by the fact that they own guns and carry them for protection. It's a good thing. Countless women are saved every day from rape, robbery, and other horrible crimes merely by being armed. Usually, just showing their gun is enough to make a criminal back off and reconsider his intentions. If not, women can and should be trained in the use of their weapons, in that terrible scenario that they must defend themselves or their families.

Women carrying guns, and being respected for it, are a natural extension of the admirable appreciation for female rights that has grown in modern American society. This is a time when women can hold jobs, serve in the military, and generally do something other than stay at home caring for children if they so wish. An essential component of this liberated mindset is that they are able and prepared to protect themselves, and show that they are not the frightened, defenseless flowers once portrayed in popular media.

__Katherine Daigle__ is an experienced public servant and a self-made woman. Katherine believes that the surest path to success is freedom from government interference, because that is what led to her own success. She has served in numerous private and public positions during her distinguished career.

PART TWELVE: ACTIVISM

We are the keepers of the flame in a dark age. If we let it die out, then the darkness falls. We are a minority. - **Daniel Greenfield**

1

STEPPING UP AS A POLITICAL ACTIVIST: FROM STATE TO NATIONAL DELEGATE

by Brian Bledsoe

As the Republican Party of Texas Convention of 2014 was approaching, the Northeast Tarrant Tea Party was holding an urgent meeting to inform people about proposals that were being considered. At one point someone suggested that more conservatives needed to be delegates because it's there where people can make a difference - not only by the numbers to be heard, but also to be there for the formation of the party platform.

At this point in my political engagement mostly consisted of attending meetings and volunteering when I was able, but I hadn't really thought of getting deeper into the process. However, it did interest me.

After the meeting, I asked what I needed to do become a delegate. They told me it was too late to become a delegate for the 2014 convention but if I'm still interested I could try to become one in 2016. That's where my journey began.

For the next two years, I continued to attend meetings, talk to party officials and local activists, and I learned more about what I needed to do to hopefully get selected as a delegate.

After a number of procedures, paperwork, networking, and people inside and outside the party who helped me, I was selected as a Texas state delegate during the 2016 precinct and senatorial convention!

Back in 2014 when I first asked about becoming a state delegate, the thought of actually being a delegate at the 2016 National Republican Convention wasn't even a thought. But the more I talked to people about it, it seemed like it could actually become a reality. Yes, it would be a long shot; I learned that trying to become a state delegate was one thing, but to go from state to national was a very wide gap.

But two aspects completely took me by surprise.

One was the cost of even attending the RNC at all. It was much more than I ever anticipated. Second was the fact that I would basically have to run a mini-campaign in order to be able to go to nationals. I'm actually glad that I didn't know about these factors earlier because I might have used them as an excuse not to run for national delegate.

So like a political candidate running for office, I sent multiple emails and had to make lots of phone calls. The first few calls felt strange; I've made hundreds of calls for various groups and campaigns but now I was calling for myself. I also had to speak at meetings about running for national delegate. I was very nervous when I made my first public announcement at the inaugural meeting of the Grapevine Republican Club. I thought I had done well but as soon as I sat down my wife informed that I had forgotten to say my name!

The excitement of being elected, as well as the honor of representing Sen. Cruz, someone who I've been a supporter of since he ran for Senator, was short lived because the issue of cost was looming. So a month before the state convention I decided to create a GoFundMe account to help cover the costs of attending the Republican National Convention in Cleveland. In the event that I wasn't elected to go to the convention, it was stated that the funds would be donated to people who were. So as soon as it was official, I posted the news about my GoFundMe account on all my social media accounts to get the word out fast. The outpouring of support the days after the convention amazed me. In one week I more than doubled what I raised in one month. Friends like Chris Dillard and Annette Kocka were sharing the page and stayed on me to keep visibility on social media. Then two weeks before the convention, I finally reached the goal and my plans were finalized to go to Cleveland.

"Uncertainty" would best describe my mindset as I arrived at my Congressional District caucus, waiting to be formally nominated as a national delegate. In the weeks leading up to the convention, I knew that there were over twenty people vying for six slots (three delegates and three alternates), and there may have been more. Many of the people wanting to be nominated were very well know activists in the community, some I really respected.

Then on May 3, 2016, just weeks before the state convention, everything changed when Senator Ted Cruz suspended his presidential campaign. Soon after his announcement, the number of people considering a delegate slot was cut in half. With the smaller number of candidates my odds were better, but still no guarantee. Because of my job as a long haul truck driver, many of the remaining candidates were able to campaign more than I could. I had very little time to reach out to the various events across the district. And many of the candidates were able to promote themselves by purchasing flyers and other promotional methods, none of which I could afford. I was truly shocked at the amount of resources others had when I walked into the room where the nominations were held. Basically all I had available were the call/email lists of all the state delegates and their network of supporters.

I barely made it –within five minutes-- to the **Kay Bailey Hutchinson Convention Center** where the 24th Congressional District caucus was taking. When I (hurriedly) walked in I noticed everyone was still talking amongst each other, but then I was instantly met with some good news. Apparently word was spreading around the room that people should vote a friend of mine, James Ashby, and myself to become national delegates. I was new to the process so I honestly had no idea of what was going on, but it turned out that I had more support than I thought.

Now that the reality of actually becoming a national delegate was becoming clearer now, I tried to get a grasp on the whole process. Thankfully, I sat next to Texas State Senator Konni Burton, who helped me as I asked numerous questions to get a better understanding of what was going on.

The first delegate slot went to James Ashby by a landslide, which was no surprise to anyone given he had Rafeal Cruz (father of Senator Ted Cruz) nominate and speak on his behalf.

So one delegate slot was taken, and all ten candidates (including myself) made our case to be selected for national delegate and we were now waiting for the results. At this point I felt at peace because regardless of the outcome, I enjoyed the experience and had exhausted all my available resources.

I thought about how two years ago I had asked North East Tarrant Tea Party president Julie McCarty how to become a delegate. She directed me to Tarrant County Republican Party chair Jennifer Hall, who guided me through the process. And then the 24th Congressional District elected me to be a national delegate representing Senator Ted Cruz.

We've all heard politicians talk about how they couldn't have run for office without everyone helping. Well, my small journey in becoming a national delegate made me really understand what they mean. Without the support of the people who I've named (as well as many who were not,) I know I wouldn't have gone to Cleveland.

All I know is that when I stepped on the floor of the Republican National Convention, I knew I wasn't alone because I felt the presence and gratitude of all the people who helped get me there - and that's a moment I'll never forget. I truly enjoyed the journey and prayerfully this is not the end of my political activist career.

Brian Bledsoe is a U.S. Army Veteran and has been a professional driver since 2005. Brian is an advocate not only for party politics but also for biblical principles, which some would either consider conservative or libertarian. He now volunteers for various organizations and campaigns, including traveling to Cleveland, Ohio as a National Texas delegate in the 2016 presidential primary at the RNC. Brian is married to his wife Dana and they have a teenage daughter.

2

POLITICS AND WEIGHT LOSS: WALK THOSE PRECINCTS!

by Kathryn Porter

Want to lose weight while helping your favorite conservative get elected to office? Candidates across the country need "boots on the ground" to reach out to neighbors and voters. Every election offers you the perfect time to kick start your physical fitness routine by volunteering to walk precincts.

All you need to do is Google your favorite candidate; visit his or her Web site to locate contact info, and express your interest to help with the campaign by phone or email.

The best part of the "precinct walking shred" is that it won't cost you anything but a good pair of walking shoes. No expensive gym memberships.

You can walk as little or as much as you'd like, assuming you have clearance from your doctor. For safety reasons, most campaigns will schedule volunteers to walk in pairs. That's a built in workout buddy for you.

Many of our elected officials could stand to learn a thing or two about political weight loss. The addiction to fees and taxes needs to stop. Burdensome regulations need to be reversed. Bad legislation needs to be repealed. It's time to trim the fat in local, state, and federal governments. That starts with a good ground game to help elect true, conservative candidates— ones who understand that the role of government is not to tax small businesses out of business, tell its citizens what kind of light bulbs to use, or enact education policy which benefits corporations and non-profits at the expense of America's children.

In the age of social media, face-to-face connections still make a difference. The ground game can make or break a close election. If you are unhappy with the direction our country is going, simply casting your vote is no longer enough. It's time to get more involved. It's time to take action through getting the right candidates on the ballot.

Regardless of whether you are looking to lose a few pounds or not, our government needs to lose more than a little weight. Instead of balanced budgets, legislators create bloated budgets, feasting on the hard earned dollars of American workers.

Help send the message that it's time for Washington— and our state and local governments— to go on a diet by getting involved at the ground level.

Join thousands of conservative across the country every election. Put your boots to the ground for some precinct walking. Are you ready boots? Start walking!

Kathryn Porter is an elected member of the Colorado GOP State Central Committee and the El Paso County Republican Party Executive Committee. As an illuminator of truth, the Colorado State Chairman banned her from being a guest at the 2016 RNC. She pledges to continue holding the CO GOP accountable. She is also an education activist and educational consultant for homeschooling families.

3
BEING THE "TOKEN" CONSERVATIVE

by Beth Baumann

Throughout my life, I've always been the "go-to" person when people want to know how conservatives feel about issues. I was always called upon in high school to demonstrate the conservative ideology – more like defend what I believe. In college, my school's newspaper advisor begged me to write the counterpoints to the ever-popular progressive views. I guess you could say I'm a rare breed, especially in the Golden State.

I grew up listening to conservative talk radio and watching Fox News. I grew up talking politics with my mom and dad. By the time I was 10, I chose to watch the news over cartoons. What was happening in our world – and particularly in our nation – intrigued me.

At 11, I helped my dad flier cars against Gray Davis and Arnold Schwarzenegger. Don't ask me what the fliers were about. I was just happy to be able to do a "big kid" job. (This was also the first time I almost got arrested – and it probably won't be the last.)

At 12, I was outside protesting the California Department of Corrections' placement of a high-profile sex offender near an elementary school. My dad and I went out there almost every weekend for a few months. At the time, John and Ken, popular talk radio hosts on KFI AM640, were hosting their show out across the street from the halfway house. I was stoked to meet them and be apart of the protest.

At 16, I was the only kid in my school with a McCain t-shirt. I broke my own rule as the yearbook Editor-In-Chief. I included my picture on the 2008 election spread we did. In a school of 3,500+ students, how could I not? I was the only one supporting the dude!

At 19, I almost got kicked out of college for standing up for my First Amendment rights by challenging my campus

Administration. I also attended my very first CPAC. I remember calling my mom, almost in tears when I met presidential hopefuls. In a lot of ways, this was my idea of a celebrity event. Or as I like to call it, the celebrity event of conservative politics.

Why do I bring all of this up? Because it paints a very clear picture of my generation and the future of our great nation. My generation is SO focused on writing every wrong in the world, of helping every single person that we forget to help ourselves. My generation is so focused on today's satisfactions and tomorrow's gratification, not the long-term impact of their decisions.

I've always held my head up high, defending what I believe in and why I believe it. I have never been ashamed to be a conservative. I have never allowed anyone to define me but me.

To those who ask me what it's like to be the only one in the room who is conservative, this is what I have to say: I am a conservative. I want limited government and free markets. I want people to have the ability to choose, to be their own person and to have responsibility for their actions. I am a conservative who sees the future of our nation slowly dwindling. So many have their hands out but very few are reaching into their pockets to give.

We're a nation on the verge of destruction. We're going broke. Our children are no longer #1 in the education system. Unemployment is at an all time high. Kids are graduating college and moving right back into their parent's houses. Our military has their hands in conflicts all over the world. We lack the proper medical care and treatment for our veterans.

We're a nation on the verge of losing who we are and what we believe me. We need more people to stand up, to be proud to be conservative. We need conservatives who aren't afraid of being the "Token" conservative like I am. If more people stand up and speak out, we can and will change the direction of our nation.

This is something that needs to be done today. It's something that needs to be done right now. Stand up and fight, my fellow patriots!

4

WOMEN IN POLITICS AND
WHY I CHOSE TO RUN FOR PUBLIC OFFICE

by Katherine Daigle

It has always amazed me that, throughout the long and checkered history of humanity's experiment with the institution of government; politics have traditionally been a man's game. Athenian democracy, marginalized women, only extending the cherished rights to vote and publicly participate only to its male citizens. As we have mercifully begun to enter into more tolerant and enlightened times, the long-standing male preoccupation with excluding females from social administration has only become more difficult to comprehend. Reading over the annals of history, I have never understood it in any period. For it is no exaggeration to state that where women have been allowed to play a part in government – and, in many cases, even despite being actively blocked from doing so – they have thrived, as have their societies.

It is no different today, in the modern United States of America, and it is here that there can be no better example of the capabilities of women as public servants. It is time to change the culture, wade into the mainstream and articulate why gender equity is a winner for everyone.

I like to think of myself as a self-made American success story. From decidedly humble beginnings, after years of hard work and schooling I now hold an MBA, allowing me to achieve success in my professional career, which has spanned the fields of law, finance, and executive business management. My family, the pride and joy of my life and my single greatest accomplishment, embody the spirit of self-determination I so cherish. My husband is an equal partner who encourages my accomplishments, while our grown daughter is a bio-scientist and will be furthering her education in medicine.

I strive to bring this dauntless tenacity to my work in

public service. An active and involved resident of Irvine, California, I have participated in a wide variety of volunteer work for the benefit of my community. From 2012, 2014, and 2016 I was blessed to have been elected as a Director of the Woodbridge Village serving more than 30,000 residents. I am a candidate for California State Assembly 74th District which includes my hometown of Irvine.

Because I want you to understand who I am, I have to tell you that throughout my life, nothing was ever given to me for free or made easy for me. I had to earn my own way and pay my own dues, most especially in the exhausting task of being a single mother when my daughter was at the age of four. In my younger days, despite holding down a job to make ends meet while I finished school, my then-four-year-old daughter still required care. I must say, I really had to dig deep, but in the end I managed not only to look after my child, but also to encourage and support her and her endeavors, as she began to practice figure skating. Frequently this meant rising in the abhorrently early morning to meet her extracurricular needs before I myself went to work for the day and her to school. I bring this up not to grumble, as I never objected about that – my little girl is worth it. But I need you to be aware that getting to where I am now was not easy for her or me those many years ago. Education is the cornerstone of every successful family

I credit that chapter in my life for my current dedication to hard work and the rewards that have graciously been bestowed upon me. This has taught me the value of self-determination, and an understanding of the potential within every American. Because I want you to hear me when I say that there is nothing inherently special about me, and I can promise you that I started from no position of privilege. It's these convictions that have allowed me to grow into a person devoted to clearing the way for people to achieve their dreams, limiting the interference of government as much as possible as they strive to pursue happiness.

I am a Republican woman because I know what people can do. I support minimal taxation, the return of taxes paid in excess, and strict limits on the size and scope of government. I believe in free enterprise and the entrepreneurial spirit, unmolested by regulation. And when it comes to schooling, I regard education as the foundation of any successful person, because it's such a huge reason that I have managed to be successful, and I strongly believe in providing for the learning of all children.

These principles, learned from the hard lessons of experience, form the basis of my journey, and they inform and inspire my involvement in politics over the course of my life. I've worked for what I have and I want to empower others to have the opportunity to do the same. I seek to motivate my fellow citizens to follow the same path of hard work and reliance on self that has brought me such bountiful blessings. I am a living example of what women can do when we work hard, and I want to help other women realize that they can do the same. There is no limit to the benefits society stands to reap when women unleash their potential in the realm of politics.

I understand the importance of the American can-do independent spirit, which made this nation great; this is why I promote it as a core value and philosophy.

And it is precisely because women have so much to offer with their talent, ingenuity, and great leadership that this motivation becomes so important. This is the essential point missed over so much of human history, and which modern society is starting to realize. For to disenfranchise women, shutting them out of the political processes that govern their own lives and those of their families, is not only to do an injustice to them but to rob civilization itself of the brilliance of its own citizenry.

One of my favorite quotes is attributed to Kerry Healey, the 70th Lieutenant Governor of Massachusetts. In it, Healey addresses the issue of women's traditional disempowerment in politics and the importance of acknowledging them: "The mounting issues facing our country are complex. If we're going to solve these problems, we can no longer afford to leave the talent of half our nation out of the conversation."

5

POLITICHICKS LAW ENFORCEMENT GRATITUDE CAMPAIGN

by Holly Woodland

"They need gratitude, not attitude!" Ann-Marie Murrell blurted out as we left the last police station on our PolitiChicks Gratitude Campaign of delivering cookies to precincts throughout Los Angeles. Our day was filled with laughter and tears as we drove from station to station. It was a day I will treasure always, spending time with a good friend and doing something that meant so much to us and to our police officers in their time of need.

The day began as I arrived at Ann-Marie's home. She was feverishly working to spread the word of our campaign. She had written the following note to place with our cookies to the officers:

On behalf of the PolitiChicks Gratitude Campaign, thank you for the hard work you do, the long hours, the training, the time away from your family. Mostly, thank you for putting your life on the line for us, and for doing all you do to keep our own families and homes safe. God bless you & yours.

I felt overwhelmed at the message, phrased so perfectly for what we were about to do. No words I could express would be more heartfelt than what she had written.

We then set out to the local grocer to purchase packages of sealed cookies: 4-dozen per precinct, plus bags of wrapped candy, and filled them into large red gift bags. We adhered the message to the outside of the bag, so it would be the first thing seen by the officers as we presented our gift.

We entered the Burbank Police Department for our first delivery and were greeted at the front desk by a young policewoman. Although Ann-Marie had contacted the stations before we arrived, not all were aware of our coming gesture. The young woman asked how might she help as we presented our gift bag.

With a professional demeanor she began to read the note, and as the realization of the words hit her, she smiled with humility and gratitude.

"Thank you, thank you!" she said as she then enthusiastically said, "Wait here!"

Soon Lieutenant John Dilibert was retrieved from the back as he entered with a big infectious smile. We continued to explain why we were there as other officers gathered around as photos were snapped and officers thanked us. We said, "No, no, we want to thank you!" as even more officers took notice of what was happening.

As we were leaving, an officer yelled out, "Tell people not to be so angry at us when we write tickets, too," reminding me that their contact with the public in the line of duty must be mostly negative. As I looked at these officers, I could see the young female officer was pregnant. These were real people, with real lives and feelings, and what was being said about them by Black Lives Matter and beyond did have an effect.

Next we arrived at the Glendale Police Department. Finding a parking space was difficult since Ann-Marie and I were excited as we arrived. The Elvis-sounding GPS Ann-Marie was using was being ignored as I rambled on in a caffeine stupor (yeah, Starbucks). The joy we felt as we went on our mission made us feel silly.

Officer Vincent W. Jackson and Officer Paul Lopez spoke with us at the Glendale station. Once again, they were surprised and deeply touched by what we were doing. Both Ann- Marie and I felt moved once again by their heartfelt and all too human reaction. The woman at the front desk, eyes welling up with tears, said, "You don't know how much this means to us. All the negativity and anger we hear from everyone hurts a lot; we are just trying to do our jobs."

We realized that even personnel working at the stations were affected by what was happening to police officers nationwide, and it comforted us knowing that so many other PolitiChicks across the country were delivering their Gratitude Cookies, too, and must be hearing the same.

Our last stop was at the Los Angeles Police Department, Rampart Area. We had to concentrate a bit more on where we were going since the area appeared more dangerous. We once again went to the front desk where a polite and professional officer was working. After reading our note, he asked us to please wait for another officer to speak with us.

Officer Mariscar soon entered from the back and approached us with a serious expression. He and other officers had read the note and well, I find it hard to write the emotion they conveyed. They told us about the violent chants they'd been hearing, such as, "What do we want – Dead Cops!" So our simple bag of cookies meant a lot to them.

As another officer had us stand together for photos, she asked that we all move closer together. I went to put my arms around the two officers next to me and could feel the vest under their uniform they were wearing. My heart sank and tears filled my eyes as I looked at Ann-Marie, both of us thinking of the anger and hatred happening in America, mostly directed against all police officers.

Mostly what we, as PolitiChicks, want to convey to the BLM-types is that you DO NOT speak for all of us! What you are inciting is hatred and violence against the vast majority of officers who will protect you and your families with their lives! Happily, the profiteers and race baiters are not the only voices being heard anymore. We, too, have a voice, but we will be using ours for love, not hate.

As we started to leave LAPD, one officer said to me, "You don't have to give us cookies or anything. A phone call with thank you means the same, just a thank you is all we have to hear." And another female officer approached us and said, "Most of the people who are out there protesting against us are people who don't work for a living and are simply doing whatever they're told to do. We know the vast majority of people out there are good; they're hard-working and they're taking care of their families, just like we are."

The difference is that police officers like the ones we met are not only taking care of their homes and families, but ours as well.

We hope you'll join us in continuing to show gratitude across the nation—either with a bag of (sealed) cookies and treats, or just by calling your local precinct and saying 'thank you.' And let's keep this Gratitude Campaign going, year-round.

Holly Woodland is a native Californian who has been in the entertainment industry for over 30 years. She is a working actress, using the pseudonym "Holly Woodland" for PolitiChicks. Holly began her career on the stages of New York before moving back to Los Angeles where she appeared in television series including Weeds, Grey's Anatomy, and she was a regular comedic sketch artist on Jay Leno's Tonight Show for several years. Holly has authored many live theatrical productions, which are currently running across the United States.

6

TAKING BACK AMERICA, ONE PERSON AT A TIME

by Abigail Adams

We, as Americans, are faced with so many crucial issues that it is truly impossible to choose the most important one. We are nearly overwhelmed, and I believe that that is precisely the objective of the Democrat Party.

Just off the top of my head: Obamacare, gun control, freedom of speech, energy (drilling for our own oil, coal mining, natural gas), rising taxes, death panels, freedom of religion, illegal immigration and open borders, corrupt no-Justice Department, crippling regulations on businesses, violations of our Constitution, Agenda 21 ... the list goes on and on.

Fear results in paralysis, but this is the time for action. Every Patriot is needed, and we are on the side of Truth. We will win if each of us learns and becomes an expert on a single issue and then reaches, teaches, and educates everybody we come across about that issue.

From personal experience, I will tell you that this method works. People listen when you have the facts to back up your opinion. Facts - not opinions; passion - not emotion.

This is our America, land that we love. Choose your issue, learn your facts, and let's go.

7

FOURTH BRANCH OF AMERICAN GOVERNMENT: WE THE PEOPLE

by Lainie Sloane

According to our Constitution, there are three branches of government:

> Legislative: Makes laws
> Executive: Approves or vetoes laws; carries out laws
> Judicial: Interpret the laws for constitutionality

Our Constitution according to Leftists is:

- Irrelevant
- Outdated
- Annoying
- Adaptable to his will
- Therefore, nonexistent

We the People: Our Responsibilities

I argue that there is a fourth branch of government, which I would venture to say, none of us were taught in school. The fourth branch is We the People because the People oversee the three branches. It is our responsibility to make sure the government is subservient to us and ensures our fundamental rights provided by the Constitution: Life, Liberty and the Pursuit of Happiness. It is our responsibility to exercise authority over the government when they do not abide by the Constitution or our will. When our government becomes oppressive, We the People are the last resort—not to be taken lightly.

Civic Duties

As citizens, we have the duty to vote, to report corruption and come against it. The Declaration of Independence states:

We hold these Truths to be self-evident, that all men are created equal, that they are endowed by their Creator with certain unalienable rights, that among these are life, liberty and the pursuit of happiness—That to secure these rights, governments are instituted among men, deriving their just powers from the consent of the governed. That whenever any form of government becomes destructive to these ends, it is the right of the people to alter or to abolish it, and to institute new government, laying its foundation on such principles and organizing its powers in such form, as to them shall seem most likely to effect their safety and happiness. Prudence, indeed, will dictate that governments long established should not be changed for light and transient causes; and accordingly all experience hath shown that mankind are more disposed to suffer, while evils are sufferable, than to right themselves by abolishing the forms to which they are accustomed. But when a long train of abuses and usurpations, pursuing invariably the same object evinces a design to reduce them under absolute despotism, it is their right, it is their duty, to throw off such government, and to provide new guards for their future security.

Democrat Leftists: Prime Examples of an Oppressive Leadership

According to the website, "Truth Seeker," authored by former Constitutional lawyer, Gerald Buess, he notes in a March 27, 2013article:

Executive Orders/Actions by the president were not designed for, nor do they give a president the authority to use as, a means to override or alter legislation or any other Constitutional violation. Executive Orders cannot defy Congressional intent.

He quotes former University of Chicago Law School Dean, Richard Epstein:

The TRUTH is Obama was not a Constitutional law professor: "under no circumstances would an offer to Obama be tenured." "The thought that the law school could have made a tenure offer to a person with no academic writing was out of the question."

Clearly as president, Barack Obama never respected or protected the Constitution.

What Happened to America?

The seeds of our destruction have been sown through our government schools and public and private universities. Our schools no longer teach the foundations of our Constitution, and if any history is taught at all, it is revisionist history. They are turning out socially engineered robots ready to embrace the government as the supplier of their needs with morals as a thing of the past.

8
THE REPUBLIC FOR WHICH IT STANDS

by Lorelei Branam Bennett

Growing up in the sixties in America, each weekday my father, smiled at us with a kiss before he went to work to earn a living for his wife and children. Mother tended to us with clean, conservative clothes, a warm breakfast, and a hand packed lunch. Then she too, kissed us with a smile as we left the house and walked with neighborhood friends, the two blocks to our public school.

Immediately after the second school bell rang we stopped whatever it was, we were doing. There was never a moment of hesitation or pause. That one ringing bell changed the tone of the moment as if a wave of honor had just washed over us. Everyone within earshot of the school building, including sidewalks and neighboring homes beyond, took a moment to pause.

From Kindergarten on, our student body was undivided and instantly responded with quiet and due respect as we pushed our chairs neatly under the desk, and stood at serious attention. Parents, teachers, staff and visitors alike, each and every one, turned to face the American flag, which proudly hung in the corner of every classroom in our school.

No one stirred in collective silence lending me to listen with all my might. I nostalgically recall the overhead speaker crackling while the vinyl recording spun around and we waited for the familiar song with the resounding words, to begin:

> Oh, say can you see by the dawn's early light
> What so proudly we hailed at the twilight's last gleaming?
> Whose broad stripes and bright stars thru the perilous fight,
> O'er the ramparts we watched were so gallantly streaming?
> And the rocket's red glare, the bombs bursting in air,

Gave proof through the night that our flag was still there.
Oh, say does that Star-Spangled Banner yet wave
O'er the land of the free and the home of the brave?
Next, we pledged our allegiance.

I remember the feeling of duty to stand straight. I held my chin high, my feet neatly together and my hand laid sincerely, over my heart, while taking an oath I didn't nearly understand:

"I pledge allegiance to the flag of the United States of America, and to the Republic for which it stands, one Nation under God, indivisible, with liberty and justice for all."

Pledging allegiance is a promise to be true to the flag that represents us as one nation under God. Yet, in this sacred pledge we are not making a covenant with the government of our country. The vow we are taking is to the *republic for which it stands*. A republic is a government that elects officials to represent their political wishes. The red stripes and blue stars embody that our institutions are of the people by the people and for the people.

It was obvious that President Obama lost sight of our pledge of allegiance. And there is no higher position to set an example, than office of The President of The United States of America.

Compromise is not always the correct political answer to the plight of democracy or problems of society. Sometimes it is time to fight back and hold ground, even if it is unpopular.

Lorelei Branam Bennett has been an active grass roots member of the GOP since her teens and has met many political candidates through the years. Lorelei received her bachelor's degree in 2010 from Florida International University's School in political science. One of her visiting professors was Sen. Marco Rubio. In addition to writing for PolitiChicks, Lorelei is also a published author of "A Little Bit of Ivey." Lorelei and her husband of almost 27 years have a son, daughter, and granddaughter.

9

THE CONSEQUENCES OF BEING A SHORTSIGHTED NATION

by Lydia Goodman

Shortsighted: Part of Speech: Adjective Definition: unmindful of future consequences Synonyms: astigmatic, blind, careless, foolish, headlong, ill-advised, ill-considered, imperceptive, impolitic, impractical, improvident, rash, stupid, unsagacious, unwary Antonyms: careful, longsighted, prudent, thoughtful, wise

We have become a myopic nation, a nation that is so divided against itself that civility, respect, strength of character, honor, and decency are words that have become almost obsolete in our quest for instant gratification (we want what we want-when we want it). There is only the "now" and how it benefits us. In our shortsightedness, we have refused to see the "forest for the trees", with no thought for the future.

Some watch cynically as our government opts to play the blame game, choosing sides, pointing fingers, and calling names, ducking back and forth with their lies-as if they were involved in a vicious game of dodge ball–with our President as the captain. Others cheer or boo from the sidelines, as each point scored by "their side" convinces them of victory over their opponent.

Then, there are those who watch these machinations silently, in a state of futility.

Look again at the definition of "shortsighted". Being shortsighted is not a matter of "unknowing" future consequences but rather being "unmindful" of them. It is a choice. Why would anyone knowingly choose to be shortsighted? There are those that simply don't care as long as nothing upsets their gravy train. Others turn their heads in an effort to avoid seeing anything unpleasant. Don't be fooled for a moment that our government and its leaders are unaware of our calculated blindness. They, in fact, count on it. The evidence is in their decision-making and their ridiculing, and a sweeping condemnation of anyone that disagrees with them.

For far too long, we have watched as our moral compass became unhinged and replaced by greed, selfishness, and above all, "self -love", instead of "love one another". We lost sight of the ideals this country was founded upon and we became filled with a complacent apathy.

Why?

"For the time will come when they will not endure sound doctrine; but wanting to have their ears tickled, they will accumulate for themselves teachers in accordance to their own desires and will turn away their ears from the truth and will turn aside to myths." 2 Timothy 4:3-4

There has been a permeating distortion of commonly shared values and morals for years. Tell us what we want to hear. Show us what we want to see. Our leaders justify their lying, cheating, stealing, aborting babies, condoning (by overlooking) horrendous acts of violence by applying situational ethics. They excuse their morally bankrupt actions and decisions-dependent on the most expedient circumstances. No more is "sin" called sin. No more is "wrong" called wrong. Again, don't be fooled. It is all about their ego, their self-esteem, and their self-gratification- an attitude that has slowly seeped down into the collective American conscious. We deserve what we want when we want it.

When did we become so blasé about our foundational principles and traditions? It began when secular humanism became our national religion. We watched as the tools of humanistic propaganda were surgically applied to our core principles in an attempt to convince us that there were no moral absolutes, to reject religious teachings, and to embrace reason and empirical evidence as "our god"-at the expense of the one true God. (Perhaps one of the greatest fallacies perpetuated by the humanists is that religion and science are exclusionary-that one must obviously deny "reason" and "empirical evidence", if one espouses a faith-based worldview.)

Our institutions, including our schools and churches, must be commended. They have done an excellent job in leading its sheep into following these same unbiblical principles, while we looked the other way–either unknowingly or unmindful. For decades, we have allowed the theology of "gradualism"-the belief that change is brought about in small, discrete increments rather in abrupt actions -to work its insidious charm into the mindset of a blind, foolish people. If our eyes had been opened, President Obama and his ilk would not have been as successful as they have been in changing the trajectory of an entire generation so rapidly. Our country was oiled and primed to accept the fashionable doctrines of "progressivism" and "secular humanism" because of the verisimilitude of our past and present leaders.

In a moment of clarity, many of us have seen the delusional effects of these false doctrines. Many of us have removed our blinders; we have stopped falling for the lies, and have started praying for the reformation of our country. We have realized that, as a nation, we have lost sight of what should be most important -our heart. It is the heart of our nation that will determine our future-not Washington.

We do have a choice. We can refuse to be "shortsighted". We can refuse to have our "ears tickled".

Ours is not a battle for today, but a war for tomorrow. We must have hope that America will once again be that "shining city upon a hill"–or there is nothing left to fight for.

10

HOW THE MEDIA EXPLOITED FEAR
IN THE 2016 PRESIDENTIAL ELECTION
(AND HOW TO TEMPER IT)

by Ann-Marie Murrell

During election week Morgan Brittany and I were in New York appearing 3 evenings on a news program called **Nieuwsuur.** The show, touted as the "60 Minutes of the Netherlands", is immensely popular albeit notoriously left-leaning. Morgan and I knew what we were up against, but were surprised when we arrived the first night to find a studio audience filled with Dutch Americans who adored Obama and Hillary Clinton and loathed Donald Trump.

Everyone treated us very respectfully, but out of the 3 nights we were on the show we were definitely the "unicorns" in the room (aka Donald Trump supporters). Seth Meyers, talk show host, SNL alumni, was one of the guests; we had fun chatting with him in the makeup room but yeah, major lefty. A few of the other guests on our panels were a Princeton history professor, a young African-American blogger, and a man who claimed to be a Republican but admitted he voted for Obama, hated Trump, and was considering changing parties (again). Another panelist was a woman who represented "Republicans for Hillary" (aka another Democrat).

Everything was light and fluffy until we were on camera and the firing squad began.

I'm paraphrasing here, but here is a sampling of some of the questions we were asked Monday and Tuesday nights (prior to election results):

(Host to Morgan): *"Are you okay with having a president who says he'll grab your p***y?"* (The host said the actual word on camera.)

"Donald Trump supporters are very angry. Will you and all of the angry Trump supporters accept it peacefully if Hillary

Clinton wins?"

"Donald Trump wants to build a wall to keep people out, and to deport families, and end work on climate change, and stop the Iran deal. How will America survive?"

Morgan and I held our own, but panel segments go pretty fast and you can only defend so much before running out of time.

When I appeared on the show Wednesday night the mood was much more somber. Morgan had to fly back home so I was on my own and the first thing I noticed was a pallor of gray everywhere. Everyone around me was absolutely morose. The studio was silent; no more live audience, probably because they were all in mourning...

The African-American blogger was back on my panel. She was genuinely distraught and told a story of how her 6-year old daughter woke up at 2 a.m. on election night "sobbing and terrified" that Trump had won. Again I'm paraphrasing but this is the gist of what she tearfully said on camera:

"My little girl is afraid that the giant wall will get built and many of her little friends will be taken away. She's afraid that all the angry people who hate people of color or anyone who's different will try to hurt all of us..."

After she made her statement the host looked at me and asked, "Ann-Marie, is this going to happen?" I said no, of course not, and explained that all the Trump supporters I personally know are some of the nicest people in the world and that no one is going to hurt children and people of color...and wow. I remember feeling completely incredulous, almost in a surreal way, that I had to even say such things--but once I got home and saw what was going on throughout social media, and protests taking place all over the U.S., and even statements among some of my own family members, I knew the fear was real.

Yep, most of the protesters out in the streets were bought and paid for and yes, the protests were a well-orchestrated plan from the beginning (see moveon.org screenshot, right). But there were definitely people participating in those protests who were genuinely afraid, having bought into the hype that the media has been perpetuating all year.

What we witnessed with all the protests that followed the

election was the fevered pitch end result of an agenda-driven media, and they are (and have always been) playing a very dangerous game with the entire world. Their goal was to terrify Americans on both sides of the political fence into believing that one person--either Donald Trump or Hillary Clinton--could end America as we know it. On the Republican side, the fear was that our Constitutional rights would end, especially the 1st and 2nd. On the Democrat side, the media insinuated (and continues to do so) that Donald Trump would revive the (Democrat created) KKK, enable and encourage rapists and evil misogynists, and every bad thing since Cain killed Abel.

There are many reasons why our country became so divided but it has very little to do with the 2016 presidential election. Problems first began 16 years ago with the seething hatred for President Bush, when protesters were on street corners almost daily burning Bush effigies. Then the divisiveness escalated to new heights (or lows) during Obama's 8 years in which Americans were promptly divided by race, class, and socio-economics. The rule of law didn't seem to exist anymore from the very beginning when Eric Holder referred to "my people" during the New Black Panther Party voter intimidation case, which he promptly dismissed. From there our entire healthcare system was changed without a vote from the American people, law enforcement was vilified to the point of police officers being publicly executed, our military and veterans were given a back seat to almost everyone, and the IRS became more powerful than ever in blatantly destroying American citizens. Black Lives Matter, funded by nefarious wealthy folks who have much to gain by destroying America, later raised the flames of racism to new heights.

So yes, there have been major problems the past 16 years or so--but where do we go from here? What can we do to build bridges instead of doing what we've seen in the past, either ignoring or torching them?

My advice, for whatever it's worth, is to work on this one person at a time. Open up a serious dialogue and genuinely listen to your friends and family members who have bought into the media hype and explain to them we're all simply pawns in a much larger game. I spent the entire election night in NY with a dear "Never Trump" friend; I listened to her concerns and tried to temper them with hope and optimism- but I never degraded or ridiculed her. I did the same with a family member when I got home, listening to her ideas about how to build bridges and help some of the millennials who are genuinely terrified of what the media is telling them about Donald Trump and Republicans-in-general.

I realize, too, that many reading this on the Republican/conservative side are also angry from years of false accusations and name-calling. As a public figure I suppose I've gotten used to it over the years; I've been called every name in the book and have received my share of death threats for speaking out. But every day citizens are unaccustomed to being publicly attacked/humiliated, and that hurt is definitely real.

What I've learned in my life is the best way to counter ugliness, hatred, and fear is to try rise above it--and that usually begins with communication. Be the bigger person; set an example.

Here are a few things all of us can do to try to mend some of the damage that's been done among friends, family, and colleagues:

Remind them that all of this is about one of the dirtiest businesses in the history of businesses: politics. In fact there has probably never been a perfectly "clean" election since politics began in ancient Greece.

Remind them there is much to gain for media talking heads to perpetuate anger, strife, and hatred. All the networks have had their greatest year ever and they do not want ratings to drop.

Remind them we're dealing with politicians who made YUUUGE campaign promises that either will or won't happen. As FDR said, "The only thing to fear is fear itself."

Remind them we live in a Republic of laws created by and for the people, and no one man has the ability to change that.

Remind them that citizens on both sides of the

aisle were angry at the establishment elites in Washington. The days of allowing governmental corruption to go unchecked has got to end, and we must remain vigilant that it happens.

Remind them that the overreaching power the Obama administration gave the IRS, to target American citizens that he disagreed with politically, is now going to be powered by Republicans. This is a perfect example of why it is always bad to give the federal government the power to enact personal revenge, and it must end immediately.

Remind them that the very nature of politics is, in a biblical sense, ugly, dangerous, and something to approach with caution:

Matthew 6:24 - No man can serve two masters: for either he will hate the one, and love the other; or else he will hold to the one, and despise the other. Ye cannot serve God and mammon.

Titus 3:9 - But avoid foolish questions, and genealogies, and contentions, and strivings about the law; for they are unprofitable and vain.

Psalms 109:8 - Let his days be few; [and] let another take his office.

Of course you can't save every relationship. Without adequate communication, once mendable bridges are sometimes burned down to the ground. Sadly some folks just can't be saved--but that, too, is biblical.

As for PolitiChicks.com, we will continue calling out political abuse from both Democrats and Republicans. We will continue watching our elected officials like hawks and will report corruption and lies from every angle.

As Editor, I encourage my writers not to fall into the mainstream media trap of fear mongering and perpetuating anger. And as a Christian woman, I will continue praying for my family, friends, and my country.

Thank you all for your work as citizen activists. Our work has only just begun.

EPILOGUE: The Dire Importance and Necessity of Conservative Political Activism

by Ann-Marie Murrell (with Daniel Greenfield)

Throughout the very contentious, divisive GOP presidential primaries of 2016, as the owner/editor of PolitiChicks.com I had to work very hard to keep my website as 'fair and balanced' as possible. So while other websites, including Drudge Report, Breitbart, and Red State, clearly promoted their favorite candidates, PolitiChicks remained one of the few that didn't draw deep lines in the sand.

This was no easy task. With dozens of writers nationwide, almost every article submitted to me was either pushing for a favorite candidate or bashing another.

Because of this, early on I put the word out to my contributors that my goal was to publish an equal amount of articles focused on each candidate along with reminders of who and what the Democrat Party is all about.

What this meant was that I also sometimes turned down articles that went too far one way or another, either bashing candidates or shamelessly praising them. I used myself as an example, reminding contributors that despite the fact that I had personally endorsed Sen. Ted Cruz and was named a National Co-Chair for Women for Cruz, I could have easily turned my website into one of those "my candidate is best" websites—but I chose not to.

Still, a few of my contributors were extremely unhappy about having any of their articles or videos rejected and went so far as saying I turned them down because I was 'anti-candidate X'. My response? Eh. Can't make everyone happy, and some people will never be happy no matter what you do.

Despite those few hurt feelings, everything else was great. I was hosting very popular "PolitiChicks Presidential Debate" parties on Facebook. I continued to fly all over the country doing speaking engagements and I was a political commentator almost every week on radio and/or television.

But then in the midst of the primaries I was diagnosed with Multiple Sclerosis and everything in my life literally came to a screeching halt. In addition to my family being thrown upside down, I also had no idea how I could keep my website going. Since becoming editor for Liberty Alliance in 2012, I had been singlehandedly doing everything regarding PolitiChicks.com: editing, publishing, queuing, sending out the daily newsletter, and much more. Because I was also suffering a bout of optic neuritis I could barely see to type.

Those were, literally, very dark days for me. While I was still in the hospital, Senator Cruz dropped out of the presidential race, making Donald Trump the presumptive nominee. So while I had no idea how to physically keep my website going, on an emotional level my heart wasn't into it anyway.

Around that time is when I learned who my real friends were, the ones who perhaps sensed I could use help and didn't wait for me to ask for it. So many stepped up in ways I will never be able to repay; others all but disappeared from my life. It was very eye opening.

A short time after I was released from the hospital, Morgan and I were scheduled to speak at an event in Southern California. Looking back now, I probably should have cancelled. I wasn't ready to speak publicly about anything, especially politics. Frankly the presidential elections were at the bottom of my list of priorities, considering my physical pain along with the emotional guilt I felt about potentially being a lifelong burden to my family.

But there I was, in front of a crowd of Republican women and men, trying to sit upright in a very uncomfortable chair. Somehow I made it through our panel unscathed--until the Q & A at the end. When someone asked me, point blank, if I was going to vote for Donald Trump, I paused. I explained that Sen. Cruz had dropped out of the race while I was still in the hospital and was still trying to process everything.

Before I could even finish my thoughts an older lady very loudly said, "Why is this woman even here if she's not going to support the Republican nominee?" Granted, Donald Trump had not even been "officially" nominee at the time but that didn't matter. I was immediately branded "evil" for daring speak my truth. A similar thing happened in another state where Morgan and I were speaking. After both of us had repeatedly encouraged the group to "never be afraid to voice your opinion" a woman very timidly stood up and said, *"I finally learned to do use my voice this year when I supported Sen. Cruz. But now, I don't like Donald Trump and I just don't know what to do."* Immediately everyone around the woman started yelling at her, criticizing her, shouting her down.

That was the first time I was ever embarrassed to be a Republican since I switched parties in 2001. Morgan and I both did our best to calm the crowd; I shared my story of getting heckled in California for the very same thing - but honestly, I doubt she will ever speak up again. After finally finding her voice, those other "Republicans" may have taken her voice away forever.

After that, I went through a bit of a dark period and it showed on my social media pages. Daniel Greenfield wrote to me and his words not only helped change my heart but also helped me refocus the entire direction of my website.

Daniel wrote,

If we were not a minority, the country would be a different place. It is time that we accepted that simple fact.

It is not a cause for despair, but for pride.

We do not march at the head of a conquering army. We are an insurgency of principles and ideas.

We are the ones who remind those at the top of our party that their victory is hollow without principles and ideas. And if they don't always listen, the time always comes when they must.

The past years have all too often made us complacent. They have convinced us that we are on the right side of history. But there is no right side of history. There is just us and what we fight for.

We do not live in an age of expanding possibilities. Instead we are the last remaining hope of our culture, our country and our civilization.

We see what most do not. And we dedicate ourselves to a

struggle that most will turn down. Victories will be few and not easy ones. And we should never become too comfortable or too convinced that this time we have it. We are the rear guard. We are all there is before the fall of darkness. We may not win. But neither will we give up.

We are not content to abandon ourselves to barbarism. We do not fight merely out of spite or anger. We do it because we believe a better world is possible. Because we can see that world when few can.

That must keep us from despair in even the darkest of times.

We are the keepers of the flame in a dark age. If we let it die out, then the darkness falls.

Our numbers are small. Take pride that you stand among us.

Trust not in men. Stand strong. Do not be dragged down by labels or false hopes. Do not feel all is lost when lies triumph. They only last for a brief while. Do not feel that you have failed or are useless. Principles are never useless. Courage is never futile.

Be proud of the task. Do not falter or despair. Do not be overwhelmed by the savage times and trials.

Have faith. Be of good courage. Raise proud banners of principle and let them fly. And though they may be stained with mud, remember that they and you are the hope of a nation.

So here we are now, heading into a new phase of American politics led by President Donald Trump. If the first week of his inauguration is any indicator, Republicans will be facing major scrutiny, further divisiveness, and perhaps continued violence led by the crazy leftists of Hollywood, media, and beyond. And yet I am personally very excited about what President Trump will do. In his first few hours as President he began working to actually fulfill his campaign promises. President Trump is surrounded by amazing, respected people and most of all, he deeply loves America. What more could any voter hope for?

NOTES

PART 1, POLITICS

1.Ben Sasse, "Senator Ben Sasse (R-Neb.) on MSNBC Defining Conservatism" video (MSNBC, 2016).

2. Jonestown: https://culteducation.com/jonestown.html

3. Infiltrate the church: https://en.wikipedia.org/wiki/Jim_Jones

4. Ambush killing Rep. Ryan and others: http://www.religionnewsblog.com/22936/peoples-temple-2

5. Huey Newton: https://en.wikipedia.org/wiki/Huey_P._Newton

6. Jim Jones' son on Oprah Winfrey Show: http://www.oprah.com/oprahshow/Mass-Murderer-Jim-Jones-Son-Speaks-Out/6

7. Hollywood Democrats consider Hillary Alternatives - March 11, 2015 Newsmax.com http://www.newsmax.com/Politics/Norman-Lear-alternatives-Hollywood-Hillary-Clinton/2015/03/11/id/629606/

8. Blue Dog Democrat, POLITICO.com, April 2012

9. "What exactly is the Tea Party", BBC, September 2010

10. Centrist definition: "Fiscal and social responsibility balanced with personal responsibility," USCentrist.org

11. Moderate definition: "views are between conservative and liberal," Quizlet.com

12. Libertarianism definition: "individual liberty, personal responsibility and freedom from government," TheAdvocates.org

13. "Pelosi's Poodles", WSJ, November 2005

14. Dr. Ben Carson addresses National Prayer Breakfast, Criticizes Obamacare - Real Clear Politics - February 7, 2013 http://www.realclearpolitics.com/video/2013/02/07/dr_benjamin_carson_addresses_national_prayer_breakfast_criticizes_obamacare.html

15. Clinton scandals: https://www.theguardian.com/us-news/2016/may/27/hillary-clinton-bill-clinton-scandals

16. FBI Director James Comey:

https://www.fbi.gov/news/pressrel/press-releases/statement-by-fbi-director-james-b-comey-on-the-investigation-of-secretary-hillary-clinton2019s-use-of-a-personal-e-mail-system

PART 2, HISTORY

1. "The Scariest Reason Trump Won", Townhall.com, May 10, 2016
2. Calvin Coolidge Speech on the 150th Anniversary of the Declaration of Independence, July 1926, TeachingAmericanHistory.com
3. The Joseph Story Distinguished Lecture: Repointing the Constitution, Justice Janice Rogers Brown, YouTube.com, October 2014
4. Thomas Jefferson, A Summary View of the Rights of British America, 1774
5. John Adams Notes for an oration at Braintree (Spring 1772)
6. Only half of protestant pastors have a Biblical worldview, (Barna January 12, 2004)
7. Agreement Between the Settlers at New Plymouth, 1620 (Avalon Project, Yale Law School)
8. Colonial Charters, Grants and Related Documents (Avalon Project, Yale Law School)
10. Magna Carta, 1215 (British Library)
11. Speech to the Constitutional Convention, June 28, 1787 (Library of Congress)
12. Summary View of the Rights of British America (1774); The Writings of Thomas Jefferson (19 Vols. 1905) edited by Andrew A. Lipscomb and Albert Ellery Bergh, Vol. 1, p. 211
13. Thomas Jefferson A Summary View of the Rights of British America, 1774
14. Federalist Papers #55 (Avalon Project, Yale Law School)
15.Federalist Papers #10 (Avalon Project, Yale Law School)
16. Federalist Papers #39 (Avalon Project, Yale Law School)
17. Thomas Jefferson letter to Marquis de Lafayette November 4, 1823
18. Speech on the Federal Constitution, Virginia Ratifying Convention, June 5, 1788
19. Thomas Jefferson, Notes on the State of Virginia, Queries 14 AND 19, 146--49, 164—65 University of Chicago Press

20. The Rights of the Colonists The Report of the Committee of Correspondence to the Boston Town Meeting, Nov. 20, 1772, Old South Leaflets no. 173 (Boston: Directors of the Old South Work, 1906) 7: 417-428

21. Constitution of the United States September 17, 1787 National Archives

22. The Declaration of Independence: A Transcription IN CONGRESS, July 4, 1776, National Archives

23. Samuel Adams letter to James Warren, February 12, 1779

24. Jay A. Parry, Andrew M. Allison, W. Cleon Skousen, "The Real George Washington" (National Center for Constitutional Studies, 2008)

25. Wayne Grudem, "Politics According to the Bible" (Zondervan, 2010)

26. David Barton, "America's Godly Heritage" (WallBuilder Press, 2013)

27. Gordon Lawrence, "Great Men Bow Down" (Sword Point Publishing, 2010)

28. Samuel Adams, "The Writings of Samuel Adams: 1773-1777" (Nabu Press, 2010, first published in 2004)

29. William Penn, "Brief History of William Penn" article (ushistory.org, 2012)

30. See Margaret Thatcher's speech in Bruges in 1988, cited by the Heritage Foundation: Charles More United States of...America or Europe? Source: http://www.heritage.org/research/lecture/2013/06/united-states-of-america-or-europe; See also: "Thatcher and Her Tussles with Europe" BBC Politics, http://www.bbc.com/news/uk-politics-11598879

31. The European Coal and Steel Community (ECSC) was an international organization serving to unify certain Continental Europe after World War II. The Treaty of Paris formally established it in 1951, which was signed by Belgium, France, West Germany, Italy, the Netherlands and Luxembourg. The ECSC was the first international organization to be based on the principles of supranationalism or what we call today "globalism." Source: CVCE European Navigator. Raquel Valls. "European Communities."

http://www.cvce.eu/obj/the_european_communities-en-
3940ef1d-7c10-4d0f-97fc-0cf1e86a32d4.html

32. *Taking Europe into 21ˢᵗ Century.* Treaty of Lisbon – official site: http://ec.europa.eu/archives/lisbon_treaty/index_en.htm

PART 3, EDUCATION

1. Common Core: The Good, The Bad, and The Downright Frightening, PolitiChicks.com, July 2013

2. Invisible Serfs Collar blog, accessed June 2013

3. Credentialed to Destroy, How and Why Education Became A Weapon, Amazon.com, accessed July 2013

4. Parents Advocating for Children and Teachers blog, Pathways of Deception: Exposing the Innovation Lab Network, April 2014

5. Performance Assessments for the Common Core, hepg.org, November 2013

6. Race to the Top, US Department of Education, http://www2.ed.gov/programs/racetothetop/index.html, accessed March 2013 2. 7. Minds, Souls, & Attitudes: Whistleblowing the Tarbiyah Project for Islamic Education Imposed for ALL Students, Invisible Serfs Collar blog, November 2015

8. Obama Executive Order Tells Schools To Cut Down On The Discipline Of Unruly Black Students, Before it's News website, August 2013

9. What We Do; Innovation Lab Network, CCSSO.org, June 2014 content/uploads/2014/01/CompetencyWorks_A_K-12

10. Competency Works, competencyworks.org, February 2013

11. Knowledge Works, knowledgeworks.org, February 2013

12. David T. Conley, epiconline.org, accessed May 2014

13. Educational Policy Improvement Center, epiconline.org, accessed May 2014

14. Bill and Melinda Gates Foundation grants, How We Work, Grants Awarded, gatesfoundation.org, accessed April 2014

15. States involved in ILN, What We Do; Innovation Lab Network, CCSSO.org, June 2014

16. Learning Strategies as Metacognitive Factors: A Critical Review, epiconline.org, April 2014

17. Linda Darling Hammond Stanford Education Speech, YouTube, accessed March 2014

18. CREATING SYSTEMS OF ASSESSMENT FOR DEEPER LEARNING, edpolicy.stanford.edu, accessed March 2014

19. Chief Education Officer Nancy Golden, education.oregon.gov, accessed April 2014

20. Record data, nces.ed.gov, accessed April 2013 25. Family Educational Rights and Privacy Act (FERPA), http://www2.ed.gov/, accessed May 2013

21. Plato in his "Republic" (c. 380 B.C.) tried to bring into existence "kallipolis" – a beautiful, noble city – thus, creating the first doctrine of socialism. People living in Plato's utopia would be taught for free by the government, the weak and old (those who cannot contribute to society) would be doomed to euthanasia (what Ms. Palin called "Obama's death panels"), the only justice would be "social" (i.e. what is for the individual benefit without primarily being for the "social benefit" is unjust – the same definition Mr. Sanders uses today), intemperate speech and art not contributing to social well-being would be banned, and children would be taken away from their mothers at birth, so as to make everyone equal (no-one knowing who their real parents are, everyone would treat everyone as their family, potentially parents or siblings). Plato saw this system as preferable to democracy ("Demos" + "kratos" = rule of the mob), which inevitably ends in tyranny. Paradoxically, as Hayek pointed out, Plato's good intentions turn sour at application every time.

22. Orwell's 1984 (prophetically written in 1948) is a dystopia, which means a dehumanized utopia, where Doublespeak (political correctness) is prescribed by the Ministry of Truth, government surveillance penetrates everywhere and everyone (Orwell created the word "thought crime"), cult of personality prevails (Big Brother), and everyone is forced into total submission. In other words, it is a picture of socialism realized and executed to a T. No-one who has not read this novel has any right to speak of socialism – simply because they do not know what they are speaking about.

23. James Madison, *Federalist No.10*, "The Federalist" J&A McLean (1787). Available online at *Wikisource*: https://en.wikisource.org/wiki/The_Federalist_(Dawson)/10

24. My reference to Joseph Conrad's "Heart of Darkness" (1899) is twofold: on the simpler and more obvious level of interpretation, I refer to permeating something dark and unknown to our civilized world; on the more sophisticated level, the two main characters – cruel and ruthless Kurtz, and the more placid but equally "imperialist" Marlow – represent two sides of the same coin: a tyrannical system where the superior one (Kurtz) rules and takes by force whatever he desires, and the subservient "intellectual" (Marlow) contemplates the "madness" of the tyrant by making up justifications and pondering causes.

25. The final reference here is to what Ernest Hemingway called "the greatest American novel" – Mark Twain's "Huck Finn." As you may recall, on the very last page of the novel, Huck states resolutely: "I've been there before – and I ain't going back!" He is referring to the "sivilization" distorted by slavery, where his best friend cannot be as free as he is, and where (therefore) his own freedom is but disguised subjugation. To my knowledge, no-one has yet read a socialist interpretation to Huck Finn, but my knowledge of socialism makes this more than a gambit of literary theory – socialism IS slavery.

26. ROPE2.0 https://rope2.org/

27. Rasmussen Report: http://education-curriculum-reform-government-schools.org/w/2014/08/new-rasmussen-poll-republicans-and-independents-oppose-common-core/

28 Gates Foundation: http://www.gatesfoundation.org/What-We-Do/US-Program/K-12-Education/College-Ready-Partners

29. Arne Duncan YouTube video: https://www.youtube.com/watch?v=L90BCEVH41U

30. Gov. Mary Fallin: https://www.nga.org/cms/home/news-room/news-releases/2013--news-releases/col2-content/national-governors-association-l.default.html

PART 4, ISLAM

1 Angela Merkel stands by her Muslim refugee stance (UK Independent, March 14, 2016)

2 Egypt, other Muslim countries rate worse for women (Denver Post, November 12, 2013)

3 Women, children and boys sexual abuse (bacha bazi) (UK Daily Mail, January 7, 2016)

4 Arabic gang-rape 'Taharrush' spreads to Europe (UK Daily Mail, January12, 2016)

5 Cologne, Germany, New Year's Eve gang rapes (BBC News, January 5, 2016)

6 Natasha Smith Tahrir Square, Egypt Rape account (UK Daily Mail, June 27, 2012)

7 Kim Barker, *Islam has nothing to do with rapes* (Co published in NY Times, Feb. 19, 2011)

8 European Churches remove Crosses for Muslim refugees (Christian Post, November 3, 2015)

9 Cologne Mayor's 'code of conduct' to prevent sexual assault (BBC News, January 6, 2016)

10 US AG Lynch to "Go after anti Muslim hate speech" after San Bernardino terror attack (ABC News, December 4,2015)

11 Democrat "hate crime" Bill (US Congress H.Res.569, December 17, 2015)

12 European Hate Speech Laws (2016 the Legal Project, Council of Europe)

13. http://www.libertiesalliance.org/2009/08/31/the-turkish-genocides/

14. http://www.ncas.rutgers.edu/center-study-genocide-conflict-resolution-and-human-rights/genocide-ottoman-greeks-1914-1923

15. http://www.nytimes.com/2016/04/23/world/europe/despite-campaign-vow-obama-declines-to-call-massacre-of-armenians-genocide.html

16. http://www.history.com/topics/armenian-genocide

17. http://www.nytimes.com/2015/04/17/world/europe/turkeys-century-of-denial-about-an-armenian-genocide.html?_r=0

18. http://www.npr.org/sections/thetwo-way/2016/06/25/483507441/pope-francis-urges-world-to-never-forget-armenian-genocide

19. http://www.history.com/topics/armenian-genocide

20. http://www.nytimes.com/2015/05/19/world/africa/boko-haram-militants-raped-hundreds-of-female-captives-in-

nigeria.html; http://www.wnd.com/2014/05/congressman-obama-policies-empower-terrorists/

21. http://www.dailymail.co.uk/news/article-3022586/Masked-gunmen-launch-attack-morning-prayers-Kenyan-university.html; http://www.cbsnews.com/pictures/kenya-reels-from-al-shabaab-garissa-student-massacre/25/

22. http://www.nytimes.com/2016/06/17/world/middleeast/isis-genocide-yazidi-un.html

23. http://www.genocide-museum.am/eng/online_exhibition_6.php

24. http://www.history.com/topics/armenian-genocide

25. http://www.nationalreview.com/article/416410/crucifixion-its-not-ancient-history-anymore-deroy-murdock

26. http://www.ncas.rutgers.edu/center-study-genocide-conflict-resolution-and-human-rights/genocide-ottoman-greeks-1914-1923

27. During his 2012 presidential campaign, Obama said: "The analogy we use around here sometimes, and I think is accurate, is if a jayvee team puts on Lakers uniforms that doesn't make them Kobe Bryant." http://www.politifact.com/truth-o-meter/statements/2014/sep/07/barack-obama/what-obama-said-about-islamic-state-jv-team/

28. U.S House of Representatives House record for December 19, 2012. Congressman Frank Wolf (10th District, Virginia) shared a dear colleague letter titled "Family Member of Benghazi Victim Supports House Select Committee on Terrorist Attack in Benghazi" where author Michael Ingmire sent a letter of support for House Resolution 824 which sought to establish a bipartisan Select committee to investigate the September 11/12th, 2012 attacks on the U.S Diplomatic Outpost and CIA Annex in Benghazi, Libya.

29. House Select Committee on Benghazi: Final Report. Released June 28, 2016. http://benghazi.house.gov/NewInfo

30. Citizens Commission on Benghazi Report, "Betrayal in Benghazi: A Dereliction of Duty." Released on June 29, 2016.

http://www.aim.org/wp-content/uploads/2016/06/AIM-Citizens-Commission-on-Benghazi-FINAL-REPORT-June-2016.pdf

31. President Barack Hussein Obama II was the 44th President of the United States from 2008 until 2016. History is continuing to be written about his Presidency at the time this article was written. By most intelligent Americans the presidency of President Obama will be considered to be a history of dividing the American people and his demonstration of a broad sympathy to groups like the Muslim Brotherhood. Considering his background as a Constitutional Professor, scholars will also look at his presidency for its broad disregard for the articles of the United States Constitution.

32. Hillary Rodham Clinton, a disgraced and terminated Watergate Committee lawyer fresh out of law school at the age of 27 in 1974. The Watergate Committee was investigating the Watergate scandal of 37th United States President Richard Milhouse Nixon. First Lady of Arkansas from January 9, 1979 until January 19, 1981 and again from January 11, 1983 to December 12, 1992. Conveniently martyred First Lady to the Presidency of 42nd United States President William Jefferson Clinton from January 20, 1993 until January 20, 2001. Martyred because of her husband's adulterous affair with White House Intern, Monica Lewinsky. Ineffectual New York Senator from January 3, 2001 to January 29, 2009. Secretary of State under President Obama from January 21, 2009 until February 1, 2013. At the time of this writing, Mrs. Clinton is the nominee for the Democrat Party for President of the United States for the 2016 election. Her failure of leadership and the policies of President Obama led directly to the deaths of four Americans in the Benghazi attack on September 11/12th 2012.

PART 5, PARENTING

1. Rose Kennedy, BrainyQuote.com

2. How College Students Think They are More Special Than EVER - DailyMail.com - January 7, 2013 http://www.dailymail.co.uk/news/article-2257715/Study-shows-college-students-think-theyre-special--read-write-barely-study.html

3. Occupy Wall Street – Wikipedia https://en.wikipedia.org/wiki/Occupy_Wall_Street
4. The Kardashians - "Keeping Up With the Kardashians" http://www.imdb.com/title/tt1086761/
5. Jersey Shore - "Jersey Shore" http://www.imdb.com/title/tt1563069/?ref_=nv_sr_1

PART 6, RELIGION
1. National Day of Prayer "Historical Summary", nationaldayofprayer.org /about
2. National Day of Prayer "Fun Facts", nationaldayofprayer.org /about
3. Barna research, "Statistics on Prayer in the U.S.", churchleaders.com
4. U.S. News & Beliefnet Prayer Survey Results, beliefnet.com, 2004
5. San Francisco General Medical Center experiment, "Statistics on Prayer in the U.S.", churchleaders.com
6. "Evidence for God from Science", GodAndScience.org (site last modified 2014)
7. John Hardwick, *"High School Class President Prays in Jesus' Name at Graduation Despite Atheist Objections"* (Christian Post, 2013)
8. Wayne Grudem, "Politics According to the Bible" (Zondervan, 2010)
9. Alvin Schmidt, "How Christianity Changed the World" (Grand Rapids: Zondervan, 2004, formerly published as *Under the Influence*, 2001)
10. Greg Forster, personal email to Wayne Grudem, January 21, 2010.
11. http://www.thelatinlibrary.com/imperialism/notes/tours.html
12. https://en.wikipedia.org/wiki/Battle_of_Tours
13. https://www.britannica.com/event/Battle-of-Lepanto
14. https://en.wikipedia.org/wiki/John_of_Austria
15. http://www.catholic.com/magazine/articles/the-battle-that-saved-the-christian-west
16. https://en.wikipedia.org/wiki/Battle_of_Vienna
17. http://www.historynet.com/turning-the-ottoman-tide-john-

iii-sobieski-at-vienna-1683.html
18. Holiday Yom Hoshoah Ve-Hagevurah Rabbi David Golinkin "Yom Hashoah: A Program of Observance"
19. Never Forget/Never Again: Huffington Post Jan 29,2015
20. Armenians Genocide: Jerusalem Post April 13, 2015
21. FirstAmendmentCenter.org, Free-exercise clause overview, September 16, 2011 http://www.firstamendmentcenter.org/free-exercise-clause
22. Heritage.org, With Liberty and Justice For All, April 30, 1996 http://www.heritage.org/research/lecture/with-liberty-and-justice-for-all
23. OregonLive.com, Sweet Cakes final order: Gresham bakery must pay $135,000 for denying service to same-sex couple, July 2, 2105 http://www.oregonlive.com/business/index.ssf/2015/07/sweet_cakes_final_order_gresha.html
24. WND.com, GoFundMe Blocks Fundraiser For Christian Baker, April 25, 2015 http://www.wnd.com/2015/04/gofundme-blocks-fundraiser-for-christian-bakery/
25. FoxNews.com, GoFundMe Nixes Donations for Bakery That Refused to Serve Gay Weddings, April 27, 2015 http://insider.foxnews.com/2015/04/27/gofundme-blocks-fundraising-oregon-bakery-refused-serve-gay-weddings
26. WashingtonTimes.com, Sweet Cakes by Melissa crowdfunder breaks record with $352K, July 14, 2015 http://www.washingtontimes.com/news/2015/jul/14/sweet-cakes-melissa-crowdfunder-breaks-record-352k/
27. WND.com, Here it is: Complete catalogue of 'same-sex marriage' violations of faith, April 6, 2015 http://www.wnd.com/2015/04/courts-conclude-faith-loses-to-gay-demands/

PART 7, HEALTH

1. Dr. Tim Shepherd, "Family Doctor: I want to take Care of My Patients" article (The Daily Signal, 2013)
2. Dr. C.L. Gray, "Cutting the Gordian Knot" (Physicians for Reform, 2011)
3. Dr. Robert Nirschl, "ABSOLUTE INSANITY': Practicing

physician slams Obamacare's damaging effects on doctor-patient relationships" article (The Daily Caller, 2013)

4. Dr. Shaun Carpenter, "Dropped Coverage: One Cancer-Surviving Doctor's Story in the Age of Obamacare" article (PJ Media, 2013)

5. Dr. Milton Wolf, "Obama's doctor cousin blasts Obamacare: 'Not a word of it is true" article (BizPac Review, 2013)

6.James Beattie and Michael Chapman, "Ben Carson Warns: 'Socialized Medicine Is Keystone to Establishment of a Socialist State'" article (CNS News, 2013)

7. Vladimir Lenin, "The State and Revolution" (Kessinger Publishing, 2004, first published in 1918)

8.Dr. Ben Carson, "Obamacare Worse Thing Since Slavery" (The Washington Post, 2013)

9. Harvard, "Top Harvard doctors: Supporting Obamacare 'makes moral and medical sense'" (Raw Story, 2013)

10.Bruce Japsen, "Doctors Still Back Obamacare's Individual Mandate Despite Emboldened GOP" (Forbes, 2013)

11. Dr. Jeffrey Cain, "Doctors Still Back Obamacare's Individual Mandate Despite Emboldened GOP" (Forbes, 2013)

12. Dr. John Noseworthy, "Obamacare lacks key cost control" (CNBC, 2013)

13. Dr. C.L. Gray, "Cutting the Gordian Knot" (Physicians for Reform, 2011)

14. Dr. C.L. Gray, "Cutting the Gordian Knot" (Physicians for Reform, 2011)

15. **The Wahls Protocol:** How I Beat Progressive MS Using Paleo Principles and Functional Medicine by Terry Wahls, M.D. Brand: Wahls, Terry/ Adamson, Eve Published on: 2014-03-13

16. World MS Day, http://www.worldmsday.org

17. National MS Society, http://www.nationalmssociety.org

18. *A Century of State and Local Spending,* USGovenmentSpending.com/stateandlocalspending; 2008

19. Living with addiction, what happens to a family when addiction becomes a part of it? Tian Dayton, PhD. 2007.

PART 8, SOCIAL ISSUES

1. NationalReview.com, UC Faculty Training: Saying 'America Is the Land of Opportunity' Is a Microaggression, June 19,2015

http://www.nationalreview.com/article/419571/university-california-microaggresions-janet-napolitano

2. TheCollegefix.com, Wisconsin University dubs 'America is a melting pot' a racial microaggression, June 30, 2015 http://www.thecollegefix.com/post/23135/

3. TheDailyBeast.com, The University of California's Insane Speech Police, June 22.2015 http://www.thedailybeast.com/articles/2015/06/22/the-university-of-california-s-insane-speech-police.html

4. The Gentle Art of Verbal Self-Defense, Suzette Haden Elgin's, Ph.D., Prentice Hall; (January 19, 2000)

5. DeborahTannen.com

6. The WashintonPost.com, UC teaching faculty members not to criticize race-based affirmative action, call America 'melting pot,' and more, June 16, 2015 https://www.washingtonpost.com/news/volokh-conspiracy/wp/2015/06/16/uc-teaching-faculty-members-not-to-criticize-race-based-affirmative-action-call-america-melting-pot-and-more/

7. U.S. Supreme Court Justice Louis Brandles (1856 -1941), quote, [Whitney v. California, 274 U.S. 357 (1927)], Truthliesdeceptioncoverups.info http://www.truthliesdeceptioncoverups.info/2013/11/justice-louis-d-brandeis-quotes.html

8. Personal interview with Michelle Rider, May 2015

9. "Fight Rages for Teenager Isaiah Rider's Freedom – His Mother Commits 'Cardinal Sin' Of Questioning Doctors", MedicalKidnap.com, October 29, 2014

10. "The Corrupt Business of Child Protective Services", Senator Nancy Schaefer, November 2007

11. "Parents of Justina Pelletier sue Boston Children's Hospital", BostonGlobe.com, February 2016

12. "Child Kidnapping and Trafficking: A Lucrative U.S. Business Funded by Taxpayers", HealthImpactNews.com, February 2016

13. *Medical Kidnapping: A Threat to Every Family in America*, Brian Shilhavy, 2016

14. Center for Medical Progress, undercover Planned Parenthood videos: http://www.centerformedicalprogress.org

15. https://www.youtube.com/watch?v=XNlMUndNaMc

16. https://twitter.com/hashtag/SorryItsABoy?src=hash

17. "The Truth About Sex Trafficking," Politico, June 2015

18. "20.9 million worldwide victims, mostly women, and 5.5 million children, according to one projection by the Polaris Project," http://polarisproject.org/facts, Polaris Project

19. "34 felony charges against human trafficking criminal Victor Rax," http://attorneygeneral.utah.gov/media-center/uag-pressrelease/34-charges-filed-in-victor-rax-case, March 2014

20. Operation Underground Railroad (OUR), www.ourrescue.org

21. Tim Ballard, http://ourrescue.org/about

22. Utah Attorney General Sean Reyes, www.seanreyes.com

23. Congressman Chris Smith (R-NJ), a bill that if passed into law would do the following (Source: H.R. 515), https://www.gop.gov/bill/h-r-515-international-megans-law-to-prevent-demand-for-child-sex-trafficking/
Child Exploitation Investigations Unit of the U.S. Immigration and Customs Enforcement the Angel Watch Center, https://www.ice.gov/news/releases/ice-authorized-create-angel-watch-center-expand-child-protection-efforts-following

24. "According to the Congressional subcommittee that oversees human trafficking," Africa, Global Health, Global Human Rights, and International Organizations, https://foreignaffairs.house.gov/subcommittee/africa-global-health-global-human-rights-and-international-organizations/

25. Former CIA agent and Homeland Security undercover operative and special agent Tim Ballard, http://ourrescue.org/about

26. "According to Reyes," *Waking to the Reality: Human and Sex Trafficking In the U.S.,* July 2015

27. "...The Abolitionists because of parallels to the movement to end slavery—have completed missions with..." www.ourrescue.org

28. The Abolitionists, a feature-length documentary, http://theabolitionistsmovie.com/

29. "...said Mazza, former president of Sony and Paramount TV, in a recent Deadline.com interview," http://deadline.com/2015/06/abolitionists-tv-series-child-sex-

slavery-rescue-documentary-1201435534/, June 2015

PART 9, MILITARY

1. God In America - John Winthrop, PBS.org

2. Ronald Reagan Farewell Speech-January 1989, PBS.org

3. James Garfield Decoration Day Address-1868, WhatSoProudlyWeHail.org

4. Ronald Reagan Farewell Speech-January 1989, PBS.org

5. Oaths of Enlistment and Oaths of Office, U.S. Army Center of Military History, History.Army.mil

6. "A De-Sexed Society is a Dehumanized Society", Stella Morabito, May 25, 2016, ThePublicDiscourse.com

7. The Writings of Samuel Adams, Volume II (1770 - 1773), FullBooks.com

PART 10, MEDIA

4. "God Was Denied Three Times at the DNC", Western Journalism: http://www.westernjournalism.com/god-was-denied-three-times-at-the-dnc/

5. Biologist E.O. Wilson: 'Humans, Like Ants, Need A Tribe", Newsweek 4/2/12

http://www.newsweek.com/biologist-eo-wilson-why-humans-ants-need-tribe-64005

6. "The Communist Takeover of America: 45 Declared Goals" by Trevor Loudon, http://www.trevorloudon.com/2013/01/the-communist-takeover-of-america-45-declared-goals/

7. "Sens. Feinstein And Durbin Specifically Try To Carve Citizen Journalists Out Of Shield Law", TechDirt.com, December 2009

8. "'60 Minutes II' Wins a Peabody Award, Raising Eyebrows", NY Times, April 2005

9. "CNN Does Not Get to Cherrypick the Rules of Journalism", Esquire, September 2014

10. "What's a Journalist", ChicagoReader.com, October 2010

11. "Inside Media Matters: David Brock's Enemies List", Daily Caller, February 2012

12. Zinsser, William. *On Writing Well: The Classic Guide to Writing Nonfiction.* New York. Harper Perennial. 2016. Print.

13. "Why Dr. Kermit Gosnell's Trial Should Be a Front-Page Story", TheAtlantic.com, April 2013

14. "DOJ Targeting Of Fox News Reporter James Rosen Risks

Criminalizing Journalism", HuffingtonPost.com, May 2013

15. "Americans living under fatwa include three women who openly criticized Islam", NY Times, March 2016

16. "Who Killed Michael Hastings", New York Magazine, November 2013

17. Thomas Paine, www.ushistory.org

18. Mickey & Friends: A Perfect Picnic, Disney 2013

19. Article Writing: 6 Rules to Getting the Perfect Format, www.hongkiat.com

20. Jules Verne, France, 1828-1905

21. George Orwell (pseudonym of Eric Arthur Blair, English author), India/British, 1903-1950

22. Huxley, Aldous (Leonard) England, 1894-1963

23. H.G. Wells (Herbert George Wells) England, 1866-1946

PART 11, 2nd AMENDMENT

1. Brigida Mack, "More woman carrying guns, experts say" article (WISTV.Com, 2011)

2.ESPN, "Jovan Belcher Kills Girlfriend and Himself" (ESPN News, 2012)

3. Chris Strauss, "Bob Costas gives anti-gun speech on 'Sunday Night Football'" video (USA Today, 2012)

4. Dan Mitchell, "New Cato Institute Study Shows How Private Gun Ownership Reduces Crime, Saves Lives" (Word Press, 2012)

5. *Shane* is a 1953 American Technicolor Western film from Paramount, based on the 1949 novel of the same name by Jack Schaefer.

6. *See* William Shakespeare "Hamlet", Act 3, Scene 2. The "mousetrap" in Shakespeare's *Hamlet* is the play-within-the-play, in which Hamlet the Prince has the players enact the murder of his father in front of Claudius, who succeeded his father and married his mother, in order to observe the Claudius' reactions and thus ascertain his guilt or innocence.

7. Military Factory, *Weapons of ISIS*, lists 45 sophisticated military weapons at their disposal (http://www.militaryfactory.com/smallarms/weapons-of-isis.asp) but, as we know, even the toughest laws limiting gun access are useless vis-à-vis the hate and zeal of the killers.

8. My quoting the obvious source here is clearly intended as

sarcasm. Communists are wont to speak in imperatives (e.g. "Make no mistake!"), which preface and conclude most of their speeches. This is political correctness in action: they prescribe you what you may and may not do or think.

9. The Online Library of Liberty, Sir William Blackstone, *Commentaries on the Laws of England in Four Books, vol. 1* (1753) http://files.libertyfund.org/files/2140/Blackstone_1387-01_EBk_v6.0.pd

10. Passed on 16 December 1689, The Bill of Rights limited the powers of the King and set out the rights of Parliament, free elections, freedom of speech, religious liberty, and prohibition of cruel and unusual punishment. The Bill of Rights 1689 was one of the inspirations for the United States Bill of Rights. https://en.wikipedia.org/wiki/Bill_of_Rights_1689

11. "All modern American literature comes from one book by Mark Twain called Huckleberry Finn. American writing comes from that. There was nothing before. There has been nothing as good since." Ernest Hemingway. *See* Quotable Quote at: http://www.goodreads.com/quotes/161912-all-modern-american-literature-comes-from-one-book-by-mark

12. "Everything we know about the San Bernardino Terror Attack Investigation So Far" LA Times, December 14, 2015

13. "Gun salesman-in-chief: 52,600 a day under Obama, more seen under Hillary" Washington Examiner, June 27, 2016

14. "Department of Justice Will Go After Anti-Muslim Hate Speech" ABC News, December 4, 2015

15. "Black Activists Call For Lynching and Hanging of White People and Cops" Breitbart.com, August 28, 2015

16. Keep Calm And Carry On World War II Motivational Poster, Wikipedia.com

ABOUT POLITICHICKS.COM

In 2011, Ann-Marie Murrell worked with Liberty Alliance and SNL's Victoria Jackson to create a popular weekly web TV talk show called "PolitiChicks". After the talk show ended, Ann-Marie continued as Editor-in-Chief and began recruiting women writers from across the United States. Over time, she helped turn PolitiChicks.com into a very popular and respected political commentary website.

Then in 2014, Ann-Marie and Morgan Brittany purchased PolitiChicks and in 2016 Sonya Sasser became a PolitiChicks spokesperson. Today, PolitiChicks.com serves as a major platform for women and men writers across the U.S. The website has hundreds of thousands of readers and followers throughout social media and many of "The PolitiChicks" are frequent guests on television, radio, and are featured speakers at major events throughout America.

PolitiChicks: A Clarion Call to Political Activism is a compilation of some of the 'best of the best' articles from PolitiChicks.com. Our goal is to encourage others to become activists, and to use whatever gifts and talents they possess to get involved in all aspects of the political process.

PolitiChicks.com understands that freedom and liberty must be maintained and protected with vigilance and with the constant support of the American people. Without that vigilance, tyranny moves in. We refuse to allow that to happen on our watch.

INDEX

43377404R00187

Made in the USA
Middletown, DE
07 May 2017